Israel Pocket Library

W9-BWH-188

SOCIETY

KETER BOOKS

This book is compiled from material originally published in the *Encyclopaedia Judaica*

Copyright © 1974, Keter Publishing House Jerusalem Ltd.
P.O.Box 7145, Jerusalem, Israel

Cat. No. 25064

ISBN 0 7065 1323 1

Printed in Israel

CONTENTS

CONTRIBUTORS

Prof. Roberto Bachi: Professor of Statistics and Demography, the Hebrew University of Jerusalem

Dr. Abraham J. Brawer: Geographer and Historian, Tel Aviv

Aharon Amir: Writer and Editor, Tel Aviv

Efraim Orni: Geographer, Jerusalem

Moshe Kerem: Lecturer in Education, Haifa University; Kibbutz Gesher ha-Ziv

Yaakov Arie Chazan: Member of Knesset: Kibbutz Mishmar ha-Emek

Shlomo Derech: Editor, Kibbutz Givat Ḥayyim

Moshe Unna: Former Member of Knesset, Kibbutz Sedeh Eliyahu

Uzi Finerman: Member of Knesset, Kefar Yeḥezkel

Dr. Israel Kolatt: Senior Lecturer in Contemporary Jewry, the Hebrew University of Jerusalem

Moshe Allon (deceased), Jerusalem

David Jutan: Histadrut ha-Ovdim ha-Le'ummit, Tel Aviv

Zalman Heyn: Ministry of Labor, Jerusalem

Herbert Allen Smith: Former Director of the Manpower Planning Authority, Jerusalem

Malka Hillel Shulewitz: Journalist, Jerusalem

Dr. Giora Lotan: Former Director General of the National Insurance Institute, of the Ministry of Social Welfare, and of the Ministry of Labor, Jerusalem

Channah Palti: Jerusalem

Doris Lankin: Legal Journalist, Jerusalem

Yaacov Shimoni: Deputy Director General, Ministry for Foreign Affairs, Jerusalem

Dr. Josef J. Lador-Lederer, Ministry for Foreign Affairs, Jerusalem

Part One
POPULATION

1 THE JEWISH POPULATION

GROWTH BY ALIYAH. In 1882, at the outset of the First Aliyah, the Jewish population of Erez Israel was c. 24,000, roughly 5% of the total, and about 0.3% of the world Jewish population. Since then there has been an almost continuous flow of *aliyah*, which brought in roughly 1,900,000 persons over a period of 88 years and created Israel's Jewish population of 2,559,000 persons at the end of 1970 —85% of the total of 2,998,000. This large movement may be divided into three distinct periods. The first (a) was during the last years of the Ottoman regime, when immigration totaled 55,000 to 70,000. The average in the years of the First Aliyah (1882–1904) was about 1,000 a year, rising in 1904–14, the period of the Second Aliyah, to about 3,000 a year. During 1882–1914, a little less than 3% of the enormous numbers of Jews who migrated overseas, mainly from Eastern Europe, went to Erez Israel. The second (b) was during the British Mandatory regime (1919–48), when *aliyah* totaled about 485,000, some 16,000 per year on the average. The peaks were in 1925 (34,000—285 immigrants per 1,000 of the country's Jewish population) and 1935 (66,000—206 per 1,000). During this period, *aliyah* constituted some 30% of the total Jewish overseas migration. The third period (c) is after the establishment of the State of Israel, when over 1,450,000 went to the new state between May 1948 and the end of 1972, or some 60,000 per year. Of these, some 687,000 immigrated between 1948 and 1951, the peak being in 1949, when about 240,000 arrived—about 266 per 1,000 of the Jewish population. During this period *aliyah* to Israel was 31.4% of world Jewish migration.

There were considerable fluctuations. Immigration tended, on the whole, to increase from period (a) to (b) and to (c), but within each period the curve of immigration was characterized by a wave-like rise and fall. This may be seen in Diagram 1, which indicates the absolute size of *aliyah* to Palestine and Israel between 1919 and 1972. Waves in immigration were largely due to the interplay of a variety of changing political, economic, social, and ideological factors in the Land of Israel and the various countries of the Diaspora: the influence of Zionism, religion, *halutziyyut*, socialist ideas, and the attraction of the independent Jewish state; the work of Jewish institutions in propagating ideologies, organizing *aliyah*, and helping the newcomers; policies regarding emigration in general, and Jewish emigration in particular, in various countries; changing immigration and absorption policies, as well as political and economic conditions, in the Land of Israel and in other countries absorbing Jewish immigration. In the later Ottoman period, immigrants came from many countries, but in the Mandatory period and since the achievement of independence, practically every Jewish community in the Diaspora was represented. While some attraction to Israel seemed to be generally felt throughout the Jewish world, the intensity of participation, as measured by the yearly rates of immigration to Israel per 1,000 Jewish inhabitants of each country, varied considerably between different parts of the world and for each region in different periods. Table 1 shows the immigration from each of the main Diaspora regions in the various periods between 1919 and 1972, as well as the percentage of immigration from the two regions in each period.

EMIGRATION. The total number of emigrants between 1949 and 1972 may be estimated roughly at 200,000. Emigration *(yeridah)* also displays wavelike fluctuations, which are, to a certain extent, connected with waves of *aliyah*, since the former is, to a certain degree, due to a backflow of the latter. The countries that have most largely attracted emigrants from Israel have been the U.S., France, and Canada.

Diagram 1. Immigration of Jews to Ereẓ Israel (1919–1972)

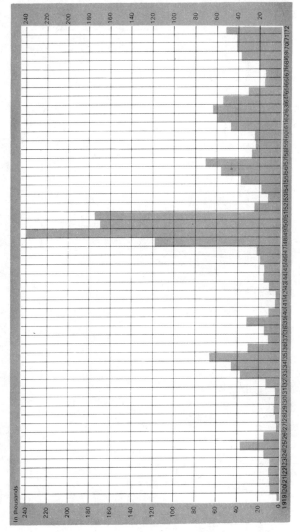

3

Table 1. Jewish Immigrants by Continent of Birth, 1882–1971

Period	Absolute numbers			Percentages		
	Asia and Africa	Europe and America	Total[1]	Asia and Africa	Europe and America	Total
1882–1919			65,000			100.0
1919–May 14, 1948	44,809	385,066	452,158	10.4	89.6	100.0
May 15, 1948–1969	696,670	577,605	1,294,026	54.7	45.3	100.0
May 15, 1948–1951	330,456	334,971	684,201	49.7	50.3	100.0
1952–1954	39,978	11,187	51,193	78.1	21.9	100.0
1955–1957	110,714	49,630	160,961	69.1	30.9	100.0
1958–1960	25,926	46,460	72,393	35.8	64.2	100.0
1961–1964	133,561	86,748	220,323	60.6	39.4	100.0
1965–1968	40,969	31,301	72,276	56.7	43.3	100.0
1969–1971	40,193	75,486	116,484	34.7	65.3	100.0

[1] Including unknown origin.

THE GROWTH OF THE JEWISH POPULATION. The most immediate demographic effects of *aliyah* were as follows. Between 1882 and 1914, the Jewish population increased by 61,000 (from 24,000 to 85,000). Immigration roughly accounted for this increase, while emigration and natural increase probably canceled each other out. Immigration failed to bring a sizable proportion of the Jewish people to the country and did not succeed in reducing the absolute size of the Diaspora (in 1914 only 0.6% of world Jewry lived in the Land of Israel). It did succeed, however, in creating a nucleus of population that was able to survive the expulsions and emigrations, diseases, and famine brought on by World War I (during which the Jewish population was reduced to some 57,000) and served as a basis for further development. During the Mandatory period, the Jewish population of Palestine increased by about 566,000 (from 84,000 according to the census of 1922 to 650,000 on the eve of independence), 71% of the growth being due to immigration and 29% to natural increase. At the end of the period, the Jews of Palestine constituted 5.7% of world Jewry.

During the period between May 1948 and May 1972, the Jewish population increased by some 2,020,000, of which about 62% was due to the immigration balance and 38% to natural increase. At the end of that period, the Jewish population of Israel (2,670,000 persons) constituted over 18% of world Jewry and was exceeded in size only by the world's largest Jewish community, that of the United States. The population increase varied considerably from year to year, largely due to the fluctuations in *aliyah*. Diagram 2 shows yearly estimates of the size of population between 1882 and 1972, by using a logarithmic scale that enables us to evaluate yearly rates of change (according to slope).

COMPOSITION ACCORDING TO PLACE OF BIRTH. Mainly as a consequence of changing sizes and origins of immigration and of differentials of fertility (which will be discussed below), the composition of the Jewish population according to country of birth has changed considerably in the course 5 of time, but has always been extremely heterogeneous. The following are some of the main aspects of this phenomenon:

Proportion of Foreign Born. With increasing rates of immigration, the proportion of persons born abroad increased from approximately 42% of the Jewish population in 1916–18 to 58% in 1931, 64.6% in 1948, and 74.8% at the end of 1951. With the subsequent slowdown of immigration, it decreased and at the end of 1971 stood at 52.8%. The percentage of foreign born is larger at adult ages (95% of those aged 45 and above in 1971). Percentages like these are exceptional, even in countries of large immigration. If conditions in Israel had been different and a considerable part of the immigrant population had not identified itself strongly with the new country, such high percentages of foreign born citizens could have produced a very unstable society, since the majority of the people acquired their cultural background in foreign countries.

Growing Diversification of Foreign Born. Whereas in the last years of the Ottoman period and the first part of the Mandatory period three-quarters of the foreign born were East European (Russians, Poles, Latvians, Lithuanians, and Rumanians, who constituted the backbone of the Zionist enterprise), their proportion in the foreign born population has rapidly decreased in recent years and fell by 1971 to 36%. Central Europeans (Germans, Austrians, Czechoslovakians, Hungarians), once a small minority, reached the considerable proportion of 18.4% in the period of Nazi persecution, but they decreased by 1971 to less than 10%. All Europeans taken together dropped from 84.9% of the foreign born in 1948 to 51% in 1971. On the other hand, those from Asian countries have increased from 12.5% in 1948 to 23% in 1971 (of which over one-third are Iraqis), while the African communities grew from 2.6% to 26% (of which four-fifths came from Morocco, Algeria, and Tunisia) in the same period.

These changes have been accompanied by a deep change
6   in stratification according to ages. While people of

Diagram 2. Jewish population in Erez Israel, 1880–1972 (logarithmic scale)

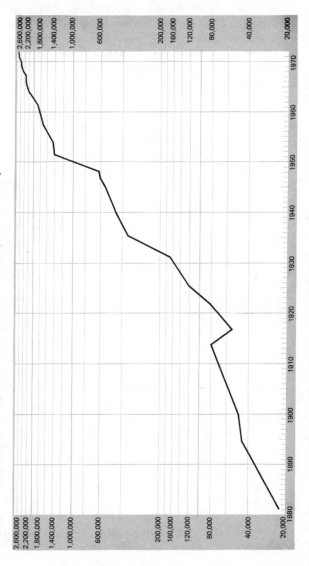

European origin still constitute the majority of the middle aged and the old, the largest group in the younger, productive ages is of Asian and African origin. Among the children, the native-born ("sabras") constitute the majority (see Diagram 3). Considering together those born abroad and their children in 1971 Jews of Asian and African origin constituted 52% of those whose origin was known, while people of European and American origins constituted 48%. The increasing variety in the composition of the Jewish population confronted the State of Israel with very complex problems arising from the need to give everyone a common cultural, political, and linguistic basis and from the lower educational standards of the Asian and African newcomers.

USE OF LANGUAGES AND LITERACY. From statistical data on the use of languages in Israel, collected in the population censuses in 1916–18, 1948, and 1961 and in various sample surveys, two dominant features of the linguistic situation in Israel are obvious: the amazing variety of languages brought by the immigrants from the countries of the Diaspora; and the important role played by the Hebrew language. The revival of Hebrew began at the end of the 19th century, when the majority of immigrants still spoke Yiddish, while the minority generally spoke Ladino or Arabic. At the end of the Ottoman period, Hebrew had succeeded in winning over some 34,000 (40% of the total Jewish population), mainly among the younger generation in "modern" localities (e.g., the new settlements and Tel Aviv). At the close of the Mandatory period, almost all those born in the country were Hebrew speakers, and those born abroad who had arrived before the age of 20 were found to use Hebrew almost to the same extent. At higher ages, it was found that the adoption of Hebrew diminished in speed and intensity in proportion to the age of the immigrants upon arrival. By 1948, 511,000 persons, 75% of the total, used Hebrew as their only or principal language. After the establishment of the State of Israel, the percentage of newcomers who knew Hebrew before arrival was far lower than that of pre-state immigrants, who were largely preselected and ideologically motivated. This decreased the proportion of Hebrew speakers in the period of mass immigration. Subsequently, however, the use of Hebrew again largely increased. Table 2 shows the changes in numbers and proportions of Hebrew speakers in the course of time. In 1966 they constituted some 70% of adults and there is no doubt that they were the overwhelming majority among the children.

Before statehood, the Jewish population was characterized by the low proportion of illiterates. This was due to the high educational level of the immigrants, who were largely of European origin, and to the fact that most of the Jewish population saw to the education of their children, although it was not compulsory at the time. Only among women in the higher age groups was the proportion of illiterates considerable. With mass immigration from Asia and Africa, the proportion of illiterates increased considerably, mainly in the higher age groups and especially among women. Due to the efforts made by the State of Israel in the educational field, the situation has improved in the course of time. Table 3 shows the classification of the Jewish population by number of years of schooling according to continent of birth, sex, age, and period of immigration. The higher standards of those born in Israel, Europe, and America, as compared with those of people born in Asia and Africa, are immediately seen. Table 4 shows the proportion of illiterates among the Jewish population from 1931 to 1971.

INTERMARRIAGE BETWEEN GROUPS OF DIFFERENT ORIGINS. The Central Bureau of Statistics of Israel publishes yearly data on marriages according to country of birth and length of stay in Israel of the bride and groom, and particularly detailed data on this point were collected in the census of 1961. The figures show that the tendency to marry people of the same origin (endogamy) is still very considerable in Israel although the percentage of those marrying out of their own group has risen to 18%.

Table 2. Persons Speaking Hebrew as Only or First Language Among the Jewish Population, 1914–66

	1914	1948	1950	1954	1956	1961	1966
Hebrew-speaking (aged 12 years and over)	34,000[1]	511,000	679,000	861,000	—	1,391,400	—
Rates per 100 of the Jewish population							
Age 2 and over	40.0[1,2]	75.1	60.0	60.9	—	75.3	—
2–14	53.7[1,2]	93.4	80.3	83.9[3]	—	92.8	—
15 and over	25.6[1,2]	69.5	52.0	52.8[4]	58.4[4]	67.4	69.3[4]

[1] Aged one year and over (estimate).
[2] Excluding Jerusalem.
[3] Aged 2–13.
[4] Aged 14 and over.

One significant feature is that endogamy differs from group to group: it is lower in smaller than in larger groups; it is lower among people having higher educational standards and in such places as kibbutzim, where the members are more integrated into the life of the community. The most relevant feature found is that endogamy decreases with the length of stay in Israel. Where both husband and wife are new immigrants, endogamy by place of birth is found to be very high, but it is generally low in marriages between veteran residents and practically vanishes among veterans belonging to smaller groups. This finding and the general decrease of endogamy in the course of time show that there is a clear tendency toward a systematic lowering of marriage barriers between different origin groups.

DISTRIBUTION OF IMMIGRATION AND POPULATION BY SEX AND AGE. Unlike most international migration processes due mainly to economic factors, modern *aliyah* was in general well balanced in regard to sex. Only in very difficult periods, as for instance in the first waves of 1919-23 and among the "illegal" immigrants in the 1940s, did the proportion of men considerably outweigh that of women. Accordingly, the distribution of population by sexes was also generally well balanced and subject only to minor fluctuations: the percentage of males at different times was: 1922—52.3; 1931—50.5; 1936—50.0; 1940—50.5; 1948—51.7; 1961—50.7; 1971—50.2. The age structure of the *aliyah* in the Mandatory period differed from that of the period of independence. Due to selection, the former was extremely abnormal in age distribution; it included a very high proportion of young people and was strongly at variance with the age distribution of the communities of origin (the Jewish population in Europe was largely characterized by a high proportion of old people). In the first phases of the Mandatory period, the Jewish population of Palestine reflected these characteristics and presented a typically strong swelling of the age pyramid in the very young age groups. The high proportion of people in young

Table 4. Proportion of Illiterates Among Jewish Population Aged 14+ (in percentages)

Year	Male	Female	Total
1931	6.7	22.5	14.1
1948	3.2	9.6	6.3
1954	8.2	21.7	15.0
1961	7.2	18.0	12.6
1971	4.4	13.5	9.0

Diagram 3. Jewish population, by age, sex and continent of birth (December 31, 1971)

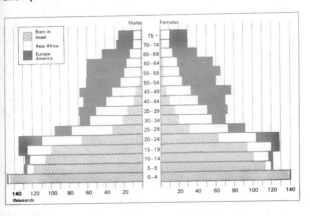

working ages was presumably a considerable asset for the economic, social, and political development of the Zionist enterprise. In the long run, however, the situation was considerably changed by the aging of the young immigrants; the low fertility of the Europeans, then constituting the large majority of the population, which set in motion a general process of aging, and the inadequate influence of the smaller, new immigration waves in rejuvenating the population. The population therefore became more regular in its distribution and lost much of its young character.

13

During the period of statehood, a considerable part of the *aliyah* was nonselective and reflected the structure of the communities of origin. This *aliyah* had a much higher proportion of children, a somewhat higher proportion of old people, and a higher proportion of those in dependent ages to those in working ages. Unlike the immigration of the Mandatory period, it contributed to a leveling-out of the age distribution of the population. It widened the base of the age pyramid and the high fertility of the oriental immigrants checked or offset the aging of the population, particularly that of the population in the working ages. As a consequence of all these processes, the Jewish population of Israel is today more regular in its age distributions than in the past; it is younger than many Western populations, but older than Eastern populations. Due to fluctuation in the number of births in the last decade, the percentage aged 10–19 is higher than the 0–9 age bracket and a much higher percentage than in the following brackets (see Diagram 3).

MARRIAGES, BIRTHS, DEATHS, AND NATURAL INCREASE. The study of the vital statistics of Israel's Jewish population is of interest from many points of view. While it has been established and expanded mainly by immigration, its future development, in the long run, will largely depend on the reproductive capacity of the immigrants and their descendants. Since Israel is a new and small country, the enlarging of its population may be of importance in order to provide a sufficiently large and differentiated basis for its economy and social structure. The demographic situation of the Jews of Israel may be significant in the light of the demography of world Jewry, which emerged from the Holocaust extremely reduced in numbers, and the fact that demographic trends in considerable parts of the Diaspora, such as aging of the population, low fertility rates, and losses due to intermarriage, are producing further population decreases. From a scientific point of view, the analysis of the evolution of marriage habits, fertility, mortality, and health standards among the various groups of the Jewish population in Israel is of interest within the larger framework of modern demographic evolution in general and that of the various branches of world Jewry in particular. Demographic patterns in the Diaspora differ considerably in relation to general environment, cultural development, degrees of religious conservatism, and assimilation of Jews into different social classes. In very broad terms, it appears that in many Asian and African communities the old Jewish customs of universal, early, and endogamous marriage, accompanied by high fertility, still tended to prevail until recently. Mortality rates had begun to fall considerably, creating a comparatively large reproductive force. On the other hand, European Jews, particularly in Central Europe, have in general had comparatively low marriage rates, rather high marriage ages, and generally increasing rates of exogamous marriage. Fertility has decreased (mainly among Central European Jews) to such an extent as in many cases to be well below replacement level, despite the generally favorable age-specific mortality rates among Jews as compared with those of non-Jews in the same countries of Central Europe. The following are some of the main features of the vital statistics of the Jewish population of Israel.

Marriage and Divorce. Marriage in Israel is almost exclusively endogamous within the Jewish community. (In regard to intermarriage between different groups of the Jewish population, see above.) Marriage is almost universal in all groups of the Jewish population: the percentage of single persons at the end of the fertility period is generally small. Only recently has there been some tendency toward increased rates of celibacy among Jewish women. In addition, the generally favorable age structure and the influx of unmarried immigrants—who often appear to postpone marriage before immigration and are afterward eager to marry—have contributed to generally high crude marriage rates among the Jewish population in Israel during periods of heavy immigration. Average age of Israel brides at first marriage is about 22, which is low by European standards, but higher than that found in oriental countries. Age at marriage is lower for Asian-African communities, such as Yemenites and Moroccans, but for some of them the marriage age is higher in Israel than it was in their countries of origin, while it seems likely that among many European communities an opposite trend has taken place. While divorce is rather frequent, though perhaps somewhat on the decrease, remarriage of divorced and widowed persons is also comparatively frequent. On the whole, marriage mores in Israel appear to have a favorable influence on fertility—certainly more so than those of European Diaspora Jews.

Fertility. Patterns of fertility differ among various Jewish population groups far more than marriage patterns. Fertility may be indicated by the average number of children born per woman in the entire reproductive period—about 15–49 (it must be remembered that an average of more than two children per couple is necessary for ensuring adequate reproduction, as some children die before reaching maturity). From the scanty statistical material available it appears that at the beginning of the 20th century, Jews in the Land of Israel still had a rather high fertility. However, in the 1920s and 1930s fertility fell rapidly (1927–29, 3.57 children per woman; 1935–38, 2.54; 1939–42, 2.33).This decrease was due to the rapid spread of birth control (by contraception and abortion), mainly among the Jews of European origin, who constituted the great majority of the Jewish population. Limitation of births was particularly strong in periods of political or economic difficulties, like that of the Arab riots (1936–39) and the beginning of World War II. In the late 1940s there was a "baby boom" among European Jews in Palestine, comparable with that which developed at the time in many Western countries; many of the births may be considered as "delayed" from previous bad times.

In 1949–50 the fertility of European Jews (see Diagram 4) reached the top level of 3.24. Later, however, it declined again (1960–63, 2.4; 1965, 2.6; 1967, probably in connection with the recession, again 2.4). In 1968, after the

Diagram 4. Total fertility rates (1948—1971)

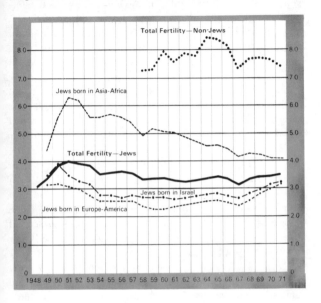

Table 5. Total Fertility of Jewish Women, 1965–68

Type of settlement	All women	Born in Israel	Born in Asia or Africa	Born in Europe or America
Jerusalem	3.6	3.3	4.3	3.2
Tel Aviv	2.3	1.9	3.3	1.6
Haifa	2.6	2.5	3.7	2.4
Other towns	3.5	3.0	4.4	2.7
Urban settlements	4.0	3.1	4.8	2.3
Villages	4.9	3.2	6.5	2.7
Moshavim	4.8	3.3	4.5	2.5
Kibbutzim	3.0	3.3	3.0	3.0
Total	3.4	2.8	4.5	2.4

17

recession, it began to increase reaching 3.14 in 1971, partly due to a change in public opinion in regard to the fertility problem. However, in general, the fertility of European Jews in Israel is not much higher than the minimum reproduction level. Fertility differentials are not large among European Jews. The main factors of differentiation are religious outlook (among religious women, particularly those observing the injunction of the *mikveh* or ritual bath, there is considerably higher fertility and less contraception and induced abortion than among others): work (working women have fewer children than others); place of residence (women in Tel Aviv and Haifa have lower fertility than in other towns), the highest fertility being found in Jerusalem, with its large proportion of religious people, and the kibbutzim (see Table 5): education (the higher the education, the lower the fertility—see Table 6); length of stay (the veteran settlers and the second generation have a somewhat higher fertility than new immigrants—see Table 7).

Jews of Afro-Asian origin somewhat reduced their fertility during the Mandatory period, mainly in places and among strata having more contact with European Jews. However, their average fertility remained higher than that of European Jews. Mass immigration brought many large families not accustomed to birth control, which considerably increased the fertility of Asian-African Jews. However, in the course of time, birth control spread among them, especially among the younger generation. Differences in fertility in this group are very large; as among the Europeans, religious outlook and work play some part, but the main differentiations are related to length of stay in the country, education, and place of residence. In the higher educational levels and in certain places, such as the kibbutzim, the differences by origin almost disappear, while women living in more secluded places, like the moshavim, have a very high fertility rate.

On the whole, the fertility of people of Asian or African origin is still rather high, and due to their large proportion

demographic problems has recently been established in the Prime Minister's Office. One of the problems facing the center is the fact that the burden of child rearing is very unevenly divided: families in poor economic and cultural conditions have considerably more children than others.

Mortality. Before World War II health conditions were favorably affected by the fact that most of the immigrants came from Europe, where the Jews, in general, had lower age-specific mortality rates than non-Jews in the same localities, and that candidates for *aliyah* were generally selected. On the other hand, the change in environment, the transition to harder work, and the presence of an Arab majority with a high mortality rate may have been adverse factors. Since World War II further adverse factors have been operative, i.e., the mass immigration of people who underwent persecution and suffered in the concentration camps and of unselected oriental immigrants with low health standards. Large-scale medical services, voluntary health insurance for the majority of the population, an exceptionally high proportion of physicians in the population, preventive services, and supervision of most mothers and children have acted as very favorable factors throughout the Mandatory and statehood periods. On the whole, the double challenge of bringing European immigrants to a prevalently oriental country (up to 1948) and bringing oriental immigrants to a prevalently European country (after 1948) has been met with considerable success. Life expectancy has steadily increased—from 54 in 1926 to 72 in 1971—and mortality has decreased at all age levels, especially among children and young people. The infant mortality rate, which in 1924 was ranked in the middle of the world list, decreased at so rapid a pace that in 1947 it was lower than that of 89 countries and higher only than that of four and had reached the record low level of 29.2 per 1,000; with mass immigration, it rose again to 51.7 per 1,000 in 1949, but afterward began to drop again and stood at 18.6 per 1,000 in 1971. The wide gulf between the mortality of children of Asian and African immigrants and that of children of European origin has been bridged to a considerable extent, and the life expectancies of these two main groups of population are now quite close.

NATURAL INCREASE. Yearly rates of excess of births over deaths per 1,000 population are shown for the period between 1923 and 1969 by Diagram 5.

GEOGRAPHICAL DISTRIBUTION OF THE POPULATION. One of the most well-known characteristics of modern Israel is the "return to the soil"—the establishment of hundreds of villages and the creation of a rural population, which are almost unknown in the Diaspora. Nevertheless, the Jewish population has been largely urban. With increasing mechanization and efficiency in Jewish agriculture, the proportion of people living on the land has been decreasing (17.3% in 1959; 10.5% in 1971). Moreover, the share of the rural population in moshavot and moshavim has tended to increase, while that in the kibbutzim has decreased. Due to industrial development in urban areas the two large conurbations of Tel Aviv and Haifa contained, respectively, 29.2% and 11.3% of the total Jewish population at the end of 1971. Great efforts have been made by the authorities to prevent the over-rapid development of these areas and the over-concentration of the population in the coastal strip. This has been done by policies designed to increase the rural population, particularly in border areas, and by establishing "development towns" (mainly in the southern and northern districts). Some of the main developments in the geographical distribution of the population are shown in Table 8, which indicates the proportion of Jewish population by size of settlement in 1953 and 1971 and the proportion of settlements of each size; Table 9, which shows the changes in the percentages of the population living in each type of settlement between 1945 and 1971; Table 10, showing the proportion of Jewish population living in each sub-district; Map 1 showing the distribution of Jewish urban settlements in 1972; and Map 2, showing density of population by sub-district in 1972.

Diagram 5. Natural increase rates per 1,000 population (1923—1969)

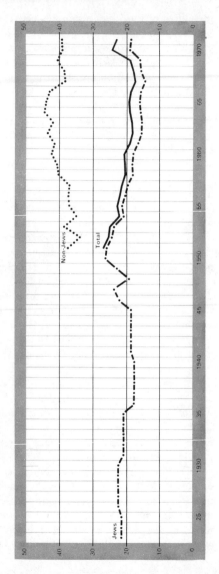

Table 8. Population (in thousands) and Settlements by Size of Settlement (1953–71)

Size of settlement	1953 Settlements[1]	1953 Population	1971 Settlements[1]	1971 Population	1953 Population	1971 Population
	Absolute Numbers				Percentages	
0—99	94	5.0	47	2.2	0.1	0.1
100—199	148	23.0	94	15.0	0.5	0.5
200—499	362	116.5	423	137.6	4.9	4.4
500—999	99	65.1	162	102.3	3.4	3.3
1,000—1,999	46	65.2	32	45.9	1.7	1.5
2,000—4,999	57	178.0	54	180.9	6.3	5.8
5,000—9,000	20	139.9	23	164.3	5.1	5.3
10,000—19,999	9	135.7	24	339.9	10.0	11.0
20,000—49,999	10	269.5	15	493.8	17.2	16.0
50,000 +	3	651.5	11	1,567.7	49.5	50.7
Living outside settlements	—	20.1	—	3.9	0.1	0.1
Bedouin tribes	3	20.1		40.1	1.2	1.3
Total	848	1,669.4	885	3,095.1[2]	100.0	100.0

[1] The number of settlements does not include Bedouin tribes, numbering 44 at the end of 1971.

[2] Including Israeli residents in the Administered Territories.

23

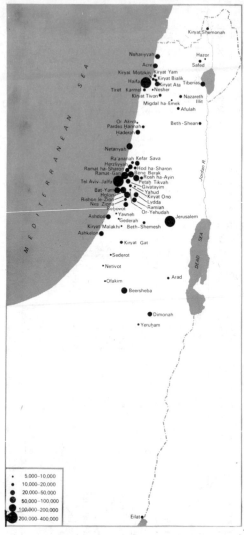

Map 1. Settlements with Jewish population numbering over 5,000.

The distribution of the population is marked by the following characteristics. Within the extremely irregular boundaries of Israel (within the 1949 armistice demarcation lines), the population is highly concentrated in certain areas, such as the Coastal Plain, and there is a very low density in the southern areas, which are largely desert. However, in the course of time there has been some tendency to modify these characteristics. The actual distribution has become a little less concentrated than it was in 1948. Population dispersal has increased, and the center of gravity has shifted considerably to the south (toward the Tel Aviv conurbation and southern development towns and zones). These changes have been largely due to the policy of attracting new immigrants to the development zones on the periphery of the country by providing housing and labor facilities in those regions. This policy has had a particularly strong effect on new immigrants from Asia and Africa.

These developments have been strengthened by the fact that there are more of the more prolific elements in the peripheral zones, while a higher proportion of the less fertile sections of the population and the older age groups is to be found in the central areas. Natural increase is

Table 9. Jewish Population by Type of Settlement (1945–71)

	1945	1948	1954	1961	1971
Urban population	84.6	83.9	76.1	84.6	89.5
Towns	64.3	64.4	64.5	69.7	73.4
Urban settlements	20.3	19.5	11.6	14.9	16.1
Rural Population	15.4	16.1	23.9	15.4	10.5
Villages	3.2	3.5	4.0	4.5	1.7
Moshavim	5.2	4.4	7.3	6.4	4.9
Kibbutzim	6.3	7.9	5.0	4.0	3.3
Other	0.7	0.3	7.6[1]	0.5	0.6
Total	100.0	100.0	100.0	100.0	100.0

Including transit immigrant centers.

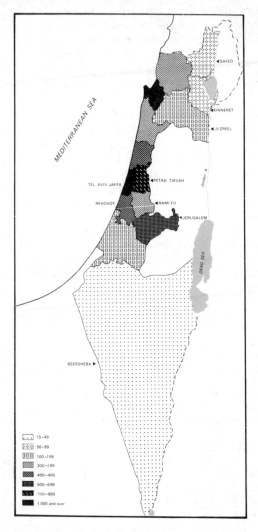

MAP LABELS: MEDITERRANEAN SEA, SAFED, KINNERET, JEZREEL, TEL AVIV-JAFFA, PETAH TIKVAH, REHOVOT, RAMLEH, JERUSALEM, Jordan R., DEAD SEA, BEERSHEBA

Legend:
- 10–49
- 50–99
- 100–199
- 200–299
- 400–499
- 500–699
- 700–999
- 1.000 and over

Map 2. Israel population density per sq. km. by sub-district

District and Sub-District	Population (Thousands)			Percentages		
	Nov. 8, 1948	May 22, 1961	Dec. 31, 1971	Nov. 8, 1948	May 22, 1961	Dec. 31, 1971
Jerusalem district	84.2	187.7	252.8	12.0	9.7	9.6
Northern district	53.4	194.3	254.1	7.6	10.0	9.7
Safed sub-district	8.9	42.6	51.7	1.3	2.2	2.0
Kinneret sub-district	14.4	35.4	38.7	2.1	1.8	1.5
Jezreel sub-district	24.1	66.6	92.2	3.4	3.4	3.5
Acre sub-district	6.0	49.7	71.5	0.8	2.6	2.7
Haifa district	147.7	322.3	400.7	21.1	16.7	15.2
Central district	106.2	380.1	513.6	15.2	19.7	19.4
Sharon sub-district	26.5	85.1	11.2	3.8	4.4	4.2
Petah Tikvah sub-district	45.9	131.8	18.30	6.6	6.8	6.9
Ramleh sub-district	1.8	63.9	80.0	0.2	3.3	3.0
Rehovot sub-district	32.0	99.3	139.3	4.6	5.2	5.3
Tel Aviv district	302.1	692.6	896.4	43.2	35.9	34.0
Southern district	6.0	155.3	317.5	0.9	8.0	12.1
Ashkelon sub-district	4.8	76.4	149.0	0.7	3.9	5.7
Beersheba sub-district	1.2	78.9	168.5	0.2	4.1	6.4
Not known	17.1	—	—			
Total	716.7	1,932.3	2,636.6[2]	100.0	100.0	100.0

[1] According to the present boundaries of the sub-districts.   [2] Including Israel residents in the Administered Territories.

therefore higher in peripheral zones and lower in the center, which increases population dispersal. These developments are offset, to some extent, by the effects of internal migration, as recent immigrants move mainly from the periphery to the center. Since the settlement of new immigrants in development areas has been the main factor in population dispersal, the latter has increased more in the periods of considerable immigration.

As new immigrants in the more peripheral areas have been largely of African and Asian origin, there has been a certain tendency toward regionalization. The immigrants of European origin, especially the veterans, are more concentrated in the large conurbations and the older settlements of the Coastal Plain, the Jezreel Valley, etc., while there is a higher proportion of people of African-Asian origin in the southern and northern regions. This regionalization explains the peculiar distribution of the population according to social, economic, and cultural characteristics (such as concentration of veteran immigrants in the central part of the country and dispersion of more recently arrived persons over more peripheral regions), higher educational standards and better economic conditions along the Mediterranean coast, and so on.

2 JEWISH COMMUNITIES ("EDOT")

A large number of Jews who immigrated to Erez Israel from a particular geographical region, country, or sometimes town or district often brought with them a characteristic cultural heritage, comprising language (in some cases specifically Jewish, like Yiddish, Ladino, Judeo-Arabic, Judeo-Persian, Georgian, or Kurdish Aramaic), religious rites and customs, habits, and traditions. They are sometimes referred to, figuratively, as modern "tribes" *(shevatim)*. Members of such a group, known as an *edah* (pl. *edot*), usually established their own synagogues, burial societies (see *ḥevra kaddisha*), and mutual aid or charitable organizations, built their own quarters or (in modern times) settled in the same villages, and tended to support each other in local or, to a smaller extent, national politics. The term *edot* often applies specifically to those groups of immigrants who came from, or trace their origin to the Islamic countries ("oriental" immigrants). The *edot* preserved their identity, to a greater or lesser extent, for several generations, their members tending to marry within the *edah,* and the tensions between them were of some importance in the history of the *yishuv* and the State of Israel (see Intercommunal Problems below). There are no accurate statistics on the sizes of the various *edot,* as census figures specify only countries of origin and language groups, which are not identical with community membership.

Communal separatism is particularly recognizable in the composition of the populations of neighborhoods and various streets in Jerusalem, in which about 100 quarters were founded up to the establishment of the State of

Israel—most of them on a communal basis—and also in greater Tel Aviv, Haifa, and some other towns. The attempt to mix various communities in the new-immigrant moshavim after the creation of the State of Israel was generally unsuccessful. It was abandoned in the 1950s, after which most of the new settlements were established on a more-or-less homogeneous basis from the point of view of origin and social mores. In the kibbutzim the percentage of non-Ashkenazim is small, but in many of them youth groups composed of immigrants from Asia and Africa have been successfully absorbed.

THE ASHKENAZI COMMUNITY. This is the largest and, socially, politically, and economically, the most important and influential community in the country. The Ashkenazim consist of Jews of European origin and their descendants, including most of North and South American Jewry. Most Ashkenazi families spoke—or at least understood—Yiddish at some point in their history. Ashkenazim first went to Erez Israel as individuals or as families from the 13th century onward, and, at the latest by the middle of the 15th century, founded their own community in Jerusalem. In the 18th century it numbered a few hundred souls, but ceased to exist, temporarily, after the first quarter of the century. In Safed, however, there was an Ashkenazi community from the 16th century, and it grew particularly after the ḥasidic immigration in 1777. Some of the newcomers moved to Tiberias, and it was from those two towns that the Ashkenazi community in Jerusalem was revived. In 1816 the *Perushim,* the opponents of the Ḥasidim, organized their own community in Jerusalem.

According to the census held in 1839 in Erez Israel, the number of Ashkenazim settled in the country was 1,714—26.2% of the total Jewish population. In the next 75 years, until the outbreak of World War I, when the Jewish population grew to about 85,000, most of the immigrants who created the "old *yishuv*" were Ashkenazim. In 1876/77 they numbered 6,800 in Jerusalem—43% of the city's Jewish population; two-thirds of them were *Perushim* and the rest

Eastern European immigrants arriving in Israel.

Ḥasidim. By the time of the First Aliyah (1882), they constituted half of the 25,000 Jews in the country, and for many years afterward the proportion of Ashkenazim among the immigrants was on the increase. It is estimated that in 1895 they numbered 25,800—63% of the 40,700 Jews; in Jerusalem they constituted 15,000 out of 28,000 Jews, in Safed 4,500 out of 6,600, in Tiberias 1,600 out of 3,200, and in Jaffa 1,700 out of 3,000. The overwhelming majority of the 2,200 Jews in the new agricultural settlements were Ashkenazim.

According to the 1916–18 census, Ashkenazim accounted for 60% of the 56,700 Jews left in the country after the hardships of World War I. They constituted the majority (about 85%) of the immigrants from the end of the war until the creation of the State of Israel (1948). At the time of the declaration of the state, more than 80% of the 650,000 Jews in Israel were Ashkenazim, but since then their proportion of the total population has been steadily on the decrease, due to the increased immigration from Asian and African countries and the comparatively low Ashkenazi birth rate. **31**

Train with Polish refugee children arriving via Teheran, February 1943. At left are Palestinian children welcoming them. Courtesy Keren Hayesod, United Israel Appeal, Jerusalem.

In the 1961 census, community of origin was not recorded, but on the basis of the information on country of origin and father's country of origin, it may be estimated that Ashkenazim constituted 52.5% of the population; by 1965 they had declined to less than half the total.

In 1948, 46.8% of the Jews speaking foreign languages spoke Yiddish as their sole language or as the first after Hebrew. By 1961 the proportion had decreased to 22.7% (273,615 persons). Other languages spoken by Ashkenazim were: German (73,195), Rumanian (69,945), Polish (51,760), English (46,615), Hungarian (43,245), Russian (21,255), Czech and Slovak (4,095), Dutch and Flemish (1,530); smaller groups spoke French, Spanish, Serb, Bulgarian, Portuguese, Danish, and Swedish.

THE SEPHARDI COMMUNITY. The Sephardim in the strict sense of the term, that is, those speaking Ladino[1] or their descendants, have the longest continuous history in the country, the origin of the community dating back to the 15th or early 16th century. It assimilated the Portuguese Jews, expelled a decade or two earlier, who are mentioned by the 16th-century travelers, the remnants of the Byzantine Jews, and, at a later period, the Musta‘rabs (Arabic-speaking Jews) and Jews from other communities, including some Ashkenazim. Individual Jews of Spanish origin were living in Ereẓ Israel as far back as the 11th century, but there was little immigration in medieval times, and, moreover, few of the Jews expelled from Spain and Portugal at the end of the 15th century made their way to Ereẓ Israel because of the insecure conditions in the country. By the end of the 15th century, however, there were many Sephardim in Safed and in 1509 there was a separate Sephardi community in Jerusalem. The flow of immigration increased after the Ottoman conquest, the immigrants receiving aid from their brethren who had settled in Turkey. The Sephardi community of the 16th century developed a flourishing social and cultural life; it included many famous talmudic scholars and served as a center for learning for the whole of the

[1] Judeo-Spanish

Diaspora. In the census of 1839 Sephardim were incorporated with the Jews from the oriental communities, but on the basis of the country of origin of Jews born abroad, it can be estimated that at least half of the total were Sephardim. With the creation of the post of *hakham bashi* (chief rabbi) of Jerusalem by the Ottoman authorities in 1842, this honored post was always occupied by a Sephardi.

During the 19th century, there were no organized groups of Sephardi immigrants, but there was increased Sephardi immigration in some years, e.g., after the liberation of Greece in 1829 and of Bulgaria in 1878. By 1877 there were 5,970 Sephardim (not including the Maghrebis—immigrants from North Africa) in Jerusalem, and it appears that 5,500 of this number, 40% of the Jewish population of the city, were descendants of exiles from Spain. Most of them were employed in various branches of commerce, but a few families from Bulgaria settled on the land at Hartuv. There was little Sephardi immigration in the 20th century until 1948, and the Sephardim, therefore, did not found their own quarters in Jerusalem like the other communities. Until 1920, however, when the Ashkenazi chief rabbinate was established, it was the *hakham bashi* (also styled *rishon le-Zion*) who was the official religious head of the entire Jewish community. In Jerusalem, the Sephardi community maintained its own community council and *hevra kaddisha*. In the 1961 census, 63,000 persons, including some Ashkenazim from South America, entered "Spanish" as their sole or second language; 31,535 spoke Bulgarian; 7,750 Turkish (young people who had been educated in state schools in their country of origin); and 2,635 Greek.

THE ITALIAN COMMUNITY. Visitors and individual settlers came from Italy in all periods and Italian Jews in Jerusalem are mentioned until close to 1870. It was only after Mussolini's anti-Jewish measures in 1938, however, that significant numbers settled in Palestine, when about 500 Italian Jews, including a high proportion of scientists and technological experts, arrived. A number of synagogues were fitted out with arks of the Law scrolls and other furnishings transferred from disused synagogues in Italy. According to the 1961 census, 5,300 persons spoke Italian, 1,650 as their first or only language. This figure, however, may have included some Jews from Libya (Tripolitania).

JEWS FROM THE MAGHREB. This term includes all the Jews of North Africa, with the exception of Egypt. Jews from the Maghreb had come to Erez Israel as far back as the 11th century, though mostly as individuals, and in 1218 a Maghrebi community was in existence in Jerusalem. Immigration increased after the defeat of the crusaders, and individual Maghrebi Jews settled in Jerusalem throughout the centuries. In 1509 there was a Maghreb community in Safed as well. From the second third of the 19th century onward, immigration from the area increased, mostly from Morocco, with smaller numbers from Tunisia. For a time there was also immigration from Algeria, but it dwindled with the spread of French culture in that country. Jews from these countries were the founders of the Jewish communities in Jaffa, where 18% were of Maghreb origin in 1905, and in Haifa. In the first half of the 20th century there was a decline in the proportion of educated and professional men among the immigrants from this area. Before World War I there were an estimated 2,000 Maghreb Jews in Jerusalem. During the British Mandate period there was hardly any immigration to Palestine from these countries, but since the middle 1950s Jews from the Maghreb have constituted a high proportion of the immigrants. The 1961 census recorded 157,680 Jews who were born or whose parents were born in Morocco, 57,530 from Algeria and Tunisia, and 48,080 from Libya, almost the entire Jewish community of which settled in Israel. Many of them were among the 122,250 persons who in 1961 recorded Arabic as their first or only language. Of the 24,300 who spoke only, or mainly, French, the majority were from Algeria and Tunisia; the majority of the 43,000 who gave it as their second language were Moroccan. Many Jews from Libya also spoke Italian. Some Berber-speaking Jews from the Atlas

Immigrants en route from Casablanca, 1950s. Courtesy Jewish Agency, Jerusalem.

mountains settled in the Adullam region. The Maghreb community in Jerusalem has its own *ḥevra kaddisha.*

IRAQI (BABYLONIAN) JEWS. It is customary nowadays to describe the Arabic-speaking Jews from southern and central Iraq, and even from parts of northern Iraq (Mosul), as "Iraqis," but their community and *ḥevra kaddisha* in Jerusalem, unlike that in Ramat Gan, are still called "Bavlim"—Babylonians. Until the middle of the 19th century, very few immigrants came from that part of the world because of the long and dangerous journey. With the introduction of steamships, which traveled down the Tigris River through the Persian Gulf and the Red Sea to Ereẓ Israel, immigration from Iraq increased. In the 30 years preceding World War I, there was a small community of Iraqi Jews with three synagogues which printed its own books in Hebrew with translation in Iraqi Jewish Arabic and booklets in the same dialect. In 1916 the community had 371 members. Between the two world wars, the Zionist idea flourished in Baghdad and Hebrew teachers were sent there from Palestine, but they were expelled in 1935 with the growth of the Arab national movement. Their ties with the *yishuv* were renewed during World War II, when many Jews served in the British forces in Iraq or went there to help in the transfer of refugees from the U.S.S.R. and Persia. In 1950 following a special immigration law almost the entire Jewish community was forced to leave, thus virtually liquidating the oldest Jewish community outside Israel. In the 1961 census, 184,130 Jews were registered as of Iraqi origin, among them 2,000–3,000 of Kurdish extraction (see below: Kurds). The Iraqi community in Israel includes people from all strata of society and of all educational levels.

JEWS FROM ALEPPO. Throughout the ages, there had been immigration from Aleppo, which was an important Jewish economic and scholastic center. Most of the immigrants, however, assimilated with the Mustaᶜrabs and later with the Sephardim. In 1862 they founded the synagogue of Aram Zoba (Aleppo) in the Old City of Jerusalem, and by 1908 eight more synagogues had been founded in the quarters outside the Old City. The second and third generations of the Aleppo community included large numbers of traders and distinguished scholars. It is difficult to estimate the number of Jews of Aleppan origin. In the 1961 census they were recorded with the 28,200 immigrants from the other cities of Syria and Lebanon.

YEMENITES. Few Jews from Yemen settled in Erez Israel before the 19th century. Noteworthy among them were R. Solomon Adani in the 16th century and R. Shalom Sharabi in the 18th. The travels of R. Jacob Saphir and the orientalist Joseph Halevy in Yemen may have stimulated Yemenite Jews to go to Erez Israel, and in 1882 a few hundred of them joined together and made their way to Jerusalem with only the clothes on their backs. The help extended to them by the Jews of Jerusalem and the Diaspora did little to alleviate their distress. In 1885 Ashkenazim active in the community purchased a tract of land for them in the village of Silwān, south of Jeru- 37 salem, which was extended over the years. In 1908 it contained five synagogues, as the Yemenites in Ereẓ Israel split into two groups: one following the traditional Yemenite *(Baladī)* version of the prayers, which goes back to the Middle Ages, and the other following the "Syrian" *(Shāmī)* rite, that of the Sephardi communities (with many deviations). In addition, special houses of prayer had to be established for the devotees of the Zohar and the Kabbalah and their opponents (the "Dor De'ah"); the Yemenites also had prayer houses in the Old City and 14 small ones in the poorer quarters of Jerusalem outside the walls. The Yemenites' reputation as diligent farm workers suggested the idea of bringing more of them to Ereẓ Israel and the plan succeeded through the efforts of Shemuel Yavnieli, an emissary of the Palestine Office in Jaffa. Three convoys arrived in 1908/09 and settled in the large moshavot of Judea and Samaria, where special neighborhoods were established for them.

The Yemenite Jews separated themselves from the Sephardim and established a separate community with a rabbi, *bet din,* ritual slaughter facilities, and cemetery plots of their own. They were outstanding for the level of their religious Jewish scholarship and their devotion to the Torah. In spite of the smallness of the community, they printed their special prayer book *(tiktāl),* R. Saadiah Gaon's translation of the Pentateuch *(Sharḥ),* and other religious books. They still preserve their traditional pronunciation and melodies in prayer and the reading of the Torah (together with the Aramaic Targum), the *haftarot,* and the Five Scrolls.

In 1916 it was estimated that there were 4,058 Yemenites in Palestine: 1,636 in Jerusalem, 859 in Jaffa, 943 in the moshavot in Judea and 620 in Samaria and Galilee. Almost all the Jews in Yemen were transferred to Israel during "Operation Magic Carpet" (1949–50), and many were absorbed in villages and development towns. In the 1961 census close to 120,000 people born in Yemen and Aden, or whose fathers were born there, were registered; at the end of 1965 the estimated Yemenite population of Israel was 150,000. The veteran members of the community have risen in the social scale and their characteristic leanness has gradually disappeared with the improvement of nutritional standards (although the adoption of the Israel diet has

Immigrants from Aden, 1949. Courtesy Jewish National Fund, Jerusalem.

made them susceptible to certain illnesses from which they were previously virtually immune).

GEORGIANS (*Gurjim* or *Geruzim*). The first Jews from Georgia (Heb. *Geruzyah*—now in the U.S.S.R.), arrived in Erez Israel in about 1860, after the development of steamboat transportation. By 1862 they had established a house of prayer in the Old City of Jerusalem and before 1914 had five more in their quarters near the Damascus Gate (abandoned in the riots of 1929) and in the Simeon ha-Zaddik quarter in the north of the city. After the disturbances of 1936 they dispersed throughout Jerusalem. They spoke Georgian in the Diaspora and are the only oriental Jewish community that did not employ Hebrew letters to write their vernacular. No scholars from Georgia settled in Erez Israel, but once in the country some members of the community turned to the study of the Torah. The Georgians succeeded in commerce, and some grew wealthy. In 1916 there were 420 Georgian Jews in Jerusalem and 19 in Jaffa. As Russian nationals they were forced to leave the country during World War I, but after the war most of them returned. Since 1916 they have not been registered as a special community in the censuses.

Since the establishment of the State of Israel, their language had been growing extinct and their unity as a community had been disintegrating, but after the Six-Day War there was a reawakening of devotion to Israel among Georgian Jews. The dramatic signed letter from 18 Georgian Jewish families to Prime Minister Golda Meir in November 1969, demanding the right to settle in Israel, was a landmark in Soviet Jewry's struggle for *aliyah*. In 1971 and 1972, some 15,000 Jews from Georgia arrived. They were religiously Orthodox and required special treatment in view of their desire to settle in closely knit groups and the fact that most of them spoke no language but their native Georgian. Several groups settled in Lydda, Ashdod, Kiryat Malakhi, and other places.

PERSIANS. It appears that the first Persian-speaking Jews who settled in Jerusalem after the destruction of the Second

Temple were Karaites, who came in the middle of the ninth century. In 1839 14 Persians were registered in Safed. In about 1815 the *Perushim* in Jerusalem were said to have hired an *'Ajami* ("foreigner" in Arabic, i.e., a Persian) to complete their *minyan*. The first Persian house of prayer in Jerusalem was founded in 1895 in the Shevet Zedek quarter (near Maḥaneh Yehudah) and eight more were established through 1908. In the same year, 80 Persian pupils studied in two *talmud torah* schools in Jerusalem. In 1916 120 Persians were registered in the city: it appears that many more of them registered as Sephardim. Before the end of the 19th century Jews came to Erez Israel from Isfahan and, especially, Meshed, and the numbers grew after the establishment of the State of Israel. The Jews from Meshed, who were descendants of forced converts to Islam, were known as *Jadīd al-Islām* "neo-Muslims." They were the richest of the Persian community and created international commercial ties in the export of rugs. Since the Ottoman period they have had two synagogues in the Bukharan quarter of Jerusalem and others lived in some of the poorer quarters. During the Mandate and after the establishment of the state, the educated and affluent among them scattered throughout the new quarters of the city. Two communities, the "Persian" and the "Iranian," were registered during the Mandate period, because of an internal dispute, but this distinction later disappeared. Jews from Afghanistan are also counted among the Persians. The 1961 census counted about 60,000 people of Iranian extraction, 22,516 of whom were born in the country. More than 37,000 of them spoke Persian, and for 16,370 it was their only tongue or their first language after Hebrew.

BUKHARANS. This term is used to denote Jews who speak a Persian dialect and whose land of origin is the present Soviet Republic of Uzbekistan. In 1827 the first Bukharans set out for Erez Israel and reached Baghdad, but it is not known if any of them actually arrived in Erez Israel. After Bukhara was conquered by the Russians, individual Bukharans settled in Erez Israel in 1868 and in the middle   41

Bukharan synagogue in Jerusalem. Photo Zev Radovan, Jerusalem.

of the 1870s a number of Bukharan families were living in Jerusalem. Following R. Yaakov Meir's journey to Bukhara in 1882 as an emissary for charitable institutions, hundreds of affluent families settled in Erez Israel, and in 1892 they established a quarter in Jerusalem ("Street of the Bukharans"), which was uncommonly spacious and elegant for the period. In most of the families some of the members kept up their businesses in Bukhara while others lived in Jerusalem and were supported by the profits of the family business (in some instances, the members abroad and in Erez Israel changed places every few years). In 1908 the Bukharans had 17 beautiful synagogues in Jerusalem, and the number had grown by 1914. During this period the affluent members of the community had books printed in their native language and in Persian, which they understood. During World War I some of the Bukharans fled and some remained in a state of poverty and deprivation. The Communist authorities in Uzbekistan confiscated the property of the Jews, and those who succeeded in returning to Erez Israel supported themselves by renting out houses.

In the census of 1961, 2,300 people were registered as "Bukharan"-speaking, but only 660 entered the language as their only or first tongue. In 1971 and 1972 a new *aliyah* started from Soviet Bukhara.

DAGESTANIS. A few hundred Jews from Dagestan, who speak Tat (an Iranian dialect), settled in Erez Israel at the beginning of the 20th century: some in Be'er Ya'akov, which was established by them, and some in Jerusalem. Their courage and command of weapons won them a reputation in Erez Israel and in the Diaspora, and some of them were outstanding in Ha-Shomer.[2] As Russian nationals they were also affected by the expulsion at the outbreak of World War I, but some of them returned during the Mandate period, especially to Tel Aviv, where they lived in the "Caucasian" Quarter. Those born in Erez Israel do not speak the language used by the community in the Diaspora.

CRIMCHAKS. The Crimchaks are Rabbanites (in contra-distinction to the Karaites) from the Crimea who speak "Judeo-Tatar." For some time before 1915 they had a small community in Jerusalem and published books and pamphlets in their native tongue, apparently for export. They also departed during World War I and in 1916 there was only one family left. After the war a few returned and established their own synagogue in Tel Aviv.

KURDS. During the 19th century, individuals from the cities and townships of Kurdistan settled in Erez Israel, and at the beginning of the 20th century, a few hundred more followed. Their language, mistakenly called "Kurd-ish," is a modern Eastern Aramaic and they consequently called themselves Targum Jews. They lived in some of the poorer quarters in western Jerusalem in huts construct-ed from discarded kerosene cans, boards, and the like (known as the "Tin Quarter," now called Shevet Zedek), although stone houses were later constructed. In 1908 they built their own synagogue. Physically powerful and trained for physical labor over the generations, the Kurds are still

[2]The early Erez Israel defense organization

dominant among the porters in the large cities. Some of them helped the Europeans of the Second Aliyah to establish settlements in Lower Galilee. The conquest of Iraq by the British liberated the Jews in the mountains of Kurdistan from their subservience to local feudal lords, but few of them left their villages. With the call to settle in Israel in 1951, however, they abandoned their property and moved to Israel *en masse*. Most of them settled on the land and their youth adjusted to the Israel way of life.

In 1916 174 Kurds were registered in Jerusalem and 222 in Galilee (together with the Urfalis, see below). In 1916, 8,560 Kurdish-speaking residents were recorded, and 3,920 entered Kurdish as their only language or first language after Hebrew. The Kurds have their own *ḥevra kaddisha* in Jerusalem.

Close to the Kurds from the point of view of language (but not in life style) are the Jews of Persian Azerbaijan, most of whom settled in Erez Israel after World War I (immigrating via various countries) and established synagogues in Jerusalem, Tel Aviv, and other places. Exact

Immigrants from Kurdistan, 1950s. Courtesy Jewish National Fund, Jerusalem. Photo Malafsky, Jerusalem.

population figures are not to be had. Most of the older generation deal in commerce, while the youth are employed in technical trades.

URFALIS. The Urfalis and residents of the other cities of Upper Urfa (in southern Turkey) speak Arabic. Jews from this area began to settle in Jerusalem at the beginning of the 20th century; their first house of prayer was established in 1904. In 1916 206 of them were registered in Jerusalem and a few more in Galilee (together with the Kurds). Settlers from two towns in the mountains north of Urfa (Jarmuk and Siverek), who came with the Urfalis, were registered in 1916 and during the Mandate period as a separate community. In 1916 there were about 200 of them in Jerusalem, where they had a special synagogue. In the same year there were several settlers from Diyarbakir, who were joined by others from the same place during the 1920s in the wake of the Kurdish revolt in their area of Turkey. They also established a synagogue in Jerusalem.

MUSTA'RABS. This term denotes Jews who adopted the language and life style of their Arab neighbors, and some of whom, it appears, were descendants of families that never went into exile. Over the years, most of the Musta'rabs were absorbed into the Sephardi community in the broad sense of the term, and only a few families remained in Peki'in. In the 20th century, even those families, except for one clan, dispersed in Galilee and Samaria.

KARAITES. As early as the middle of the ninth century C.E., a movement to settle in Jerusalem and mourn the destruction of the Temple arose among the Karaites in Babylon and Persia. In the first generation of the tenth century, the Karaite community in Jerusalem was stronger and larger than the Rabbanite one, but the crusaders destroyed it in 1099. In 1540 Karaites settled for a short period in Hebron. In the middle of the 18th century some settled in Jerusalem and established a synagogue, which continued to exist (but never had a *minyan* of worshipers) until the fall of the Old City in 1948. After the establishment of the State of Israel, about 2,000 Karaites went from **45**

Egypt and settled mainly in Ramleh, Ashdod, Beersheba, and the moshavim of Maẓli'aḥ, near Ramleh and Ofakim in the northern Negev. The determination of their status, as Jews according to halakhah or as a separate religious community, has raised difficult problems.

INDIAN JEWS. Over 20,000 Indian Jews have settled in Israel since 1948. They include members of two closely knit communities: the Bene Israel, who speak Marathi, and Cochin Jews who speak Malayalam. Through 1954, 1,200 of the Bene Israel settled in Israel, and in 1965 their number had grown to 7,000. Because of their remoteness from the Jewish world and their ignorance of rabbinical laws of marriage and divorce, the halakhic problem of recognizing their right to marry within the Jewish community arose on their arrival in the country. In 1970, there were about 3,400 Cochin Jews in Israel, many of whom settled in development towns throughout the country and in moshavim in the Judean mountains.

3 MINORITIES

OTTOMAN PERIOD. In spite of the fact that there are no detailed statistical data available for the Ottoman period, it is possible to sketch the main demographical characteristics of the non-Jewish population in the 19th century and the beginning of the 20th century. Economic standards were, on the whole, very low, the population living largely on primitive agriculture. Urban development was limited; only a small part of the Muslim population lived in the towns, and in the few larger ones the proportion of Christians and Jews was considerable. As health services were almost nonexistent in most of the country and the government took very little interest in the health and welfare of the population, it may be assumed that mortality was high and offset the high birth rate to a considerable extent. Under those conditions, the population increased slowly. A rough estimate for the year 1914 indicates that the total population of the area that later became Palestine under the British Mandate was 689,000; 604,000 non-Jews and 85,000 Jews.

BRITISH MANDATE PERIOD. During this period demographic conditions changed quickly. In the first years of British administration, the situation of Muslims in Palestine was quite similar to that of those in other countries in the Middle East, such as Egypt. Mortality was still high; malaria still predominated in certain regions of the country; trachoma was widespread; and epidemics of typhoid, measles, etc. were frequent. Child mortality was particularly high in 1927–29; for example, 41% of Muslim children died before reaching the age of five.

With improving health conditions, better security,

economic development, and improved communications, however, mortality quickly decreased: the death rate of Muslims dropped from 30 per thousand in 1924–28 to 21 in 1939–41, while the average life expectancy increased from about 37 in 1926–27 to 47 and the child mortality up to the age of five fell to 29%. In the later years of the Mandate, mortality is known to have continued to decrease, but no reliable data are available (as the village heads who were responsible for reporting were also responsible for food distribution and were thus interested in concealing deaths). The fall in mortality was particularly marked in areas where the Arabs lived in closer contact with the Jewish population and could enjoy the services of Jewish physicians and medical institutions, as well as the benefits of more rapid economic development.

Marriages during the Mandatory period were practically universal among the Muslim population and were contracted at a very young age. Remarriages of divorced and widowed persons were also frequent. Nuptial mores were on the whole very favorable to fertility, which was high, as measured in terms of children per woman in the entire productive span, and tended to increase during the period, due probably to improved health and economic conditions. Among the Muslim population, the fertility rate was 6.1 children per woman in 1927–29, 7.6 in 1939–41, and 8.1 in 1942–43. Among the Christians, marriage was less universal and fertility was lower on the average.

Although no data are available on internal migration, it is known that a considerable movement took place toward the Coastal Plain, which developed more quickly under the impact of Jewish enterprise. The towns that increased their non-Jewish populations most were Jaffa, Haifa, and Gaza. In the interior of the country there was a very considerable development of the non-Jewish population only in Jerusalem; Hebron and Nablus each passed the 20,000 mark toward the end of the Mandatory period. On the whole, Judea and Samaria remained predominantly rural, having an urban population of less than 25% throughout the

Mandatory period. Emigration from Palestine was, on the whole, very limited, while in periods of more intense economic development there was some immigration, mainly to find work, from neighboring countries. Under the impact of the large and growing natural increase, the main feature of the demographic evolution of non-Jews in the Mandatory period was the very considerable increase in population: the non-Jewish population almost doubled itself between 1922 and 1948. This corresponds to an average increase of 2.5% per year, which was exceptional at the time for underdeveloped countries.

IN THE STATE OF ISRAEL: 1948–67. The tension in the late months of 1947 and the beginning of 1948, followed by the invasion from Arab countries and the War of Independence, brought about dramatic changes in the political and demographic situation. The territory of Mandatory Palestine was divided into three parts. In the part that passed under Israel rule, the non-Jewish population was drastically reduced by the flight of Arabs, who took refuge in various Arab states. The number of Palestinian Arab refugees has been assessed at different levels by different research workers, institutions, and political agencies. The difficulty in establishing the true figures stems from lack of accurate data for the end of the Mandatory period (the last census taken by the British authorities was in 1931), the fact that applicants for assistance from the United Nations Relief and Works Agency included many who were not refugees, and the inability of the UNRWA to keep accurate records of deaths, migration, and so on. Despite the difficulties, however, it may be roughly reckoned that the Arab population before the disturbances of 1947–48 and the war of 1948 in the part of Palestine that passed under Israel rule was of the order of magnitude of 750,000. It is known that after the departure of the refugees about 156,000 Arabs remained in Israel.

The economic and social conditions of Israel's Arabs improved quickly and the death rate decreased to the same level as that of the Jewish population. Marriage among **49**

Muslims remained practically universal although a little more delayed than during the Mandatory period, and re-marriage was still frequent. The fertility rate remained extremely high (eight or nine children to each woman on the average). Only among the Christian Arabs have signs of increasing birth control appeared in recent years. Emigration was practically nil. Under the impact of all these facts, the natural increase of Arabs in Israel has been very high by international standards (see Diagram 4), and the Arab population doubled itself between 1948 and 1967. The reunification of Jerusalem added 53,834 Muslims, 10,970 Christians, and 1,053 others (census of Sept. 27, 1967) to the population.

Table 11 gives some details on the changes in the non-Jewish population of Israel classified by religion. Its structure by sex is well balanced and the age structure is very young (Diagram 6). Table 25 shows the geographical distribution of the non-Jewish population by regions. While the Muslim population has largely retained its rural character, the Christian population is largely urban.

Diagram 6. Non-Jewish population, by age, sex, and group of population (December 31, 1969)

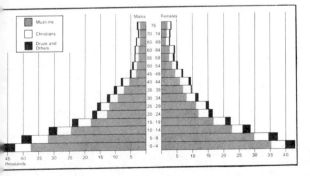

4 INTERCOMMUNAL PROBLEMS

A basic factor in the relationship between the "communities" in Israel is the long-standing dominance of the large and important Ashkenazi community in the economic, social, cultural, and political spheres. As a result the various *edot* did not undergo a process of mutual acculturation; instead, the non-Ashkenazi communities tended to assimilate with the Ashkenazi community and adopt its values and way of life. To the extent that the process of assimilation was impeded, inter-community tension developed and was made much more acute by the fact that the distinctions between the communities were largely superimposed on the existing economic and educational stratification: on the whole, the Ashkenazim were better educated and more prosperous, while there was a higher proportion of poverty, under-education, and illiteracy among the Sephardim and other oriental communities, particularly the new immigrants from African and Asian countries. The closing of the gap between "the first Israel" and "the second Israel" became a central problem. The alleviation of intercommunal tension through the "integration of the exiles" *(mizzug galuyyot)* became a major aim of national policy. At the same time, the opinion was widely held that the tension would be alleviated with the disintegration of the communities themselves and the disappearance of communal allegiances, and that as long as the communities themselves continued to exist there would not be a sense of a united people in Israel. This process of disintegration, however, proved a much more lengthy and complicated process than was initially envisaged.

Group of sabras. Courtesy Keren Hayesod, United Israel Appeal, Jerusalem.

During the period of the British Mandate, when a large Ashkenazi majority was created by the mass *aliyah* from Europe and the comparatively small *aliyah* from Asian and African countries, intercommunal tension was expressed primarily in the relations between various Ashkenazi groups, such as "Russians," "Poles," and "Galicians," but especially between these three groups together (Eastern Ashkenazim) and those from central Europe (Western Ashkenazim). This situation even led to the crystallization of specific political groups (such as the Aliyah Ḥadashah Party established by immigrants from "Central Europe" —actually from Germany).

The sting of this tension became blunted, however during the first few years after the founding of the state due to the arrival of thousands of immigrants from the Islamic countries, as the differences between the newcomers and the Ashkenazim obscured the much finer distinctions between the groups within the Ashkenazi community. Among the Ashkenazi community no one group was outstandingly superior in the economic, political, and educational spheres: immigrants from Eastern Europe had molded the main institutions of the country and its pre-1948 ethos and they were dominant in the political leadership of the Zionist Organization, the *yishuv,* and afterward of the state, and in their contribution to the shaping of social values. Immigrants from Germany were distinguished in the liberal professions and economic life and those from Western Europe and America were prominent in the technological and scientific developments after 1948. The confrontation between Ashkenazim and non-Ashkenazim, on the other hand, took place under conditions of obvious inequality.

Until the establishment of the new *yishuv,* the communal frameworks were accepted as the basis of public life and there was no conscious aspiration to merge the *edot.* This aim was a product of the modern nationalist movement and the new *yishuv,* and since the builders of the new *yishuv* were Ashkenazim, the idea of "merging" was conceived as the assimilation of non-Ashkenazim to the way of life and value system of the Ashkenazim. At the same time the secular character of the new *yishuv* widened the gap between the two groups by undermining the religious base common to Jews of all communities.

Under the Ottoman regime, the Jews of the new *yishuv* did not hold commanding economic and political positions in the life of the community; indeed, these hardly existed at all until the institution of the Mandatory regime. When the new *yishuv* acquired such positions during the 1920s, political and communal organizations began to develop among the Sephardim, but they reflected, for the most part, the aspirations of affluent businessmen and products of a Western education, themselves candidates for rapid assimilation to the Ashkenazi way of life.

The problem of intercommunal relations became of central importance with the large immigration after the establishment of the state, which created a situation of numerical equality between Ashkenazim and non-Ashkenazim. The immigrants from Islamic countries, especially from areas that had had all but no contact with Europe 55 (such as Yemen) or countries from which it was mainly the poorer strata who came without the communal leadership (such as Morocco), quickly became an economic, social, and especially cultural proletariat in Israel. They felt uprooted in their new surroundings, where the dominant social forces demanded that they abandon their traditions and culture and assimilate unconditionally into modern Israel society, which was basically Western. Consciously or unconsciously, the authorities and the prevailing public opinion in the country tended to regard the older generation of new immigrants from Islamic countries as a lost generation that would eventually die off, and their main concern was to help the younger generation throw off the burden of its paternalistic traditions. Israel society, however, was successful in many instances only in shattering the patriarchal family structure, which was the principal framework of the immigrants from Islamic countries, and thus destroying old values without simultaneously transferring its own value system as an integral part of the new-comer's personality. In effect, this resulted in the creation of a segment of society that was socially displaced, living on the fringes of two cultures and attracted to the glittering commercial aspects of modern materialistic culture. The non-Ashkenazim developed psychological sensitivity toward what the Ashkenazim said and did, and this sensitivity sharpened intercommunal tension.

There was still a considerable backlog in the complete absorption and integration of the immigrants, however. The houses built for them during the mass influx were small, often hopelessly inadequate for the many large families. While the immigrants were improving their skills, the veterans were making even faster progress and still largely monopolized senior administrative and managerial posts.

The major complaint of many of the immigrants from Islamic countries was that their absorption into Western society was not being sufficiently accelerated, that they were being prevented from enjoying its social and material fruits to the same extent as the Europeans, and that prejudice was being displayed toward them.

These differences were, first of all, a matter of income. In 1968/69, the net monthly income of an average family of Asian or African origin was 79% of the income of one of European or American origin. Since the former family consisted, on the average, of 4.9 members, compared with 2.9 for the latter, the difference in *per capita* income was much larger (see Table 12). However, there was some improvement; taking gross monthly incomes, the percentage went up from 72% in 1966 to 75% in 1971.

Jews from the Islamic countries also suffered more from over-crowding, although the figures showed marked progress. While the percentage of all families living more than three persons to a room fell from 12.3% in 1966 to 7.4% in 1971, that for families from Asia and Africa dropped during the same period from 27.2% to 15.4%—a distinct narrowing of the gap. Length of time in the country significantly affected the figures; for those who came from the Islamic countries in 1955 or later, the percentage dropped from 27% to 17.1% while for pre-1955 arrivals, it fell from 27.4% to 14.5%.

Table 12. Average Monthly Income of Urban Family, by Continent of Birth of Household Head

	European– American Origin	Asian– African Origin
Average monthly income (before tax)	991.9	724.7
Direct taxes	181.2	82.1
Net monthly income	810.7	642.6

Source: Survey of Family Incomes, 1968/69

There were also serious disabilities in education, where the great differences in family background could not be quickly counterbalanced by governmental action.

In the early years it was felt that a common education would eliminate differences, but cultural deprivation was perpetuated even under equal educational facilities. Factors at work here were differences in home background and living conditions (Oriental families could not provide the same atmosphere for study), the Western outlook of the schools and the teachers, and the concentration of better teaching facilities in the large cities (whereas the oriental communities were largely in the development areas). There was thus a high dropout rate among pupils of oriental origin.

In the 1970/71 school year, while pupils of Asian-African origin made up 60.1% of those in grade 7 (normally 12-year-olds), the percentage dropped to 50% in grade 8, 30.2% in grade 12 (the last in the post-primary school) and 12.6% in the universities.

However, steady progress was evidenced, for example, by the fact that whereas 13% of secondary school pupils in 1956 were of Afro-Asian origin, the percentage increased to 26% in 1961/62 and 43.6% in 1970/71.

Conscious efforts were steadily made to help such children, not only by special tuition and scholarships, but even by lowering pass standards for children of Afro-Asian background so as to encourage them to continue their education.

A wide variety of governmental measures were devoted to the narrowing of the gap; in fact, a large proportion of state expenditure on health, housing, education and social services automatically helped to improve the conditions of the "oriental" communities, since they comprised most of the poorer strata. These measures included: family allowances, grants to low-income families, maternity grants, old-age pensions and survivors' pensions through the National Insurance Institute; social welfare payments of various kinds, crèches, youth clubs, hostels, etc.; sub-

mob outbreaks, the most serious of which occurred in 1959, especially in the Wadi Salib quarter of Haifa. However, attempts to establish political parties on a communal basis proved failures. Almost all the political parties made a habit of including in their election lists a token number of candidates from the "oriental" communities and every government had one or two members from these communities.

In the 1960s there was a slackening in intercommunal tensions. This was partly a result of the integration of children of all the communities in the school system.

The incidence of intermarriage between Ashkenazi and Sephardi-oriental communities has risen less sharply than was forecast in the early years of the State but it has nevertheless shown a consistent increase: from 8.6% of all Jewish marriages in 1952 to 14.5% in 1960 and 17.6% in 1970.

Further, army service, in which members of all communities meet under conditions of equality, also helped to blur intercommunal distinctions and the common experiences of the Six-Day War and its aftermath had a powerful influence in the same direction.

In 1971, however, there was some recrudescence of intercommunal tension, owing mainly to the emergence during the cease-fire of domestic problems that had been overshadowed by concentration on defense. There was some unrest among children of the first wave of mass immigration whose parents had been incompletely integrated and who had become school drop-outs and juvenile delinquents. A group of them adopted the name "Black Panthers" and held demonstrations which erupted into spasmodic violence. One of their grievances was the contrast between the skimpy immigrant housing, now overcrowded, which was all the country could afford in the early 1950s, and the roomier dwellings now allotted to new immigrants from the Western countries and the U.S.S.R. The Government budgeted more money for housing, social services and education, and at the end of 1972 the tension seemed to be subsiding, but the problems of poverty, of which the oriental communities had more than their share, still awaited comprehensive solutions.

Attempts to draw parallels with community problems in other countries are misleading. There are no racial distinctions between the *edot* in Israel: there is a feeling of common national (and, obviously, religious) affiliation; there is not legal discrimination against the members of any community; and no one in Israel is interested in perpetuating the gap between the communities. On the contrary, every effort has been made to work toward the fullest integration. Basically, the communal problem in Israel is only the outcome of a sudden confrontation of two cultures, the first sure of itself and the second in stage of decline, and of the high correlation between communal affiliation and social and educational attributes. These factors reinforce each other, it is true, but the weakening of one also tends to weaken the other. The sense of communal affiliation is on the decrease among those born in Israel; and immigrants from Islamic countries are rising in social status, being exposed to the dominant culture in the country, and in integration with the Ashkenazim without feeling it necessary to create a parallel leadership of their own.

Part Two
URBAN AND RURAL ISRAEL

5 TOWNS

ANTIQUITY OF TOWNS IN THE COUNTRY. The history of most towns and urban centers goes back long before the Arab conquest of the 7th century C.E.; many even date from the second or third millennium B.C.E. Until the founding of Tel Aviv in 1909, the only exception was Ramla, which was built in 717 C.E. by the Omayyads to replace nearby Lydda as the Arab capital of the country. On the other hand, numerous ancient towns ceased to exist after the Moslem occupation, and urban settlement completely disappeared from whole districts, whether through slow decline and dilapidation as in the Negev, or through deliberate and systematic destruction, as in the Coastal Plain. Even the towns of the hill regions were abandoned or degraded to the rank of villages. Other centers, particularly those sacred to Christianity, lay vacant and neglected through centuries, and revived in the late 18th century after the Turks had conceded Europeans the right to settle there and erect religious institutions (e.g., Nazareth, Bethlehem, Ramallah).

ECONOMIC FOUNDATIONS OF ANCIENT TOWNS. In this part of the world, as everywhere else, trade and commerce formed the principal economic basis for country towns in antiquity. Peasants of the surrounding villages brought their produce to town to barter it against wares of local tradesmen. It appears, however, that during all periods of history farming also constituted an important occupation for city dwellers, whether as a principal or subsidiary source of income. This fact was undoubtedly the result of the precarious security situation through most periods of history: many farmers preferred to live within fortified towns without forsaking their holdings, even if this meant dwelling at a considerable distance from their fields and gardens. In towns near crossroads, trade was lively: local produce was exchanged for wares brought by the caravans, often from great distances, and traders arriving from different directions exchanged goods at these meeting places.

Of a different character were the harbor towns of the Mediterranean and Red Sea shores, where fishing, seafaring, and shipbuilding constituted additional lines of occupation. In some cities, such as Gaza, Ashkelon or Eilat, merchants who traveled along continental highways met traders who plied international sea routes, and these contacts livened commerce and formed the basis for specialized trades.

URBAN CENTERS FOUNDED BY ZIONIST SETTLERS. The urban centers founded by Zionist settlers before Israel's statehood had at first been planned as villages but developed into towns and cities because of particularly favorable conditions. Most of these lie in the central section of the Coastal Plain, e.g., Ḥaderah, Netanyah, Petaḥ Tikvah, Rishon le-Zion, Reḥovot. Since all these moshavot had, in their early days, fairly large areas of cultivable land sufficient for many farmsteads, they soon needed additional hands. Laborers, finding more or less permanent employment in agricultural work, took up residence there. This increase necessitated more economic, social, and cultural services. This, in turn, created additional employment and a further population growth. Some of the trade shops in the moshavot eventually grew into small or medium-sized factories and sold their produce to other parts of the country, and even abroad. Some enterprises, however, had been planned from the start to attain a wider scope. The first of these were the large wine cellars built by Baron E. de Rothschild at Rishon le-Zion and Zikhron Ya'akov. Reḥovot, where the Agricultural Research Station of the Jewish Agency (now of the State and the Hebrew University) and the Sieff Institute—today the Weizmann Institute—were founded, became an important center of 63 learning and at the same time broadened its economic scope and foundations to absorb additional population.

A separate chapter are the satellite towns and cities of the Tel Aviv conurbation (Ramat Gan, Bene Berak, Ramat ha-Sharon, etc.) although these, too, began either as farming villages or as garden suburbs. Different from all of these centers, however, is Afulah, which is also the only one outside the Coastal Plain, in the Jezreel Valley: although planned to become the urban center for its region, for a long time it did not fulfill this hope. Until 1948 it numbered hardly 3,000 inhabitants since the farmer settlers of the Valley preferred Haifa, still at a convenient distance for them; only now, as a result of industrialization and development, has Afulah grown to about 17,000 inhabitants.

NEW TOWNS AND CITIES. Since the State of Israel was created, more moshavot in the Coastal Plain have attained town status (Nahariyyah, Herzliyyah, Kefar Sava) or at least assumed an urban or semiurban character (Zikhron Ya'akov, Ra'anannah, Nes Zionah, Gederah). Country towns formerly inhabited by Arabs exclusively (Ramleh, Mejdal = Ashkelon, Beersheba, Bet She'an) or partly (Safed, Tiberias) were in 1948 abandoned by all or many of their inhabitants and later repopulated by Jewish immigrants. This necessitated the creation of entirely new economic foundations for such towns and often a remodeling of their town-planning blueprints.

In a third group are those towns laid out in the period of statehood to serve as centers of regional settlement projects or to fulfil special economics tasks. Thus, Eilat was built as Israel's gateway to the Red Sea and Indian Ocean; from the start it was also envisaged to become a first-rate tourist center. Dimonah was initially intended to serve as a residential quarter for laborers of the Dead Sea Works and the Oron phosphate mines, and after a short time it was provided with large textile factories and other industries to form a broad basis for its economy. Arad was established to house further employees of the Dead Sea Works, and thereupon to become a large center of chemical and other industries. Ashkelon was founded as a site of industry, recreation, and tourism in the Southern Coastal Plain; Ashdod as Israel's second-largest port on the Mediterranean seaboard; Kiryat Malakhi as a semi-urban center in closely settled rural surroundings of the Southern Coastal Plain; Kiryat Gat as the urban center of the Lachish Region. Bet Shemesh was built to absorb greater numbers of settlers in the Jerusalem Corridor area, particularly on an industrial basis. In the north, new urban and semiurban centers include Migdal ha-Emek and Yokne'am on the circumference of the Jezreel Valley, Kiryat Nazareth in Lower Galilee, Karmi'el on the border of Lower and Upper Galilee, Ma'alot in Western Upper Galilee, and Kiryat Shemonah and Ḥazor in and near the Ḥuleh Valley. All these settlements are planned to draw industry and productive service to hitherto underpopulated regions and to create a closely interlocked rural and urban economy and a more balanced distribution of population over all parts of Israel.

The growth of exaggerated population concentrations in one or several huge centers is a complicated problem today in many countries; in Israel, this is aggravated by the small size of the country and by its special security situation. Some countries have been aided in this respect, to a certain degree, by a difference in wage levels between regions of dense and sparse population which attracts enterprises to the latter. In Israel, however, this factor is absent; on the contrary, commodities are often more expensive at outlying places like Eilat, so that workers there must be paid certain premiums. To attract investors and settlers to new towns and cities, other means must be used, such as cheap building land and housing, loans, subsidies and tax exemptions. Such a policy is successful, particularly where enterprises also find geographical advantages such as markets and raw materials close at hand to even out high transport costs and other overheads. This explains, in part, why larger enterprises often show greater readiness to go to 'development towns' than do small undertakings. Proximity of raw materials, for instance, has been decisive in attracting to Beersheba industries of ceramics, insecticides and other chemicals; to Kiryat Gat, Kiryat Shemonah and Bet She'an—cotton gins and spinning mills; to Afulah and Kiryat Gat—sugar factories, to Ramleh and Bet Shemesh—cement plants, etc. The Sharon, the Southern Coastal Plain and the Jezreel, Kinneret and Huleh valleys are seen as the natural location of food-processing and preserve plants. Markets explain placing of garages and machine shops for farming equipment in centers of developing agricultural regions, e.g., Kiryat Gat, Beersheba, Kiryat Shemonah, etc.

Industries which can be drawn with relative ease toward development regions are those of comparatively low transport costs; a case in point are diamond-cutting and polishing plants now found in many new towns, from Eilat in the south to Kiryat Shemonah in the north.

Tourism and recreation have greatly aided the progress of veteran towns, and of villages which have become towns or cities during the period of statehood (Tiberias, Safed, Nahariyyah, Zikhron Yaakov, Netanyah, Herzliyyah) as well as of new centers, e.g., Eilat, Ashkelon, Caesarea.

In the early years of statehood, housing was a decisive criterion in settling new immigrants in towns abandoned in the War of Independence as well as in new development centers, even if the immigrants could not be given immediate employment. In the first stages of development, public works and investment (such as construction of houses and roads, land reclamation, etc.) provided the livelihood for most of the newcomers. Incidentally, these activities in most cases constitute the necessary groundwork for industrialization of a new center. When factories are opened in development towns, a growing percentage of the local labor force gains permanent employment in partly skilled or skilled work.

TEL AVIV-JAFFA. There is archaeological evidence of Jaffa's uninterrupted inhabitation at least since the Neo-lithic Period, i.e., for 7,000–10,000 years. Since the end of the 19th century, Zionist immigrants settled in Jaffa and soon Jaffa was regarded as the Zionist center of the country.

In 1909, two societies set up by Jaffa Jews, 'Aḥuzat Bayit' and 'Naḥlat Binyamin,' chose the barren sand dunes north of Jaffa for the suburb they planned to build, simply because plots there were offered at a reasonable price. Characteristically, the dominating building of early Tel Aviv was the Herzliyyah Gymnasium, situated at the north end of Herzl Street, the first Hebrew secondary school in the country.

With its swift growth in the 1920s and 1930s, Tel Aviv expanded from the Jaffa border northward and around 1935 it reached the south bank of the river Yarkon. The distance between the southern and northern end of the city increased and soon exceeded 5 km. (3 mi.) while the width between the shore and the easternmost houses measured only a few hundred meters. Medium and large industrial enterprises in need of adequate building space preferred the smaller agglomerations which had meanwhile come into being on Tel Aviv's circumference (Ramat Gan, Bene Berak, Ḥolon, etc.); these, in turn, grew into small or medium-sized cities. Only on the southeast rim of Tel Aviv and near the border of Jaffa did somewhat larger factories of the metal, food and other branches concentrate. The bulk of the city's economy was based on commerce, on cultural activities (the city served as the seat of all Hebrew dailies and theaters, of most publishing houses, etc.) and on its being the administrative center of the Jewish population of the country (seat of the Histadrut, the political parties, etc.). All of these institutions concentrated in the south of Tel Aviv, along Herzl Street, Allenby Road, and their side streets.

With the outbreak of World War II, conditions changed gradually and the municipal area expanded eastward; this development quickened after 1948. On April 24, 1950, Jaffa was united with Tel Aviv and the municipal area thus enlarged to 4,242.5 ha (over 10,000 acres). Although the 67 incorporation of Jaffa, with its destitute quarters dilapidated structures and winding lanes, demanded great efforts in reconstruction, the new areas thus added to Tel Aviv opened vistas in rational planning. Since statehood, the city's residential and commercial quarters have tended to expand principally northeastward. Building quality has improved perceptibly since the 1950s; since the early 1960s, multistoried structures began to go up, particularly in the center of the city. The focus of social and commercial life, too, has shifted northeast, from Allenby Road to Dizengoff Square and Dizengoff Road. Tel Aviv's water-front has, with its large hotels, become the primary center of tourism in the country. The quarter on Jaffa Hill was in the 1960s transformed into an attractive center for artists and entertainment.

A comprehensive reconstruction scheme has been drawn up for a modern banking and commercial center to extend, mainly along the shore or at a small distance from it. The entire 13-km. shore-front between Herzliyyah and Bat Yam is also slated for redevelopment, with certain areas to be won from the sea.

Tel Aviv's border today, contiguous with satellite towns almost in its entire length, merges with them into a solid built-up area for 12 km. (7 mi.) to the east, and even larger distances from north to south. In the east, the satellite chain stretches through Givatayim and Ramat Gan to Bene Berak and touches upon Petaḥ Tikvah. In the south, the cities of Bat Yam and Ḥolon link up with Jaffa. In the southeast, only the fields of the veteran farming school of Mikveh Israel form a curtain of green between Jaffa and the small industrial or semi-industrial centers of Azor, Bet Dagan, etc. In the northeast, Ramat ha-Sharon forms the continuation of Tel Aviv's new suburbs and connects them with the town of Herzliyyah. The communities of Ra'anan-nah, Hod ha-Sharon, Kefar Sava, Petaḥ Tikvah, Yehud, Lydda, Ramleh, Rishon-le-Zion, Nes Ẓionah with Reḥovot form an outer ring. The inhabitants of the conurbation proper numbered in 1971 over 800,000, and together with the outer ring well over one million, i.e., 30 or 40% respectively of the total population of the State of Israel (within its pre-1967 borders), while the conurbation occupies only 0.8%, and together with the outer ring 3%, of the country's area.

Similar to developments in other world conurbations, a migration has been noticeable, since the early 1960's, from Tel Aviv proper to the satellite towns, particularly to the south, where Bat Yam has increased its population by an annual 7.0%, and Holon by 6.2%. While the growth of the eastern satellites has been more modest (Bene Berak 4.1%, Givatayim 3.6%, Ramat Gan 2.2% annually), Tel Aviv's population has dropped in a decade by more than 10,000 to number 382,900 (thereof 6,900 non-Jews) at the end of 1969. The city fathers, however, expect this trend to be reversed in the future, and predict for Tel Aviv (in its present boundaries) 650,000 inhabitants by the year 2000.

HAIFA. Haifa Bay is the most convenient for shipping and development of port facilities of all sections on Israel's Mediterranean coast. This is particularly true today of the southern part of the bay, where Mount Carmel protects the shore from the prevailing southwesterly winds and the water is deep enough for ships to drop anchor close to the shore. Haifa seems to have begun its existence only in the Second Temple period and, except for the last fifty years, was at best a small town ranking a poor second to Acre.

Since the beginning of the present century, the construction of railways (Haifa–Damascus in 1905, Haifa – Lydda – Egypt, completed in 1919) and of roads made Haifa an important traffic hub. The advantages of Haifa's deep-water anchorage were recognized and led to the construction of the large, modern port completed in 1934. The Kirkuk - Haifa oil pipeline was laid and the Haifa Oil Refineries were installed between 1936 and 1939.

Before World War I Jews began to acquire land on the Carmel slope, particularly on the broad level step 40–60 m. (180–200 ft.) above the sea, where a site was prepared for **69** the Technion (Israel Institute of Technology) and where in 1920 the modern Jewish quarter Hadar ha-Carmel was founded. The early 1930 s saw the forming of the nuclei for the garden suburbs atop Mount Carmel—the French Carmel at its northwest extremity, the Central Carmel, and Aḥuzah further to the southeast. With the construction of the port and dredging of its bottom, a strip of land was added to downtown Haifa. Room was thus provided for the port installations as well as the broad King's Way thoroughfare. The area became a center of banking, wholesale trade, and enterprises connected with the port's activities.

The first step toward comprehensive town planning for Haifa was taken in 1928. At that time the Jewish National Fund's acquisition of the first strip of land adjoining the bay shore almost up to Acre gave scope for allocating areas to different functional tasks. The southern section, near the mouth of the Kishon Stream, was earmarked for small, medium and large industry, as it is nearest to the city and to the port (which was then about to be built) and could be most easily linked by branch lines to the railway. The oil harbor was built there in the years before World War II. Between 1952 and 1956 the Kishon harbor was built to serve Israel's high-sea fishing fleet. Inside the industrial zone, most factories giving off obnoxious fumes were placed furthest from the city to the east, where they were last in the chain of dominant wind direction.

North of the industrial zone the Kerayot (garden cities) were laid out, at first with small, one- or two-family homes, and later superseded (particularly in the last decade) by large apartment houses. The Kerayot originally meant to house workers of the industrial zone, soon took up other strata, among them many people employed in Haifa City or within the Kerayot.

In the years of statehood, several changes have been introduced into this basic blueprint. West of the former agricultural zone and south of Acre, more and more industrial enterprises take up the dune strip, while to the east, residential quarters are pushing north. Simultaneously, growing parts of Mount Carmel are included in the town planning scheme. The residential quarter of Hadar ha-Carmel climbs the slope and links up with the zone of apartment houses, villas and hotels on the mountain crest. Sections of Mount Carmel further east are included in Haifa with the spread of residential areas such as Neve Sha'anan and Kiryat Remez and the large campus of the Technion ('the Technion City'). On the mountain top southeast of Aḥuzah, the Haifa University campus, designed by world-famous architect Oscar Niemeyer, has taken shape. Sections of Mount Carmel, with their abundant and variegated vegetation, have been set aside as nature preserves.

Downtown Haifa spreads west: modern residential quarters occupy the level space between the port area, the Carmel Cape, and the Carmel slope. The city also expands beyond the cape and spills over into the narrow Carmel Coast. Here, an arrangement resembling that of Haifa Bay becomes noticeable—a manufacturing zone occupies the low area west of the Haifa–Tel Aviv railway and highway, and the houses climb the slope of Mount Carmel.

Haifa numbered, at the end of 1969, 214,500 inhabitants within its municipal boundaries, while the Haifa-Acre conurbation exceeded 300,000. The port, whose capacity is steadily increasing, the docks and expanding shipbuilding trade, and notably heavy industry, for which Haifa is becoming the primary center of the country, together with the region's assets for tourism, which are not yet fully exploited, warrant a further rapid population growth.

JERUSALEM. Jerusalem is one of the most important spiritual centers of the world: this significance forms the basis for its life today, in spite of all geographical, economic and political drawbacks.

As a result of the gradual population rise, space between the walls of the Old City became even more crowded in the 19th century, particularly in the narrow Jewish Quarter. Jews were therefore the first to found new quarters outside the walls. In 1858 Mishkenot Sha'anannim was built west of the Old City. At about the same time, churches began to establish hostels and other institutions outside the walls for the benefit of the growing flow of Christian pilgrims. The New City spread mainly toward the northwest along the road leading to Jaffa, which was then the only port in the country.

At the end of the 19th century, the first garden suburbs made their appearance: those of non-Jews (e.g., German Colony and Greek Colony, Katamon, etc.) preceded modern Jewish quarters (Reḥavvah, Bet ha-Kerem, Talpiyot, etc.). In all these it was attempted to plan streets, water, sewage and electricity networks along rational lines. The British Mandate authorities aimed to preserve Jerusalem's beauty and historical treasures. All outer walls had to be built of the fine local stone, rules limiting the height of structures were issued, and care was taken to retain open spaces and preserve the skyline. On the other hand, the Mandatory authorities rejected industrialization as not befitting Jerusalem's character.

In the first years of Israel's statehood, the most pressing tasks were repair of the enormous damage caused in the War of Independence battles, absorption of thousands of new immigrants, and preparation of a new outline scheme fitting in with the border which then divided the city between Israel and Jordan: at a later stage came zoning into residential, commercial, administrative, cultural and industrial units. With the Hebrew University campus and the National Museums as pivotal points, a large center of Government institutions, of local administration, and cultural and commercial institutions was laid out. This whole complex is thus situated between the older quarters in the east and the expansion belt of residential suburbs in the west and the southwest. The huge Hadassah Hospital is today the extreme point of westward expansion.

As elsewhere in the country, the large new suburbs in the west and southwest were laid out as self-contained neighborhood units. The frontier which surrounded Israeli Jerusalem left the west as the direction for expansion.

Industry is now regarded as an element indispensable to Jerusalem's economy. Owing to the city's geographical position, light industries are easiest to develop here. In addition to the enlarged existing industrial area at Tel Arzah in the northwest, a second, at Givat Shaul in the west, is developing rapidly. After the War of Independence, a single highway to Tel Aviv in the northwest was open: the railway line became usable again after border corrections in the Israel-Jordan armistice of 1949. Since then, additional roads, which converge on the city from the west and southwest, were constructed.

Immediately after the Six-Day War, all military installations, fences and shell-proof concrete walls which had separated the two parts of the city were removed, and the connecting streets and roads paved and opened. Within the Old City, reconstruction of the Jewish Quarter and its historic synagogues was begun, and institutions of religious study moved in, their pupils forming the nucleus of the Old City's renewed Jewish community.

Jerusalem's boundaries were redrawn, giving the capital a municipal area exceeding 100 sq. km., the largest in the country. According to the census of May 1972, there were 304,500 inhabitants in Jerusalem, of these 78,100 were non-Jews.

One of the main problems of the Jerusalem master plan lies in reconciling the quest for a continuous built-up area with the necessity to preserve and enhance numerous historical sites, sacred to three world religions. Both inside and outside the Old City walls, gardens have either been laid out or are blueprinted, while other areas to the east and south have been earmarked as public open spaces or sites for preservation and reconstruction. Overcrowding in the Old City could possibly be remedied by resettling some of the inhabitants elsewhere in the city. However, the Old City is not to be viewed as a museum piece, but should continue to serve as a residential and, to an extent, commercial area, with the additional development of tourist facilities.

The existent main thoroughfares have become totally 73

inadequate. A network of new broad roads has been blue-printed in order to provide alternative approach routes from all directions, enabling vehicular traffic to cross the municipal area to destinations beyond it without clogging Jerusalem's main arteries.

The Hebrew University has seen the return of its original campus atop Mount Scopus, where an intensive restoration and building program was launched in 1968, comprising lecture halls and dormitories for thousands of students.

In view of the growing need for tourist accomodation and services in Jerusalem, large sums of public and private capital are being invested in hotel building, and suitable sites have been earmarked for these purposes throughout the city. The capital is also attracting increasing numbers of industrial enterprises, particularly of the electronics and other science-intensive branches, for which new areas have been set aside in the south and northeast.

New housing developments call for the largest share of both space and investments. While the southwest (Kiryat Yovel, etc.) continues to serve as the sector of intensive apartment building, and vacant lots elsewhere are increasingly being used for new constructions, a concentrated effort is now being directed toward the favorable terrain in the northeast beyond the former armistice line. New residential quarters like Ramot Eshkol, under construction since 1968, promise to provide accommodation for tens of thousands of citizens, both Jews and non-Jews.

6 THE KIBBUTZ

The kibbutz or kevuẓah (plural: kibbutzim, kevuẓot) is a voluntary collective community, engaging mainly in agriculture but also industry, in which there is no private wealth and which is responsible for all the needs of the members and their families. The kibbutz movement in Israel in 1971 numbered 86,300 people in 229 kibbutzim and kevuẓot organized in several federations according to social, political, and religious outlook. The first kevuẓah was founded in 1909 at Deganyah by a group of pioneers, who, after working at first as employees of the Palestine Land Development Company, undertook collective responsibility for the working of the farm. Another group, which started work at Kinneret in the same year, became an independent kevuẓah in 1913. By 1914 there were 11 kevuẓot established on Jewish National Fund land under the responsibility of the Zionist Organization, and the number grew to 29 by the end of 1918. The early kevuẓot had small memberships based upon the idea that the community should be small enough to constitute a kind of enlarged family. During the Third Aliyah, after World War I, when larger numbers of pioneering settlers *(ḥalutzim)* arrived, Shelomo Lavie and others proposed the establishment of large, self-sufficient villages, combining agriculture with industry, for which the name "kibbutz" was used. The first of this type was En Harod, founded in 1921, and many others followed. Later, however, the distinction between the two terms almost disappeared. The kibbutzim and kevuẓot combined to establish federations in accordance with their social character, political affiliations, or religious outlook: Ḥever ha-Kevuẓot, founded in 1925 (later merged in Iḥud   75 ha-Kevuẓot ve-ha-Kibbutzim); Ha-Kibbutz ha-Arẓi ha-Shomer ha-Ẓa'ir, and Ha-Kibbutz ha-Me'uḥad, both founded in 1927; and Ha-Kibbutz ha-Dati, founded in 1935. (For separate accounts, see below.)

The kibbutzim received their manpower mainly from the pioneering youth movements abroad and, in their turn, provided the movements with a practical ideal of pioneering settlement on the land in order to make a major contribution to the building of the Jewish National Home and create a model and a basis for the socialist society of the future. They played an important part in expanding the map of Jewish settlement and safeguarding the growing community. In the late 1930s many were set up overnight on the Tower and Stockade plan so as to forestall official obstruction and Arab attack. The kibbutzim served as bases for the Haganah defense force and later the Palmaḥ, its commando section. Most of the new villages established under emergency conditions during and immediately after World War II, especially in the Negev, were kibbutzim. By the establishment of independence, they numbered 149 out of the 291 Jewish villages in the country.

In 1948 and 1949 the momentum of kibbutz expansion continued: out of 175 new villages founded during the two years, 79 were kibbutzim. The Jews from Muslim countries and survivors of the Holocaust who arrived in enormous numbers during the early years of the state were not favorably disposed to the kibbutz idea, however, and most of them preferred to settle in moshavim. Youngsters born or brought up in Israel, including the second or third generation from older kibbutzim and graduates of Youth Aliyah and Israel youth movements, became more prominent among the founders of new kibbutzim, especially in the Negev and, after the Six-Day War (1967), in the Golan Heights and the Jordan Valley.

The Character of the Kibbutz. The kibbutz is a unique product of the Zionist labor movement and the Jewish national revival. It was not conceived theoretically as an escapist or utopian project; it was developed by Jewish workers inspired by ideas of social justice as an integral part of the Zionist effort to resettle the homeland. Ever since its inception, the kibbutz movement has played a pioneering role in the economic, political, cultural, and security activities required to carry out that purpose. The movement is composed of people from different countries and backgrounds, and of varying political beliefs. Some communities were inspired by A. D. Gordon's[3] ethical Jewish socialist philosophy, which emphasized the importance of identification with nature and of physical labor as the supreme human value. Others cherished the tradition of the Gedud ha-Avodah of the early 1920s, which regarded itself as a militant constructive task force. Others, again, do not regard themselves as a part of the socialist movement, while a number of kibbutzim (mostly organized in Ha-Kibbutz ha-Dati) have been established by religious Jews and combine communal life with the fulfillment of the laws of the Torah.

In the early 1950s differences of opinion over Marxist theory and support for pro-Soviet policies led to a split in Ha-Kibbutz ha-Me'uḥad, and one section joined with Ḥever ha-Kevuẓot to form Iḥud ha-Kevuẓot ve-ha-Kibbutzim. Ha-Kibbutz ha-Arẓi Ha-Shomer ha-Ẓa'ir, believing that the kibbutz as an economic unit cannot be divorced from its political ideals, regards itself as a political unit as well. Over the years, each of the federations has been associated to a greater or lesser degree with one of the Israel parties. With the passage of time, many of the initial differences between one type of kibbutz and another have disappeared. Most of the small, purely agricultural ones have grown and established industries, and there is no difference today between the small kevuẓah and the large kibbutz. With the intensification of Soviet hostility to Israel, the attitude to the U.S.S.R. has, to all intents and purposes, ceased to be a dividing factor, especially since the Six-Day War. There is an increasing trend toward inter-

[3]Socialist philosopher: lived in Deganiyyah, died 1922

Carpentry factory at kibbutz Ḥamadyah, 1970. Courtesy Keren Hayesod, United Israel Appeal, Jerusalem.

kibbutz activity and cooperation in all spheres, ranging from education to economy.

The movement has been supported since its inception by Zionist and Israel government agencies with long-term leases of national land, technical advice, development projects, and long-term financing. Through a special corps, Naḥal, composed of youth movement graduates, the Israel defense forces train nuclei of future kibbutzim and help in their establishment. Sites for new kibbutzim have been chosen in the light of national settlement and defense policy, often at the expense of economic viability. Many of them are in border areas and play an important part in the regional defense system.

Organization. The basis of kibbutz administration is a

Vegetable fields at kibbutz Yotvatah in the Arabah, 1969.
Courtesy Keren Hayesod, United Israel Appeal, Jerusalem.

weekly general meeting of the membership, which formulates policy, elects officers, and supervises the overall working of the community. Candidates for membership are usually accepted after a year's probation. Kibbutzim are incorporated cooperative enterprises, and generally speaking members transfer all assets, other than personal effects, to the kibbutz. If a member decides to leave he is entitled to his personal effects and, in line with a recent decision of the movement, to a cash grant proportional to the time he has been in the kibbutz. Uniform national bylaws governing individual rights in the kibbutz have been approved.

Affairs of the kibbutz are conducted by elected committees, the principal one being the secretariat, which usually consists of a secretary, treasurer, chairmen of some of the key committees, the production manager, and others. There are committees in charge of education, cultural activities, questions of principle and personal problems of members, economic planning, coordination of work, and nominations. Elective positions, including managerial ones, are rotated every year or two.

The kibbutz federations provide financial assistance to their member villages through independent loan funds and national negotiation with financial and governmental institutions. They offer technical advisory services ranging from economic analysis to the planning of communal kitchens and laundries. Central purchasing and marketing services cut costs for individual kibbutzim and a special department deals with kibbutz-based industry. They operate their own psychological clinics for children (including a school for disturbed children) and, in cooperation with institutions of higher learning, offer courses in specific branches of technology, agriculture, and kibbutz management. Cultural activities range from movement-wide choirs and amateur orchestras to regional schools for adult education on a non-university and university level. The kibbutz federations are joined together in Berit ha-Tenu'ah ha-Kibbutzit ("Kibbutz Movement Alliance"), which coordinates their activities in the many areas in which they cooperate. The three major ones jointly operate Israel's largest teachers' training college—Seminar ha-Kibbutzim. They sponsor educational and sociological research and are investigating the possibility of establishing a kibbutz-sponsored university.

Each federation operates an ideological center, where seminars are conducted, and publishes bulletins and journals of letters and opinion. Berit ha-Tenu'ah ha-Kibbutzit has established a company for the production of television material on kibbutz topics. Each federation negotiates with its kibbutzim for manpower for general movement activity, not only within the movement itself but in the Zionist and labor movements and in government service. There is an increasing degree of regional cooperation cutting across federation boundaries. This includes regional secondary schools, youth and cultural activity, and large regional economic and industrial complexes—including plants for canning, poultry slaughtering and dressing,

Cotton fields at kibbutz Neveh Ur in the Jordan Valley, 1969.
Courtesy Keren Hayesod, United Israel Appeal, Jerusalem.

packing and fodder preparation, cotton gins and large silos, trucking and hauling cooperatives, and large regional garages.

Social and Educational Aspects. The kibbutz movement believes in personal labor and places equal value on all kinds of work. In the course of time people take up more or less permanent jobs, but there is a great deal of work mobility. With economic expansion and the increasing technical complexity of the kibbutz economy, it has become necessary in many instances to hire outside labor in contradiction to the movement's socialist principles. It is hoped to solve this problem in the course of time with increased population and efficiency. Another problem which the movement is trying to solve is the absorption of the increasing proportion of members pursuing academic or professional careers, often outside the kibbutz, while retaining their membership.

The kibbutz provides a complete spectrum of services to its members, ranging from razor blades to housing and from honeymoons to financial aid for dependents living outside, with complete medical coverage. Each kibbutz has a communal dining hall, laundry, and a tailor shop. With the rise in the standard of living, increasing allowance has been made for individual tastes and for spending in accord with personal inclination on clothing, furnishings, cultural activities, hobbies, vacations, and so forth.

In all but some dozen kibbutzim, children live in children's houses, which include sleeping quarters and play and study rooms, where community living is taught from the very earliest age. They are part of an organized children's community, living, eating, and studying together; in some ways they constitute a miniature kibbutz, conducting their own affairs, with the advice of teachers and group leaders, and in many kibbutzim operating their own small farms. Children "graduate" from one house to another as they advance in age. Mothers—especially, of course, when nursing—visit their children frequently during the day, and after work the children are with their parents. People working with children are trained in kibbutz-sponsored

Babies' house of kibbutz Manarah in Upper Galilee, 1969.

Courtesy Keren Hayesod, United Israel Appeal, Jerusalem.

courses, ranging from intensive three-month seminars to full-fledged kindergarten and teacher training. The kibbutz school differs from the city school in its emphasis on agriculture and on work as an integral part of the curriculum. It is considered an extension of the children's society, so that the teacher-pupil relationship is close and informal. All kibbutz children continue through secondary school; the increasing number who intend to go on to higher education are prepared for the matriculation examinations. A number of kibbutzim, principally among those belonging to the Iḥud, have changed the system to provide for children sleeping in the homes of their parents. Advocates of the change believe that it enhances the psychological security of the child, as well as improving the position of the woman and the family in the kibbutz. The effect of the kibbutz and its educational system on its

Communal dining hall, kibbutz Ayyelet ha-Shaḥar, 1969. Courtesy Keren Hayesod, United Israel Appeal, Jerusalem.

children has been extensively studied. Research has not shown significant indications of maternal deprivation, though some psychologists have found some signs of this at the younger ages. They feel, however, that this is overcome at a later age by the powerful supporting environment.

There are some kibbutzim in which the third, and in a few even the fourth, generation has reached maturity, and a goodly number in which the kibbutz-born are now the dominant group. Over 75% of the latter have remained in the kibbutz, despite the attraction of the cities. Though only 4% of the total population of Israel, their percentage among army officers is three or four times as high. A quarter of all the casualties in the Six-Day War were soldiers from kibbutzim. More direct and practical than their parents, and less given to hairsplitting ideology, it is the young people who are the principal force pushing toward the ultimate unification of the movement.

Some sociological studies have shown that although there is no material basis for social stratification, elements of such stratification do exist on the basis of social prestige or kinds of work. There are some differences in personal possessions as well, due to outside sources of income such as gifts, reparations from Germany, or inheritances, which are not always handed in to the kibbutz in their entirety, though very large sums of money received by beneficiaries of reparations have been handed over to the kibbutzim. Women have been disappointed at times in their relationship with the kibbutz community. The idea of freeing women from household chores so that they can work at other tasks was one of the prime aims of the movement, but this becomes increasingly difficult as a kibbutz grows older and pressure is generated for increased work in child care and household services. Kibbutzim are now attempting to improve the personal and family status of women by improving physical conditions of work in the services, by raising the work level of a profession through training and study, and, in some cases, by reducing working hours for **84** women with families.

The kibbutz movement has been, and still is, a major factor in the activities of the Zionist movement and the State of Israel. Its influence has been both moral and practical, ranging from settlement and security functions (including settling new areas since the Six-Day War), to the absorption of immigrants and Youth Aliyah children, and the provision of leading personnel for Zionist and government service. The number of kibbutz members in the Knesset and among army officers is far beyond their proportion of the population. This influence is indicated by such diverse statistics as the fact that its production accounts for 12% of Israel's gross national product, and that more than 20 members of the Knesset are kibbutz members. In recent years, the movement has been increasing in size at the rate of about 2–3% a year. Although it has become an established institution, it has demonstrated a capacity for changing with the times.

Iḥud ha-Kevuẓot ve-ha-Kibbutzim (Heb. "Union of Collective Settlements") was founded in 1951 through the unification of Ḥever ha-Kevuẓot and Iḥud ha-Kibbutzim, which had split off from Ha-Kibbutz ha-Me'uḥad (see below). In 1971 it comprised 76 communities, with a total population of about 26,900. Ḥever ha-Kevuẓot was the federation of the smaller, purely agricultural collective settlements, many of whose members believed in the ethical socialist concepts of A. D. Gordon, and most of whom belonged to Mapai, the Israel Labor Party; it included such long-established villages as Deganiyyah and Geva. The Iḥud ha-Kibbutzim settlements also leaned toward Mapai. The Iḥud is considered the most liberal of the three major kibbutz federations, allowing for more diversity and imposing less social or political discipline. In more than a dozen of its villages, for example, children sleep in the parents' homes, though most of the other kibbutzim regard the dormitory system as a part of the movement's educational methods. A number of Iḥud kibbutzim also allow for more latitude in the spending of personal funds. In 1953, the non-socialist kibbutzim of Ha-No'ar ha-

Wedding procession at kibbutz Sa'ad in the northern Negev, 1961. Courtesy Keren Hayesod, United Israel Appeal, Jerusalem.

Ẓiyyoni, associated with the Independent Liberal Party, joined the Iḥud on condition of educational and political autonomy. In 1971 there were 5, with a population of 1,500.

Each kibbutz elects its representatives to the national executive, and the national secretariat consists of members drafted from the kibbutzim. The movement operates a loan fund, purchasing services, and departments for economic planning and assistance, social and ideological problems, education, youth work, military security, manpower, and immigrant absorption. It delegates members for work in youth movements both in Israel and abroad, in Zionist and political affairs, in the labor movement, and in government service. It conducts a variety of seminars and courses in cultural and technical subjects. It cooperates with the other kibbutz federations in operating Seminar ha-Kibbutzim for training teachers, and at its convention in 1969 it decided actively to encourage university education for members. The kibbutzim conduct their own elementary schools and regional secondary schools, attended in some areas by children from moshavim and Kibbutz ha-Me'uḥad communities as well.

In 1971/72, the agricultural output of its kibbutzim totaled IL310,000,000, and their industrial output IL 195,000,000.

The movement publishes a weekly bulletin, *Iggeret la-Ḥaverim* (1951–); a quarterly journal, *Niv ha-Kevuẓah* (1930–); a bimonthly journal of opinion, *Shedemot* (1948–); and a periodical for educators, Iggeret le-Ḥinnukh (1952–). It organizes regional and national cultural activities, such as discussion circles and the federation's choir. The youth of the movement are affiliated as a group to Ha-No'ar ha-Oved ve-ha-Lomed, the Histadrut's youth section. the Iḥud has a special relationship with a number of youth movements in Israel and abroad, sending youth workers to them and receiving reinforcements from them. Among these are Ha-No'ar ha-Oved ve-ha-Lomed, Ha-Ẓofim, Iḥud ha-Bonim, and La-Merḥav.

Ha-Kibbutz ha-Arẓi ha-Shomer ha-Ẓa'ir, founded in 1927, comprised 76 kibbutzim throughout the country in 1971. Its ideological basis is a belief in the kibbutz as an instrument for fulfilling the Zionist ideal, furthering the class struggle, and building a Socialist society. Its founding members, who belonged to the Ha-Shomer ha-Ẓa'ir ("Young Guard") youth movement, came from Poland and Galicia in 1919, and in 1920 established the movement's first kibbutz, which settled at Bet Alfa in 1922. By 1927 there were six Ha-Shomer ha-Ẓa'ir kibbutzim, four of which founded Ha-Kibbutz ha-Arẓi. In the 45 years that followed, the population of its villages grew from 249 members and 19 children to over 30,000 persons, of whom some 16,000 were members and 10,000 children.

Ha-Kibbutz ha-Arẓi ("The National Kibbutz [Movement]") regards the kibbutz as an autonomous unit of social life, comprehending all spheres of economic, social, cultural, political, and educational activity, which are developed on principles laid down by the movement as a whole—both as an instrument for the realization of **87**

Zionism, the class struggle and the building of socialism, and as an end in itself: the archetype of the socialist society. Through continual democracy in all fields, the movement strives to develop a common outlook on life that unites all its members (the so-called "ideological collectivism"). Its ideology is founded on pioneering Zionism paving the way for mass *aliyah,* the kibbutz way of life, integration of settlement work with political activity, Jewish political independence combined with Jewish-Arab cooperation, and the defense of Israel's security coupled with unremitting efforts to achieve peace.

From the start, Ha-Kibbutz ha-Arẓi favored a union of all workers, including those in the cities, based on Zionist pioneering and socialist principles. Since such a union failed to materialize, a Socialist League was formed in 1936 as its political partner. In 1946 they combined to form the Ha-Shomer ha-Ẓa'ir Party, which in turn, joined with two other groups in 1948 to found Mapam, the United Workers' Party, of which Ha-Kibbutz ha-Arẓi with its constituent kibbutzim is an integral part.

Members of Ha-Kibbutz ha-Arẓi have played a prominent part in the struggle for Jewish independence. They formed the first Tower and Stockade settlement, Tel Amal (Nir David) in 1936; many of them joined the supernumerary police, the Jewish units in the British army, and the Jewish Brigade; and they made an important contribution to Aliyah Bet ("Illegal" Immigration) and the founding of the Palmaḥ.

Ha-Kibbutz ha-Arẓi regards the education of its members' children as a matter of central importance. It trains them for active and creative participation in collective life, employing youth movement traditions and progressive educational methods. There are independent children's communities, covering the first six years of schooling, in almost every kibbutz, as well as 25 schools serving the kibbutzim, with youth communities covering the 7th–12th school years, and a teachers' training seminar at Givat Ḥavivah. The aim of the movement's educational institutions is to inculcate a general philosophy of life, and not mere booklearning. Some 4,800 of their alumni have become kibbutz members and in 1967 the first group aiming at the formation of a new kibbutz was founded. Members of the older kibbutzim serve an additional year in newer kibbutzim after completing their army service.

Although Ha-Kibbutz ha-Arẓi had as its primary objective the development of agriculture, most kibbutzim now also have industrial plants. In 1968, the movement's agricultural output was valued at IL 168,000,000 ($48,000,-000), or 9.9% of agricultural output in the country, and the industrial output at IL98,500,000 ($28,000,000). Ha-Kibbutz ha-Arẓi publishes various periodicals for its members. It maintains a publishing house, Sifriat ha-Po'alim, founded in 1931, which has issued about 1,000 books, and the Moreshet Institute for research on the Holocaust, established in 1962. The highest authority in Ha-Kibbutz ha-Arẓi is the triennial convention, which has committees that meet annually. The convention chooses an executive council, which appoints a secretariat. Younger members have their own sectional organization.

Ha-Kibbutz ha-Me'uḥad (Heb. "The United Kibbutz [Movement]"), founded in 1927, is a national organization of kibbutzim united by a common concept of the kibbutz and a common approach to the building of a labor society in the Land of Israel. The ideology of the movement is based on the following principles: the kibbutz should be a large settlement, with no predetermined limit to the number of members; it should be open to all comers and should not restrict itself to the graduates of any particular youth movement; it should engage in all forms of essential production, both agricultural and industrial; it should play a role in the integration of newcomers to the country by aiming at a membership representing a wide range of geographic origin. The first kibbutz with these aims was En Harod (founded in 1921 by Gedud ha-Avodah, "the Labor Legion") and when the Kibbutz Me'uḥad movement was founded, at a conference **89**

in Petaḥ Tikvah in 1927, it was based on En Harod, groups of newcomers, and local youth from the moshavot. Other kibbutzim joined in 1929, and a second conference, held at Yagur in 1936, further elaborated the movement's principles. It exercises authority over the kibbutzim of the movement in matters of ideology, each kibbutz being autonomous in administration and finance. From its foundation, it regarded Yiẓḥak Tabenkin of En Harod as its spiritual and ideological leader. During the Mandatory regime Ha-Kibbutz ha-Me'uḥad played a large part in the defense of the *yishuv,* the organization of "illegal" immigration, and the struggle for independence, with a special role in the creation and maintenance of the Palmaḥ. The movement's kibbutzim are scattered all over Israel, and it prides itself that their location has always been determined by the country's pioneering needs. Thus the first Jewish settlement to be established on the Golan Heights after the Six-Day War was founded by Ha-Kibbutz ha-Me'uḥad, conforming to the principle, adopted at the 1955 conference held at Givat Brenner, that "the natural borders of Ereẓ Israel are those of the historic homeland of the Jewish people, and this is the area for *aliyah,* settlement, and the realization of the Zionist program."

Most of the movement's members belonged in the 1940s to the left-wing faction of Mapai. When the latter split in 1944, Ha-Kibbutz ha-Me'uḥad was the nucleus of the newly formed Si'ah Bet (B Faction), later Aḥdut ha-Avodah, which joined with Ha-Shomer ha-Ẓa'ir in 1945 to form Mapam, though a minority remained in Mapai. Owing to the fact that its members came from a variety of youth movements, there was never a dearth of internal political and social controversy in the movement and its kibbutzim. Differences came to a head as a result of the growing intensity of the struggle between Mapai and Mapam and the decision of the Mapai minority to set up its own cultural and educational institutions. At a meeting of the movement's council, held at Na'an in 1951, kibbutzim with a Mapai majority seceded and formed Iḥud ha-Kibbutzim, which joined with Ḥever ha-Kevuẓot to form Iḥud ha-Kevuẓot ve-ha Ki-bbutzim. Four kibbutzim (one of them En Harod itself), which were evenly divided between Mapai and Mapam, were each split into two separate settlements.

Members of Ha-Kibbutz ha-Me'uḥad have figured prominently among the founders and leaders of the Israel labor movement and the Haganah, officers in the Israel forces in the War of Independence, authors and artists, Knesset members and cabinet ministers. Always a strong advocate of the unification of the labor movement, it supported the formation of the Israel Labor Party, which was joined by practically all its members. Ha-Kibbutz ha-Me'uḥad has a chain of economic enterprises and cultural and social institutions: Keren ha-Kibbutz and Mishkei ha-Kibbutz, its major financial and economic instruments; Efal, a center for higher education and leadership training; *Mi-Bifnim* ("From Within"), an ideological quarterly; and *Ba-Kibbutz,* a weekly. It also publishes periodicals for youth and others dealing with education, culture, etc. Ha-Kibbutz ha-Me'uḥad publishing house issued 700 original works up to 1968. The movement maintains a museum and research center for the study of the history of the Holocaust, Beit Yiẓḥak Katznelson, at Kibbutz Loḥamei ha-Getta'ot, and an art museum, Ha-Mishkan le-Ommanut, at En Harod.

In 1972 it comprised 62 settlements, with a population of some 26,000. One of these, Givat Brenner (population 1,660), was the largest kibbutz in the country. In the 1960s the population of the settlements grew by an average of 3.5% per year. The area under cultivation is 12,500 acres (50,000 dunams), and the number of industrial enterprises is 45, with a turnover of about IL 50,000,000.

Ha-Kibbutz Ha-Dati (Heb. "The Religious Kibbutz"), the union of Ha-Po'el ha-Mizrachi kibbutzim, was established in 1935 by four religious pioneer groups consisting of members of Baḥad ("League of Religious Ḥalutzim") from Germany and the Mizrachi Pioneers from Poland. Most of its development took place before

Israel's independence. Seven pioneer groups were founded before 1940 and another nine before 1948. Ten groups were able to establish kibbutzim: three in the Beth-Shean valley (Tirat Zevi, Sedeh Eliyahu, En ha-Naziv), three in the Hebron hills (Gush Ezyon), three in the neighborhood of Gaza (Be'erot Yizhak, Sa'ad and Kefar Darom), and Yavneh. Two more were founded in 1948—Sheluhot in the Beth-Shean Valley and Lavi in Lower Galilee. Six of the villages, which were situated at the edge of the Jewish area in a completely Arab district, were totally destroyed during the War of Independence and many of the adult population were killed. They were reestablished later, three of them as moshavim shittufiyyim. After a lengthy period of stagnation, most of the religious kibbutzim recovered in the 1960s and are now among the most flourishing in the country. One new kibbutz, Alummim, was founded in 1966, and at the end of 1971 Ha-Kibbutz ha-Dati had 11 member

Children's dining room at kibbutz Ayyelet ha-Shahar in Upper Galilee, 1969. Courtesy Keren Hayesod, United Israel Appeal, Jerusalem.

Chicken coop at kibbutz Manarah, 1969. Courtesy Keren
Hayesod, United Israel Appeal, Jerusalem.

settlements with a total population of 4,000, including
Naḥal outposts on Mount Gilboa and at Kefar Ezyon.

PRINCIPLES. Ha-Kibbutz ha-Dati was based, from the
beginning, on the idea of combining religious practice with
labor—*Torah va-Avodah*. Its founders believed that the best
means to this end is the communal group, within the
framework of which the community can carry out religious
precepts in daily life; this attitude was in contrast to the
general view of Ha-Po'el Ha-Mizrachi of the time. While
implementing the general kibbutz principles of communal
production and consumption, equality, self-labor, and
pioneering, it also emphasizes the importance of Jewish
religious tradition. Its religious socialism is founded on
prophetic concepts of social justice and talmudic principles of human relations and good government; as regards
the attitude to contemporary problems, its way is that of
religious socialism. It regards democracy as a basic value of
the kibbutz, and not merely as a corollary of equality. In its
view, communal ownership is important not only for   93

economic reasons but as an expression of religious and human attitudes.

PUBLIC ACTIVITIES. Ha-Kibbutz ha-Dati aims at establishing a self-contained religious society as a major instrument for bringing about religious renewal under present conditions of national renascence and the resettlement of Erez Israel. It has developed an approach of its own to the celebration of Independence Day, army service for girls, public prayer, *shemittah,* and so forth. It aims at establishing groups of kibbutzim in the same area, with a view to developing regional activities in education and economy in accordance with its principles.

Ha-Kibbutz ha-Dati has influenced public life in Israel in various ways: it was among the founders of Youth Aliyah and of various religious youth villages, yeshivot, and other educational institutions, and it provides help and guidance for the Benei Akiva youth movement. Politically, it expresses its independent view within the frameworks of Ha-Po'el ha-Mizrachi and the National Religious Party, having been instrumental in the establishment of La-Mifneh, the left-wing faction in these movements. The association publishes a journal, *Ammudim* (called *Alonim* 1938–49, *Yedi'ot ha-Kibbutz ha-Dati* 1951–56), which appears monthly and is devoted to questions of the religious public and the state, apart from purely internal affairs.

7 THE MOSHAV

The moshav (or moshav ovedim) is a cooperative small-holders' village combining some of the features of both cooperative and private farming. The idea was evolved during World War I in the quest for a form of settlement that would not only express national and social aspirations on the basis of collective principles like the kibbutz, but also provide scope for individual initiative and independent farm management. The idea was mooted in articles published in various periodicals and was given definite shape in a pamphlet *Yissud Moshevei Ovedim* ("The Establishment of Workers' Villages," 1919) by Eliezer Joffe, who formulated the social and economic principles on which the moshav should be based: nationally owned land, mutual aid, cooperative purchasing and marketing, and the family as the fundamental unit. These principles were further developed in the writings of Yiẓhak Vilkanski (Elazari-Volcani), the agronomist, who dealt with the economic structure desirable for the moshav and regarded it as the appropriate answer to the needs of mass settlement. This evaluation was fully vindicated after the establishment of the State of Israel, when tens of thousands of new immigrant families were settled on the land in hundreds of moshavim.

At first the moshav economy was based on mixed farming, which, it was expected, would supply most of the farmer's needs and give him greater stamina to withstand agricultural fluctuations and crises than the single-crop farm. It would also permit the work to be spread out evenly over the year, a point of particular importance since the settler and his family had to cultivate the farm by themselves without the aid of hired seasonal labor.

Kefar Yeḥezkel, one of the first two moshavim to be established in Ereẓ Israel. Courtesy Government Press Office, Tel Aviv.

Milestones of Moshav Settlement. The first two moshavim were founded in 1921, Nahalal in September in the northern Jezreel Valley and Kefar Yeḥezkel in December in the eastern part. Most of the members had formerly lived in kibbutzim (Deganyah, Kinneret, Ḥuldah, and Merḥavyah). Within ten years another eight moshavim were founded, most of them in the Jezreel Valley. At the beginning of the 1930s, the movement was given a new impetus by widespread settlement in the Ḥefer Plain by the Hityashvut ha-Elef scheme, intended to settle 1,000 families on the land in the Sharon and Judea, and by the establishment of the first moshavim in the south. The landholdings were small compared with those of the first moshavim, as it was assumed that incomes would be supplemented and the farms consolidated by work outside the moshav in fruit groves and construction projects. During the Arab rebellion of 1936–39, more moshavim were established all over the country, especially in the valleys and in the south, as Stockade and Watchtower settlements. At the end of

World War II, a number of moshavim were established by demobilized soldiers from the Jewish Brigade and other Jewish units in the British army. In 1948, when the State of Israel was established, there were 58 moshavim in the country.

Most of the new immigrants who arrived in large numbers immediately after the establishment of the state differed in many respects from the pioneers who had settled on the land after spending years in training and preparation. They consisted mainly of families with many children, elderly persons, even entire communities brought over en masse. The moshav ovedim, with its family structure, was felt to be the only medium of settling these immigrants on the land. Hundreds of veterans from the older moshavim came forward to recruit new immigrants for settlements, to set up moshavim, and particularly to instruct and guide the new settlers. In the period 1949–56, 250 new moshavim were established, with a population that approached 100,000 in 1971.

The Moshav Movement (Tenu'at ha-Moshavim). The moshav movement was founded in the mid-1930s to cope with the problems of the existing moshavim, to mold and preserve their social structure, and to help establish more moshavim. The movement developed a series of economic, financial, and service institutions to advance these purposes. These include: Keren ha-Moshavim, a mutual assistance fund; the Ein Ḥai Bank; Tagmulim la-Moshavim, a savings and pension fund for members; Bittu'aḥ Hadadi, a mutual insurance company; Matam (Mishkei Tenu'at ha-Moshavim—Moshav Movement Farms), which provides low-priced, high-quality products; Bank le-Mashkanta'ot (Mortgage Bank), which provides loans for private and public building in the moshavim; and regional purchasing organizations, with some 30 to 50 moshavim in each, to organize marketing and supplies. The latter have set up enterprises, in cooperation with local councils, to lower the cost of services and supplies, and improve production facilities. Examples of these enterprises are citrus-canning plants, fodder plants, slaughterhouses, fruit-packing plants, egg-sorting warehouses, and cold storage plants. The movement has departments for education, culture, social activities, internal arbitration, advice and training in farming and organization, and absorption of new settlers. It also has a youth section, and it publishes periodicals.

In 1971 there were 215 moshavim, with a total population of 77,000, affiliated to Tenu'at ha-Moshavim. Other moshav movements were: the Union of Religious Cooperative Movements of Ha-Po'el ha-Mizrachi, with 56 moshavim and a membership of 24,000; the Farmers' Union (Ha-Ihud ha-Hakla'i), with 33 villages and 10,000 people; and the cooperative Agricultural Center of the Herut Movement and Betar, with eight moshavim and 1,600 people. There were also 13 moshavim with 4,000 people affiliated to Ha-Oved ha-Ziyyoni; nine, with 2,500, to Po'alei Agudat Israel and Agudat Israel; six, with 1,500, to the Farmers' Federation (Hitahdut ha-Ikkarim); and seven unaffiliated moshavim, with 3,400 people making a total of 347 moshavim with a combined population of about 124,000—97,000 living in 270 moshavim founded after the establishment of the State of Israel in May 1948 and 26,500 living in 77 veteran moshavim.

Organization of the Moshav. Each moshav is organized as a cooperative society for agricultural settlement and constitutes a unit of local government administered by the management of the society. The moshav operates in accordance with the Cooperative Societies Ordinance, 1933, under the authority of the Registrar of Cooperative Societies; its accounts are audited by the audit unions for agricultural cooperation. Its activities are governed by a general set of regulations which serves as a pattern for those of the individual moshavim. At an annual assembly of members, each moshav elects its management, which comprises a managing committee, a control board, and committees for economic, social, educational, and cultural activities. Disputes between members or between a member and the management are submitted for arbitration and decision to the social committee or a judicial committee of the parent movement. The moshav helps its members to obtain credit, purchase seed, fertilizer, and fodder, and to market their produce. It maintains farming equipment and vehicles (sometimes together with neighboring moshavim), workshops, cooperative stores, etc. It provides members' children with primary and post-primary education in local or regional schools, and fosters cultural activities; members receive medical care in local clinics.

The society erects all the public buildings and installations including pumping installations, central irrigation network, supply stores, dairies, refrigeration and sorting plants, schools, clinics, and sports facilities. It finances its investments partly by direct taxation of members and partly by loans based on a general mutual guarantee by the members. The general assembly decides on the annual budget, composed of the local government budget (covered by direct taxes) and the administrative budget (covered partly by taxes and partly by levies on items of income and on various types of production outlays). In the 1960s the moshav set itself new goals: securing production rights in nationally planned branches of agriculture (dairy farming, poultry farming, orchards, etc.); the encouragement of new crops, notably for export purposes; and the protection of members' interests in taxation and social security. The expansion and social developments of the moshavim have given rise to the need for a legal basis for their life and activities. The draft Cooperative Societies Law submitted to the Knesset contains a special chapter dealing with the legal framework of the moshav. This is designed, in accordance with existing conditions, to safeguard established principles and ensure that the moshav and the moshav movement will continue to develop as an efficient and healthy unit of the national economy and society.

The Moshav as an Example to Developing Countries. In recent years the moshav and its way of life have attracted the interest of some leaders and many students from Asia, 99

Africa, and Latin America. Thousands of them have come to Israel to study the methods of the moshav, which they regard as a possible solution to the problems of organizing agriculture in their own countries. The moshav movement has been host to students and has organized study courses for them. It has also provided Israel's technical assistance program to these various developing countries with many instructors to establish and advise settlements of the moshav type in these countries. Today there are scores of such settlements in Africa, Asia, and Latin America, with moshav members from Israel as instructors. The moshav movement, together with the Israel Ministry of Foreign Affairs, has also established a volunteer movement for foreign service, and many young men from moshavim have served, and are serving, as volunteers in developing countries, living and working with the local population.

Moshav Shittufi. The moshav shittufi is an alternative form of settlement combining features of the kibbutz and the moshav. The originators of the idea wanted to combine the advantages of both forms of settlement, while avoiding what they regarded as overemphasis on collectivism in the kibbutz and on individual farming in the moshav. They therefore separated production from consumption, adopting the productive system of the kibbutz and the preservation of the family unit in the moshav. The village's lands and installations—sometimes including industrial plants—are collectively owned and operated, as in the kibbutz, but each family has its own home and is responsible for its own cooking, domestic economy, and the care of children, as in the moshav. Mothers generally work outside the home for two or three hours a day five times a week. From the proceeds of the moshav shittufi's farming and other enterprises, each family is allotted a sum to meet its own needs, while the village as a whole provides education for the children, medical services, cultural activities, and the like.

The first two moshavim shittufiyyim— Kefar Ḥittim in Lower Galilee and Moledet in the Gilboa district—were founded in 1936–37, and after World War II many of the demobilized soldiers who settled on the land chose this form of settlement. In 1971 there were 27 moshavim shittufiyyim with a total population of 5,700. Ten belonged to Tenu'at ha-Moshavim, six to Ha-Oved ha-Ziyyoni, four to Ha-Po'el ha-Mizrachi, four to the Ḥerut movement, two to the Farmers' Union and one to Po'alei Agudat Israel. To coordinate their activities, the moshavim shittufiyyim maintain an inter-movement committee.

Part Three
LABOR

8 JEWISH LABOR ORGANIZATIONS

THE HISTADRUT UNTIL 1948. Since the late 19th century sporadic labor associations arose in agriculture and in the printing, clothing, and building trades, as well as groups limited to a particular locality or place of work. The Teachers' Association was founded in 1903, but its aims were only partially those of a trade union. The first abiding Jewish trade union organizations in Erez Israel were the two regional associations of agricultural workers founded in Galilee and Judea in 1911. In 1913 a clerical workers' union was set up. In 1919 a railroad workers' union, including both Jews and Arabs, was founded; it later took in the postal and telegraph workers.

Founding of the Histadrut. The founding of the Histadrut, the General Federation of Labor, in 1920, was not primarily the result of the development of these early trade unions, but rather the outcome of strongly held ideas about the unity of the Jewish workers in Erez Israel and their mission in the building of the country as a workers' commonwealth. Ahdut ha-Avodah, founded in 1919 at a labor unity conference in Petah Tikvah, aimed at establishing one body, organized on a trade union basis, which would deal with all the interests of the workers including ideological and political activities. However, it did not achieve the support of all the workers, especially those in the Ha-Po'el ha-Za'ir party, which rejected its socialist definitions. The newcomers of the Third Aliyah, belonging to the He-Halutz, Ze'irei Zion, and Ha-Shomer ha-Za'ir movements, who arrived in 1919 and 1920, were opposed to the authority of both Ha-Po'el ha-Za'ir and Ahdut ha-Avodah, which had set up competing labor exchanges, contracting companies, and medical services and each of which claimed to represent the workers, especially in the vital area of agricultural settlement.

Joseph Trumpeldor's appeal (at the beginning of 1920) for the unification of the workers to deal with their common interests and the threat by a conference of ḥalutzim, which met on Mount Carmel in autumn 1920, to set up a separate workers' organization pushed the parties into agreement on the convening of a general conference of workers in December 1920. Eighty-seven delegates, representing 4,433 voters, participated. (Aḥdut-ha-Avodah had 37 delegates, Ha-Po'el ha-Ẓa'ir 26, "newcomers" 16, pro-Communist 6, and others 2.) The very fact that delegates were chosen by general elections (although they were held on a party-list system) constituted an agreement to establish a general organization and not just an interparty coordinating body, as Ha-Po'el ha-Ẓa'ir wanted, but there was much controversy at the founding conference over the character of the organization. The leaders of Aḥdut ha-Avodah (Berl Katznelson, Shemuel Yavni'eli, and others) wanted to endow it with the widest possible powers in political activities, cultural affairs, and defense, while Ha-Po'el ha-Ẓa'ir, led by Yosef Sprinzak, wanted to preserve the power of the parties. The differences were resolved by a compromise: the founding conference decided to establish the General Federation of Jewish Workers in Palestine (Ha-Histadrut ha-Kelalit shel ha-Ovedim ha-Ivriyyim be-Ereẓ Israel), which, according to its constitution, "unites all workers in the country who live on the fruits of their own labor without exploiting the labor of others, for the purpose of arranging all the communal, economic, and cultural affairs of the working class in the country for the building of the labor society in the Land of Israel." With the founding of the Histadrut the He-Ḥalutz Organization in Palestine announced its dissolution. Gedud ha-Avodah, the Labor Legion, which had been set up in 1920 to carry out pioneering tasks on a cooperative basis, joined the Histadrut but later developed into an opposition group.

Early Activities. In the early years, the Histadrut devoted itself to creating work and encouraging immigration by building up an independent labor economy. Agricultural settlement was to be the highroad to this goal, but the shortage of national lands and public funds for the purpose, which delayed the start of the Zionist Organization's operations, pushed the workers into public works and building. The Histadrut set up an Immigration and Labor Center, which received immigrants and tried to find them work on a contract basis—groups of workers undertaking jobs and sharing the proceeds. The contracting offices which the different parties had set up before the establishment of the Histadrut were unified into the Office for Public Works and Building, which received government and other contracts. Cooperative contracting seemed the right way not only to build an independent labor economy but also to compete in the unorganized labor market.

Within the framework of the Histadrut's Office for Public Works and Building, various subcontracting groups from different backgrounds, organized according to different principles, were formed. Some came from the youth movements and some from particular cities abroad, while other groups were organized ad hoc for the purpose of a particular job. Some worked as partnerships, while others divided up the income either in equal parts or with higher shares for the skilled workers. Some of these groups became well enough organized to be ready to establish agricultural settlements. The Histadrut was careful to keep all these groups open to new immigrants and tried to limit the advantages of the skilled workers.

In the organization of its basic units, the Histadrut gave preference to *"kibbutzei avodah"* and *"havurot"* (collective work groups), which undertook subcontracting jobs, the urban cooperatives, which were regarded as stages on the road to an independent workers' economy, and trade union organizations, which were seen as a correlative to the capitalist economy. Of the trade unions themselves, the Histadrut favored those set up on an industrial, rather than a narrow craft basis, despite the very small scope of industrial enterprise at the time. The industrial basis was regarded as a safeguard against separatist tendencies among the skilled workers and as training for the running of industries in the future. In accordance with this policy, a National Union of Public Works and Building Employees was established in 1922; it was also intended to exercise democratic control over the Office of Public Works and Building. There was opposition to this policy from skilled workers as well as from the Communists and other left wing adherents, who regarded the building of a workers' economy as utopianism and exploitation of the workers. Bank ha-Po'alim (the Workers' Bank), which was founded in 1921, was intended to be the credit institution for the Office of Public Works and for the contracting groups; its long-range goal was to help to build the independent labor economy. The basic capital of LP50,000 was invested by the Zionist Organization, which bought the founding shares. A Histadrut delegation which went to America to raise money from the half million Jewish workers there in the summer of 1922 did not succeed in its mission due to anti-Zionist opposition. The supply organization, Hamashbir, which furnished the workers of the Office with consumer goods on credit, was also included within the framework of the Histadrut. Medical aid was provided by Kuppat Ḥolim (the Workers' Sick Fund), which had been founded in 1913, split in 1919, and was reformed.

Labor Economy versus Class Struggle. At the Second Convention of the Histadrut, which took place in February 1923, the debate between the advocates of the independent labor economy and those who defended purely trade union interests continued. The former view was favored by the great majority of the 130 delegates, representing 6,581 voters. Aḥdut ha-Avodah, which had 69 delegates, more than half the total, regarded it as a Palestinian form of the class war and Ha-Po'el ha-Ẓa'ir, with 36, as the Jewish national way to the building of a people's socialism and a just society. The left-wing opposition, on the other hand, argued that this was "the socialism of poverty" and demanded a class-war policy which would assume the evolution of a capitalist economy and the adaptation of the immigrants to its existence. At that conference, the Histadrut completed its constitution and decided to join the Trade Union International in Amsterdam, against the opposition of the left, on the one hand, and Ha-Po'el ha-Za'ir—which opposed all international ties—on the other.

From 1922 to 1927 the policies of the Histadrut, under the vigorous leadership of David Ben-Gurion, were guided by three central principles: the building of the Land of Israel as a socialist economy under workers' control; maximum economic self-sufficiency, the workers supplying their own needs in order to accumulate capital; and the syndicalist idea of identity between management and labor. These aims found expression in the legal-economic framework set up by the Histadrut to safeguard its social principles and run the labor enterprises which were under the control of the workers. Hevrat ha-Ovedim, the General Cooperative Association of Jewish Labor in Palestine, which was identical in membership with the Histadrut and the legal owner of its assets, ensured its influence in its subsidiary companies by means of founders' shares. One of the subsidiaries was Nir, the Cooperative Society for Agricultural Settlement, which was established to control and develop the workers' agricultural settlements, and to whose members its shares were sold. A second was Solel Boneh, the Cooperative Society of Jewish Workers for Public Works, Building, and Industry. By means of preference shares without voting rights, the two companies were able to raise external capital.

The grandiose plans of Hevrat ha-Ovedim, which was licensed by the authorities in 1924, were only partially realized, however. Solel Boneh over-expanded its activities in order to give as much employment as possible and went bankrupt in 1927; its failure caused difficulties for Ha-mashbir, which had given it credit in kind. The Zionist

Organization did not recognize Nir as the representative of the agricultural settlements in signing contracts, and there was also internal criticism of excessive control over the individual settlements. For all practical purposes the Histadrut remained in control only of its central institutions and not of the cooperatives or the communal settlements. During the economic recession of 1923, large-scale public works were stopped, investment and credit were severely limited, and unemployment rose to 1,500–2,000. These developments increased the Histadrut's responsibilities in the distribution of work and assistance and its leadership proposed the building of the economy by the workers' own resources as a defense against the retreat from Zionism. The planting of tobacco in the villages marked an improvement in the employment situation in 1924. The idea of moving to the countryside suited the aspirations of many workers at that time, and collective contracting groups began to form in the villages. In 1925, the urban employment situation picked up with the beginning of the Fourth Aliyah.

The leaders of the Histadrut regarded the building of a workers' commonwealth as first and foremost a question of agricultural settlement. There were still groups of workers—some of them formed before World War I—that had been supported by the Palestine Office of the Zionist Organization and wanted to settle on the land. The decisions of the London Conference in 1920 favoring settlement on Jewish National Fund land by self-employed farmers or groups suited the principles of the workers. The Histadrut represented the candidates for settlement in contacts with the Zionist institutions, which left the choice of the social form of each settlement up to the settlers themselves. Gedud ha-Avodah adopted the idea of the "large commune" conceived by Shelomo Lavie. Workers' groups from the youth movements or from particular cities also formed collective settlements. Some workers formed organizations for cooperative smallholders' settlements (moshavei ovedim). Groups of all these types settled in the Jezreel Valley in the early 1920s.

In 1923 En-Harod, the first "large" kibbutz, split away from Gedud ha-Avodah in a dispute over economic autonomy, and in 1927 formed the Ha-Kibbutz ha-Me'uḥad (United Kibbutz) movement. In the same year Ha-Kibbutz ha-Arẓi (Countrywide Kibbutz) of Ha-Shomer ha-Ẓa'ir settlements was founded. Gedud ha-Avodah split; some of its members became Soviet-oriented Communists and left the country for the U.S.S.R., while the others joined Ha-Kibbutz ha-Me'uḥad. The kibbutz movements represented their settlements in dealing with the Histadrut, while the latter's Agricultural Center presented to the Zionist Organization on behalf of the settlers matters dealing with priorities in allocation of land, budgeting, and development of various branches of farming. It also protected the social structure of the settlements—especially in periods of economic difficulty—mediated in disputes between settlements, and looked after agricultural training—especially of women in special training farms. In 1926 it founded an Office for Agricultural Contracting.

Organization in the Cities. Despite the emphasis on the building of an independent agricultural economy, the Histadrut did not neglect job opportunities in the cities. It set up labor exchanges which fixed conditions and priorities for applicants for employment. With the development of industry, in addition to building, and the creation of regular jobs, the trade unions began to develop at the expense of the labor communes of the earlier period. The idea of combining the labor commune with workers' neighborhoods and small auxiliary farm plots or other forms of cooperative economy was not realized on a large scale. The Jewish National Fund did not supply the land nor the Zionist institutions the funds for this purpose. The independent workers' economy was limited for the most part to the countryside. Despite the absence of legislation or regulation and the competition of cheap labor, the Histadrut gained many achievements, including recognition of its right to represent the workers in collective bargaining, the conclusion of wage agreements, and the beginnings of social benefits. On the question of allocation of work only through the labor exchanges, the Histadrut ran into opposition from religious workers who did not belong to it (some of whom formed Ha-Po'el ha-Mizrachi in 1923) and employers who, on one occasion, in 1925, announced a lockout. These conflicts brought on the intervention of the British police. The Va'ad Le'ummi tried to mediate on behalf of the *yishuv,* but ran into difficulties, partly because of the absence of a representative employers' organization. The main Histadrut institution in the towns was the local labor council, which, in practice, set up the various trade unions and coordinated the activities of the other Histadrut institutions in the locality. Elections to the councils were held on a personal basis, which led to complaints of discrimination from the smaller parties, and at the Third Convention proportional representation was introduced.

The ramified activities of the Histadrut swelled the size of its staff and led to complaints of bureaucracy. To bridge the gap between members and officials, the family wage system, under which all the Histadrut's employees were paid on the same scale, wages depending only on whether the official was married and the number of his children, was adopted at the Second Convention. Breaches of the system in the direction of professional scales were condemned at the Third Convention and a watchdog committee was set up.

Despite its very limited funds, the Histadrut did not abandon its activities in the field of education and culture, which were conducted both by central institutions and local branches with the idea of creating a "workers' culture." These activities included instruction in Hebrew, publications, libraries, theater performances, periodical literature, and, from 1925, the daily newspaper *Davar.* From 1923 an autonomous "workers' trend" in the Hebrew educational system began to take shape. To overcome the effects of the split in the Jewish labor movement in the Diaspora, the Histadrut tried to set up an organization which would unite all groups supporting labor in Palestine, and the Labor Palestine Committee was founded in 1923. The Palestine

Workers' Fund (Kuppat Po'alei Erez Israel—Kapai), which had been founded before World War I by the World Union of Po'alei Zion, was transferred to Histadrut authority in 1927.

New Policies After the Third Convention. The Histadrut's membership grew more rapidly than the economy as a whole, or even than the number of workers, but it did not succeed in taking in the religious workers: a section of Ha-Po'el ha-Mizrachi joined in 1925 but left again in 1927. The growth of the Histadrut was noticeable at its Third Convention, which took place in 1927, at the height of an economic crisis, when it had 22,500 members—a fivefold increase since 1920, though the Jewish population of the country had only doubled in the period. The majority of the membership, nearly 70%, was urban. Of the 201 delegates, Aḥdut ha-Avodah had an absolute majority with 108, and Ha-Po'el ha-Za'ir had 54.

Communist influence made itself felt, mainly among the unemployed, and the Zionist parties combated it not with the ideal of an independent workers' commonwealth, but by a many-sided policy of activating all public and economic factors. The Histadrut leadership called on the Mandatory government to adopt a policy of aid and encouragement to agriculture and industry, and urged the Zionist Organization to conduct its settlement activities with a view to establishing productive enterprises. The advantages of private capital investment were recognized, and willingness was expressed to conclude collective agreements on working conditions. The economic institutions of the Histadrut were reorganized, maintaining their autonomous character, and a Control Commission was set up. The convention defined its policy toward Arab workers as the establishment of autonomous trade unions allied with the Histadrut in a federation to be called the Alliance of Palestinian Workers (Berit Po'alei Erez Israel). In view of the economic crisis and the financial retrenchment carried out by the Zionist Organization, the Histadrut leadership agreed in the late 1920s to the enlargement of the Jewish

Agency in the hope of raising larger sums for agricultural settlement and decided to seek a more influential role in the Zionist Organization.

In 1928 the employment situation began to improve and there was a shift in the structure of the economy, followed by a change in the structure of the Histadrut. The leading source of employment was no longer building, but large national industrial enterprises like the electric station at Naharayim, the Dead Sea Works, and the Athlit quarries. About 20% of the workers employed in building Haifa port were Jewish. There was development in medium-sized industries, handicrafts, services, and particularly transportation. Many found employment in the large citrus-based moshavot. The 1929 Arab riots also had the effect of increasing the use of Jewish labor, even if only for a short period. As a result, the Building Workers' Union decreased in size and trade unions based on regular membership and more skilled workers developed. There was an improvement in labor relations and efforts were made to sign collective agreements.

The Histadrut intensified the struggle for Jewish labor in the moshavot, despite the opposition of the left wing (Ha-Shomer ha-Za'ir and Left Po'alei Zion) who were against the demand for 100% Jewish labor; a Histadrut company for agricultural contracting (Yakhin) was set up. The workers in the villages for the most part regarded hired labor only as a stage on the way to independent settlement; some of them organized themselves into groups ready to set up kibbutzim or moshavim. The Jewish National Fund bought land in the Kishon region and the citrus areas for the scheme to settle 1,000 wage-earners' families on the land. Keren Hayesod's funds were not sufficient, so the settlements were financed partly by workers' savings and partly by Histadrut investment, in the main through the Nir Company. The Histadrut's Agricultural Center determined the order of priority for settlement, had a say in the apportionment of land, and exercised a considerable degree of authority.

Expansion of Activities and Influence. In the early 1930s the Communist challenge to the Histadrut, which had been based on unemployment and the failure to develop an independent socialist economy, weakened. Mapai, the Palestine Labor Party, founded in 1930 by the unification of Aḥdut ha-Avodah and Ha-Po'el ha-Ẓa'ir, was supported by some 80% of the membership and there was no longer any large opposition party. The minority parties, Ha-Shomer ha-Ẓa'ir and Left Po'alei Zion, concentrated on the demand for class militancy in the *yishuv* and in the Zionist movement and for closer cooperation with the Arab workers. The leadership rejected any limitation of Jewish workers to skilled occupations and stood firmly on the need to penetrate all branches of the economy, state and private.

In the Jewish-owned economy it demanded the employment of Jewish labor only, as the Arab workers had ample scope in the governmental services and also in Arab enterprises which were closed to Jews.

The Histadrut was strengthened by the immigration of members of He-Ḥalutz, which, since its Third Convention in Danzig, regarded itself as a source of reinforcements for the ranks of labor in Palestine. The growing influence of the Histadrut parties in the Zionist Organization had the effect of increasing immigrant quotas and allocations for agricultural settlement. Opposition to the status of the Histadrut in the *yishuv* in those years came from the Revisionist workers' organization, Histadrut ha-Ovedim ha-Le'ummit, the National Labor Federation, founded in the spring of 1934, which opposed the integral character of the Histadrut and its control over labor exchanges and job opportunities. The Histadrut leadership rejected all demands for the limitation of its all-inclusive character, and was ready to agree in principle to a labor exchange not exclusively run by the Histadrut only on condition that a single body be responsible for the organized allocation of work and that the Histadrut's influence in the representation of the workers not be weakened. In the early 1930s there were

violent clashes over these controversies. In the autumn of

1934 Ben-Gurion and Vladimir Jabotinsky, the Revisionist leader, reached agreement on avoidance of violence and the regulation of the relations between the two federations, but the agreement was rejected by a Histadrut referendum. The development of joint labor exchanges began in the second half of the 1930s and continued all through the 1940s, ending only with the establishment of state labor exchanges in independent Israel.

Despite the contraction of the Histadrut's comprehensive economic ambitions, it continued, with some success, to strengthen the labor-owned enterprises, although most of the Jewish sector of the economy was based on private capital. The labor economy was reorganized in 1927–34 according to directives laid down at the Third Convention. These demanded that the economic institutions be put on a sound financial basis; that each enterprise operate on a scale appropriate to its own economic, financial, and organizational capacity; that a regularly constituted authority should be developed for each enterprise, participating in its management and responsible for the economic consequences of its activities; and that each enterprise have complete internal financial autonomy within the framework of the overall authority and control of Ḥevrat Ovedim.

Contracting ceased to be the central branch of the labor sector. Solel Boneh was replaced by a Public Works Center under the control of the Histadrut Executive Committee, while contracting offices were set up under the local labor councils. Solel Boneh was reestablished in 1935 and absorbed the local contracting offices between 1937 and 1945. Some of its veteran employees were granted permanent status and special privileges. Bank ha-Po'alim expanded its turnover and capital through deposits and sale of shares. In 1926 Tnuva was established to market agricultural produce and took over the sales department of Hamashbir. It was divided into regional branches—Haifa, Tel Aviv, and Jerusalem—and was under the control of the settlements that sold their produce through it. In 1928 the Cooperative Center was founded to organize the cooperatives in manufacturing and crafts, transport, and other services; the transport cooperatives were particularly successful, but Histadrut control was fairly lax. In 1930 Hamashbir was reorganized as Hamashbir Hamerkazi, a cooperative wholesale society with defined functions, and was placed under the authority of the kibbutz movements and consumers' cooperatives in the towns and moshavim. A Housing Center was set up in 1930 with all its shares held by Hevrat Ovedim. In 1935 it became Shikkun, Workmen's Housing Ltd. It represented tenants' cooperative societies in their dealings with the Jewish National Fund, acquired and developed land, and prepared building plans. The building was done on public land and the apartments were cooperatively owned.

Problems of Prosperity. Between 1927 and 1933 the proportion of urban to rural workers shifted to the advantage of the countryside: the percentage of town workers fell during the period from 70% to 56.9%. The period of prosperity from 1933 to 1935 increased the demand for labor and stepped up wages, but led to developments which the leadership regarded as dangerous and incompatible with labor principles: for example, the renewed concentration of workers in the building trade and in the cities, with a decline in economic activity in the rural areas; employment of hired labor by cooperatives and contracting groups; letting and selling of apartments built with public funds at inflated market prices. There were complaints about the rise of a privileged bureaucracy, isolated from the public it served. All of these questions were taken up at the Fourth Convention of the Histadrut in 1933–34. The number of Histadrut members had risen to 33,815; 22,341 participated in the elections. Of the 201 delegates, 165 belonged to Mapai. The Histadrut leadership regarded the expansion of the labor market through private capital investment and increased demand as a desirable but economically unstable phenomenon, while the status of hired labor (as against labor economy) and the rise in workers' consumption were seen as socially undesirable. It

114

was believed that the Histadrut should concentrate its efforts on stepping up savings during the period of prosperity in order to invest the proceeds in the building of an independent workers' economy, especially in agriculture. Since 1928 the Histadrut had been trying to build up its own credit facilities for agricultural settlement by selling shares in Nir. In 1934 it was decided to reorganize Nir as a limited company in order to secure funds from the private market.

The emphasis on increasing immigration and work on the land brought a renewed struggle for the employment of Jewish labor in the moshavot and citrus groves. The Histadrut called on the workers to go to the villages despite the higher wages in the towns and demanded that the grove owners provide them with employment. Efforts by the Zionist Organization to mediate did not help very much, but the outbreak of the 1936 Arab riots completely changed the situation. Under Katznelson's leadership, the Histadrut began to widen its cultural activities and its work among the youth, laying greater emphasis on its ideological character. In 1934, after Ben-Gurion had joined the Jewish Agency Executive, he was succeeded as secretary-general by David Remez.

Enhanced Role in National Leadership. The Arab revolt of 1936, which transformed the life of the *yishuv,* also had an important influence on the activities of the Histadrut. Its political and communal activities widened: it had a political office in London to foster relations with the British Labor Party and the Trade Union International, and its representatives gave evidence before the Peel Commission. In its political appearances the Histadrut attacked the Communist interpretation of the Arab revolt as the uprising of an oppressed people against colonialist domination, emphasizing the progressive structure of the new Jewish society and the economic advantages accruing to the Arabs from Jewish settlement. Its support, as a workers' organization, for increased immigration, despite unemployment, was of great importance.

In the Jewish community itself, the Histadrut used its

moral authority and its organizational and economic resources to strengthen the defense of the settlements and road communications, but it opposed retaliation against Arab civilians as practiced by the "dissident" underground organization Irgun Ẓeva'i Le'ummi (I.Ẓ.L.). In the united Haganah (defense) organization, which was based from 1937 on parity between labor and non-labor, the Histadrut represented the labor sector. Its authority over the pioneering and settlement organizations made it a leading factor in the establishment of the stockade and watch-tower settlements, while members of He-Ḥalutz and the Histadrut took the initiative in setting up the organization for clandestine "illegal" immigration. Although more men had to be employed in defense—as policemen and watch-men and in building fortifications—1936–40 was a period of recession and unemployment. Building activity slowed down and the demand for labor fell, despite the growth in citrus cultivation. The Histadrut established a Work Redemption Fund to which every worker contributed several days' pay to support the unemployed. Public works were started through public companies established in partnership with the Jewish Agency. Expansion into new fields, such as fishing and shipping, was encouraged. In that period the organizational structure of the Histadrut was strengthened. In 1937 it introduced the "unified tax"—a single membership fee to cover the cost of organization, mutual aid, and health services—thus integrating trade union membership with membership of Kuppat Ḥolim.

In the late 1930s, the Mapai leadership tried to achieve unity with Ha-Shomer ha-Ẓa'ir and its urban partner the Socialist League, hoping to avoid ideological and political controversies that would weaken the Histadrut's capacity for common political action. The ideological conflicts were already too deep, however. Ha-Shomer ha-Ẓa'ir regarded the Histadrut as a class organization dedicated to the class struggle and refused to accept national authority in labor affairs. It wanted to establish joint Arab-Jewish trade unions and believed that the Zionist goal could be achieved by class partnership with the Arab workers in the framework of a binational state, which would accept the Zionist demand for free immigration. It also developed a leftist orientation in international affairs. It strongly opposed any ideological or cultural activity on the part of the Histadrut. Although the Histadrut had established a publishing house, Am Oved, in addition to its daily organ, *Davar,* Ha-Shomer ha-Za'ir set up its own publishing house, Sifriyyat ha-Po'alim, and newspaper, *Al ha-Mishmar.*

The period of World War II presented the Histadrut with difficult problems, both as a labor organization and as a Zionist body. At the beginning of the war period, the employment situation worsened because of a decline in investment and building, a shortage of raw materials and industrial goods, and marketing problems, especially in citrus. In November 1939 there were 18,000 unemployed; in January 1941 there were still more than 10,000. Only in 1941 did the tide begin to turn, owing to recruitment to the armed forces, which reduced the numbers looking for work, and increased economic activity, first in building army camps, bridges, and fortifications and later in the economy as a whole. The scarcity of imported goods created favorable conditions for the development of local agriculture and industry, while the British Middle East Supply Center regulated the supply of raw materials.

The war situation changed the character of trade union activities. In 1943 the Mandatory government issued a decree forbidding strikes and introducing compulsory arbitration. The rise in the cost of living made it necessary to adjust wages, which were linked to the cost-of-living index. During these years the trade unions achieved seniority payments, annual vacations, and employers' contributions to Kuppat Holim for their members. Trade-union negotiations became more centralized, with the development of larger enterprises and the growth of the Manufacturers' Association. The trade unions developed in different directions and along 117 flexible lines on countrywide industrial and craft foundations; in all cases care was taken to preserve the authority of the center over the sectional organizations.

Agricultural worker in Ereẓ Israel, 1940. Courtesy Keren Hayesod, United Israel Appeal, Jerusalem.

The Zionist character of the Histadrut and its organizational and economic power made it the center for discussion and decisions on the *yishuv's* war effort. The Histadrut supported enlistment in the British army, with emphasis on the defense of Palestine by Jewish units. The entry of the Soviet Union into the war, in June 1941, overcame the hesitations of some of the pro-communist groups about the war. The Histadrut's control over the labor market made it easier for it to put pressure on those who shirked enlisting. It also agreed to demands, strongly supported by the left groups, to recruit members for the Haganah and the Palmaḥ. The kibbutzim and other settlements were put at the disposal of these units as places of work and bases for military exercises. The Histadrut also developed and encouraged independent activity in the rescue of European Jewry and "illegal" immigration.

The great possibilities for marketing and investment during the war increased the strength of the Histadrut's economic sector, whose long-range aims had been curtailed since 1927. Initiative, technical and management capacity, and capital, which had accumulated in the contracting and supply companies, were invested in industry. Enterprises were also set up in partnership with private capital on a 50-50 basis. At first Solel Boneh and Hamashbir took up branches closest to their own field of operations—building materials and food products—and then expanded into other areas. The management of the enterprises became more and more independent of the central institutions of Ḥevrat Ovedim and the Histadrut's control over the cooperative sector was weakened. Efforts to renew Nir ha-Shittufit to take the initiative in labor settlement did not succeed: the kibbutz movements preferred their own separate funds. On the other hand, the Histadrut's credit and social insurance institutions developed successfully.

Controversies and Splits. The war period created political and ideological problems which led to disagreements and splits in the Histadrut. In the elections to the Fifth Convention in 1941, 88,198 members voted out of the total **119** eligible membership of 105,663. Out of 392 delegates, Mapai had 278 and Ha-Shomer ha-Ẓa'ir and the Socialist League 77. A non-socialist group, 'Ha-Oved ha-Ẓiyyoni, returned 14 delegates. At the convention, which met in 1942, there were outstanding differences between the left, which believed that Zionism might be realized with the support of world Communism, and the majority in Mapai, which stood first and foremost for the enhancement of the *yishuv's* own strength. The definition of Zionist aims in the Biltmore Program (1942), which demanded the establishment of Palestine as a Jewish commonwealth, sharpened the controversy. Ha-Shomer ha-Ẓa'ir continued to support the binational solution and the disagreement came to a head over the question of the instructions to be given to the Histadrut delegation to the conference of the World Federation of Trade Unions, in which the Soviets participated, in 1945. These controversies weakened the Histadrut's capacity for political action, but it was united in its opposition to the 1939 White Paper and to the "dissident" underground organizations (I.Ẓ.L. and Loḥamei Ḥerut Israel).

Both prewar unemployment and wartime prosperity aroused tensions within the Histadrut over such matters as the relations between workers and unemployed, hired labor in the contracting companies and the cooperatives, and conflict between the bureaucracy and the membership. In 1944 Mapai split and a minority group, Siah Bet (B Faction), later Ha-Tenu'ah le-Aḥdut ha-Avodah, adopted an independent stance in the Histadrut. It called for more "class independence" and opposed Ben-Gurion's program, which had been followed since the beginning of the 1930s, of emphasizing the Histadrut's leading role in the *yishuv* and the Zionist movement, even to the extent of giving up separate labor activities.

The elections to the Sixth Convention in 1944, in which 106,420 of the 151,860 eligible voters participated, showed that Mapai still had a majority, though a much reduced one: 216 out of the 401 delegates. Ha-Shomer ha-Ẓa'ir and

Posters for the Histadrut elections of 1944. Courtesy Central Zionist Archives, Jerusalem.

Left Po'alei Zion had 83 delegates, Ha-Tenu'ah le-Aḥdut ha-Avodah 71, and Aliyah Ḥadashah, a new non-socialist group (mainly immigrants from Germany and Austria), and Ha-Oved ha-Ẓiyyoni 12 each. The Mapai leadership tried to win greater support among the urban workers and achieved a decision to set up national unions of factory, transport, and building workers, in addition to the existing national unions of agricultural, clerical, engineering, railroad, and postal workers. They also tried to reduce the influence of the left-wing parties on the pioneering and youth movements in the Diaspora and succeeded in getting the Histadrut to decide on a united pioneering movement under its sponsorship. The period between the end of World War II and the War of Independence was not, as some had feared, one of economic depression. Investment capital and increased consumption raised the demand for labor and enhanced the power of the Histadrut. During the struggle against British rule and the War of Independence, the economic and organizational strength of the Histadrut provided a solid basis for the military strength of the Haganah.

121

THE HISTADRUT IN THE STATE OF ISRAEL. Achieving independence obviously necessitated a reconsideration of the role of the Histadrut in national life. Some thought that the State could now perform most of the functions the labor movement had assumed during the Mandatory period and that the Histadrut should become purely a trade-union body, dealing only with wages and working conditions. The great majority of its leading members, however, believed that it should continue to combine the defense of the workers' standard of living with the provision of social services, the building of a labor economy, and cultural activity. According to this view, which was held by Mapai and Mapam (founded in 1948 by the union of Ha-Shomer ha-Ẓa'ir, Left Po'alei Zion, and Aḥdut ha-Avodah), its centralized structure must be preserved in order to prevent particularist tendencies and exorbitant claims by pressure groups, to influence the allocation of the labor force to those places and trades in which it was required by national needs, and to mobilize public capital and labor potential in development areas which did not attract private enterprise.

In an address to the Eighth Convention of the Histadrut in 1956, David Ben-Gurion expressed this view:

> During the period of the British Mandate, the Histadrut fulfilled governmental functions in the consciousness of a historic function and in the absence of Jewish governmental organs. On the founding of the state, the continuation of these functions is a superfluous burden on the Histadrut and a serious injury to the state . . . The Histadrut is not a rival or competitor of the state, but its faithful helper and devoted support. The labor movement, therefore, has a dual additional aim after the rise of the state: (a) to mold the character of the state and make it fit to carry out to the full the mission of national and social redemption, and to strengthen and organize the workers for this purpose; and (b) to initiate pioneering activities in the educational, economic, and social spheres which cannot be carried out by compulsion, law, and the governmental machine alone.

Thus, while the Histadrut's school system and the labor

exchanges it ran in cooperation with the other labor federations were taken over by the state, the labor economy in agriculture, industry, and services, and social-welfare agencies, such as Kuppat Holim and the provident and pension funds, were considerably expanded. At the same time, the Histadrut continued to carry out its trade-union functions, coordinating the wage claims and policies of the various sections and reorganizing its structure by establishing additional national trade unions. In several of the enterprises for which it was jointly responsible together with the Jewish Agency, such as the Mekorot Water Corporation and Zim Israel Navigation Company, the government supplied a steadily increasing share of the development capital and took over a larger part of the control.

The membership of the Histadrut has risen much faster than the growth of the population: from 133,140 (not counting housewives) at the beginning of 1948 to 448,390 in 1958—68% of the labor force—and 722,249 in 1969—78% of the labor force. Together with housewife members, the total grew from 180,600 in 1948 to 988,207 in 1969. The "population" of the Histadrut (including members' families) increased sixfold during the same period: from 267,912 to 1,631,607; with the religious labor federations, the total was 1,827,300 in 1969—64.4% of the country's population.

Political Forces in the Histadrut. In the elections to the Seventh, Eighth, and Ninth Conventions of the Histadrut, held in 1949, 1956, and 1960, Mapai kept its absolute majority with 57.6%, 57.4%, and 55.43% of the total vote. In 1949, Mapam had 34.43%, and when Ahdut ha-Avodah seceded from it, the two left-wing parties together had 27.15% in 1956 and 30.95% in 1960. There was thus no serious challenge to the traditional view of the Histadrut's structure and functions, which was supported by all three parties. The small Ha-Oved ha-Ziyyoni (Progressive) and General Zionist Workers factions, which were in favor of limiting the Histadrut's activities, obtained less than 9% of the votes between them at their peak and, although 123 represented in the federation's executive organs, had little influence on its policies. Mapam, Aḥdut ha-Avodah, and the Communists (who rose from 2.63% in 1949 to 4.09% in 1956 and dropped again to 2.80% at the Ninth Convention), however, hindered Mapai's efforts to ensure wage restraint by proposing higher rates of increase than the majority thought practicable and conducting sporadic agitation among the workers outside the framework of the Histadrut's governing institutions.

At the Tenth Convention, in 1966, there were three new features in the political set-up. Mapai joined with Aḥdut ha-Avodah to form the Alignment (Ma'arakh), which gained only a bare majority, 50.87%. Rafi, which had broken away from Mapai under Ben-Gurion's leadership, also contested the elections gaining 12.13%. Perhaps the most significant new departure, however, was the Ḥerut Movement's decision to take part in the Histadrut elections despite its close association with the Histadrut ha-Ovedim ha-Le'ummit, National Labor Federation, to which many of its members belonged. Together with its Liberal partners in the Ḥerut-Liberal Bloc (Gaḥal), it formed the Blue-White Workers' Association (Iggud Ovedim Tekhelet-Lavan), which emerged as the second-largest group with 15.21%, Mapam (without Aḥdut ha-Avodah) obtaining 14.51%. However, Rafi, although many of its members believed in the absorption of Kuppat Ḥolim into a state health service and were not very enthusiastic about the labor economy, did not press its views; at the beginning of 1968 it merged with Mapai to form the Israel Labor Party and thus joined the Alignment.

All the country's political parties, except the religious ones, took part in the elections to the 11th Convention in 1969, at which the Israel Labor Party combined with Mapam in a more comprehensive Alignment, obtaining 62.11% of a reduced poll. The Ḥerut-Liberal Bloc increased its strength to 16.85% and the Independent Liberals (formerly Ha-Oved ha-Ẓiyyoni) improved to 5.69%, while Ha-Oved ha-Dati, which had formed a part of the 1965 Alignment, gained 3.06% and the two Communist lists 4.04% between them. The presence of representatives of the Free Center, a splinter group which had broken away from Ḥerut (1.99%), and Ha-Olam ha-Zeh (1.33%) reinforced the Gaḥal challenge to the leadership—without, however, undermining the Alignment's control.

The post of secretary-general of the Histadrut, which is one of major influence in national affairs, was held by a succession of personalities of ministerial caliber: Pinḥas Lavon (1949–51 and 1956–59), Mordekhai Namir (1951–56), Aharon Becker (1959–70), and Yiẓḥak Ben-Aharon (from 1970). The last belonged to the Aḥdut ha-Avodah wing of the Israel Labor Party; all the others were members of Mapai.

The Labor Economy. The labor economy expanded rapidly during the first decade of the state, the numbers employed rising from 60,000 in 1949 to 174,000 in 1960, i.e., from about 6% to 9% of the population and almost 25% of the labor force. During the second decade, its growth was slower: in 1971 it employed 223,000, about 22% of the labor force; there were plans, however, for a renewed drive in the field of industry. Labor enterprises thus played a notable part in the provision of employment for new immigrants. In agriculture there was a considerable increase in the number of kibbutzim and an even larger one in the moshavim, the numbers employed in Histadrut agriculture rising to 84% of the national total in 1971. The Histadrut also played a large part in establishing industries in the new villages and towns and in extending transport, marketing, and shopping services to the development areas, especially in the early years, before government incentives to private industry began to take effect. Its role was conspicuous in construction, road building and other public works, harbor expansion and construction, and the extension of the area under citrus, previously the preserve of the private farmer, in which the share of the labor settlements grew to about 50%. Solel Boneh, the biggest Histadrut enterprise, was reorganized in 1958, despite some opposition, on the initiative of 125

Pinḥas Lavon. It was divided into a Building and Public Works Company, which had 22,200 employees and a gross product of over IL375 million in 1970, an Overseas and Harbors Works Company, operating in Africa, Asia, and the Middle East, and Koor, an industrial holding company but later independent, which had 13,000 employees and a gross product of IL770 million. Tnuva, which handles over two-thirds of all farm produce and is increasingly active in exports, had a turnover, counting subsidiary food industries, of over IL890 million in 1970. In the same year Hamashbir ha-Merkazi and its 550 affiliated consumers' cooperative enterprises had a total turnover of some IL533 million; the gross product of its industries totaled IL108 million. The Cooperative Consumers' Alliance had some 1,500 branches all over the country, including supermarkets in the large towns. Producers' cooperatives did not expand in the same degree, except for the passenger-transport companies Egged and Dan. Bank Hapoalim became the third-largest bank in Israel with over 150 branches throughout the country. Hundreds of cooperative housing societies raised the standard of workers' housing and enabled thousands of wage-earners to buy their own houses.

The kibbutzim, moshavim, and industrial and service cooperatives were troubled by the problem of hired labor, which was incompatible with their basic socialist principles. Rapid expansion made it impossible for their owner-members to dispense with the employment of outside labor, which raised serious question of social inequality. The problem was raised frequently at conferences of the Histadrut and its constituent bodies, and efforts were made to work out a solution by mechanization, automation, and assistance to hired workers to become full members of the cooperatives.

In 1955 the Histadrut decided on the establishment of joint management-labor advisory councils in some of its enterprises, but little was done by the managers to put the decision into effect. With the expansion of the centrally run concerns, which employed tens of thousands of workers, it was felt that they were beginning to lose their specific character as labor enterprises and that the employees saw little difference between them and private plants. The 86th Council of the Histadrut, in 1964, decided that the principle of workers' participation in management should be put into practice in the labor industries. A central department for labor participation, consisting of representatives of Ḥevrat ha-Ovedim and the Trade Union Department, was set up to carry out the decision. Workers' representatives were to be elected to the management of each plant to serve for not more than three years running. In these plants, the workers were also to receive a share in the profits. The Tenth Convention of the Histadrut in 1966 confirmed the decision, declaring: "The place of the Histadrut economy in the building and development of the country largely depends on the identification of the worker with his enterprise and his participation in the responsibility for its management and maintenance." Up to 1970, joint management had been established in 15 enterprises.

Wages Policy. The structure of employment in the Israel economy has had an important influence on the Histadrut's wages policy. About half the wage earners—the highest percentage in any country outside the Communist world—are employed by the public sector: the civil service, local authorities. Jewish Agency and its institutions, Histadrut enterprises, and so forth. In addition, a large part of industry and agriculture is subject to government influence through subsidies, loans, licenses, and various incentives. Thus, some three-quarters of the workers are employed in undertakings over which some measure of public control is exercised in the national interest. In the public and semi-public sectors, a responsible labor organization like the Histadrut cannot be concerned merely with increasing the amount the worker takes out of the undertaking in the form of wages at the expense of the employer's profits, since exorbitant demands may have to be met, in the last analysis, from the pocket of the local taxpayer or the contributor to pro-Israel funds from abroad.

Furthermore, some 90% of wage earners are organized in the Histadrut or the religious labor federations which cooperate with its trade union department. The Histadrut also has a central strike fund, which can assist the workers in an authorized trade dispute even in a weakly organized sector. This gives it a much greater bargaining power than exists in other countries, even in times of slack employment, and certainly in normal times, when there is no significant shortage of jobs. Moreover, it does not represent a downtrodden class, but one of the major elements in the building of the country, whose representatives not only wield considerable power in the trade-union field and control an important sector of the economy, but, through the labor parties, have held a dominant position in parliament and government throughout Israel's history.

This massive power implies a great responsibility, to which the Histadrut's leadership has always been acutely sensitive. Its power has enabled it to lay down and, to a large extent, to enforce, an all-inclusive wages policy covering all industries and services, but lack of restraint in exercising it might have been disastrous to the economy. The Histadrut's wages policies have, therefore, always been based on the assumption that, while using its power to maintain and improve the workers' standard of living, organized labor must share in the responsibility for the future of the economy, since no one is more interested in its stability and progress.

C-o-L Allowances and Labor Contracts. At its Seventh Convention, in May 1949, the Histadrut decided to press for the maintenance of the cost-of-living allowance system in order to preserve the real value of wages, while supporting the introduction of methods conducive to greater productivity, such as the institution of work norms with premiums for output above the norm, while assuring the worker of a fair minimum wage. In 1951, the cumulative cost-of-living allowances were merged with the basic wage and the Histadrut demanded wage increases of 10–15%. In

1953 it was decided not to claim a further increase in the

basic wage; pay was to rise only in accordance with increases in the cost-of-living and by increased premiums earned by greater productivity, with exceptions in backward undertakings. The same general policy was maintained in the following two years.

In 1955 the government appointed a committee headed by Israel Guri, chairman of the Knesset Finance Committee, to consider salaries in the civil service and public institutions, particularly the claims of senior administrative officials and members of the liberal professions that the differentials between their pay and that of lower-grade employees had been narrowed by the effect of the cost-of-living allowances. The committee recommended a general pay increase, with increased differentials for higher and academic grades, and its recommendations were carried out.

In 1956 the Histadrut decided that, in view of the grave security situation, one-third of the increases granted to the senior civil servants should be frozen for the time being, while other workers should get a graduated increase of 5-15%. The full rates were paid in 1957 and the frozen amounts were repaid during that and the two following years. In January 1957, the basic wages were again consolidated with the accumulated cost-of-living allowance and it was decided that collective agreements between workers and employers be signed once in two years. In 1958 there was no change in basic wages, but seniority increments were raised, employees belonging to the professions were given a special annual grant to cover the cost of professional literature, and the wages of professional and administrative staffs were increased to cover overtime payments.

In 1959 and 1960 a number of changes were instituted: the addition of another grade at the top of the scale in industry and construction; higher family allowances for industrial workers; a special holiday allowance to cover hotel or recreation home expenses; an increase of 2% in employers' contribution to building workers' pension **129** funds; and the preservation of seniority allowance on promotion for civil servants (who had previously started at the basic salary for the new grade).

At the Ninth Convention, in the latter year, it was decided in principle that further general increases in wages should be linked with rises in the net national product, and in 1962 the Histadrut established an independent institute, staffed by economists and statisticians, to produce objective figures on the level of national productivity which would serve as criteria for future wages policy.

In 1961 the problem of salaries in the public service again became acute. In the course of time, special salary scales had been instituted for employees belonging to various professions: physicians, technicians, engineers, journalists, social workers, and so forth. There were 20 different scales, resulting in many inconsistencies and frequent claims by those who felt themselves unfairly treated in comparison with members of other professions. Toward the end of 1961, the government appointed another committee, headed by the governor of the Bank of Israel, David Horowitz, to propose a reform of the system. In the meantime administrative staffs were paid advances on account of the wage increases expected after the conclusion of the committee's work. The Horowitz Committee reported in 1963, recommending the institution of a single scale for the entire civil service, with the exception of teachers, regular army, police, and prison staffs, and drafted conversion tables for the transfer of all employees to the new scale. The government and the Histadrut, however, felt that automatic conversion would perpetuate the inequalities between the various scales, and it was decided, instead, to carry out a comprehensive job evaluation so that each employee's grade should be decided according to the work he was doing. The determination of the grades of the various classes of employee was a prolonged process, lasting several years. Owing to pressures exerted by staff representatives and the grant of an 18% increase to professional workers in 1965 the total civil service wage bill increased by one-third

In 1963 it was decided to make no change in the existing labor contracts, in order to support the government's policy of economic stabilization following the devaluation of the Israel pound in 1962, but in 1964 the Histadrut decided, in view of a rise in productivity, that wages should be raised by 3% in that and the following year. In addition, family allowances of IL6 per month for each of the first three children were instituted through an equalization fund (the fourth and subsequent children were already covered by the family allowance scheme of the National Insurance Institute; see Social Security, pp.218 ff.). In 1965 these allowances were taken over by the Institute and financed by a levy on employers of 1.8% of wages. In 1966 the existing labor contracts were further renewed without change for a period of two years.

In view of the burden of increased defense expenditure after the Six-Day War (1967), the Histadrut made no further wage claims when these agreements expired, so that wages were largely frozen for a period of two years. In 1970 it was felt that complete restraint could no longer be justified and that increased productivity during the past four years warranted a wage increase of some 8%. However, in view of the security situation and the drastic increase in the adverse balance of payments, a package deal was concluded between the Histadrut, the government, and the employers' organizations, providing for a 4% rise in the cost-of-living allowance and another 4% wage increase to be paid in government bonds, while the government undertook not to raise taxes and the employers not to increase prices, as well as to invest a further 4% of wages on government bonds. A committee representing the three parties was appointed to supervise the implementation of the agreement.

Strikes. During the past decade the Histadrut's centrally imposed wages policies were under constant pressure from various groups of workers who felt that they were entitled to higher wages and, in most cases, manned services, where a stoppage would produce considerable inconvenience to 131 the public, such as the ports, the posts, or electricity supply. The tendency toward decentralization, as well as the strong loyalties of the workers to their directly elected local or sectional committees at the expense of their allegiance to the more distant central organs of the Histadrut, made wildcat strikes easy to call and difficult to control. In 1967–1972 the majority of the labor disputes, claims, and stoppages—many of which took the form of slowdowns, working to rule, or similar measures—were not officially recognized. Attempts by the Histadrut and local labor councils to impose discipline were generally unsuccessful, and most of the unofficial disputes ended in compromises, which gave the strikers at least part of their demands.

There were considerable and irregular fluctuations in strike statistics over the period. The number of strikes rose from 45 in 1948 to a peak of 90 in 1955, fell to 46 in 1958 and 51 in 1959, rose to 135 in 1960 and reached a peak of 288 in 1965 and 286 in the following year, falling in 1967 to 142 and in 1968 to 101. The number of strikers during the years 1949–56 varied between 7,308 in 1950 and 12,595 in 1952; it fell in 1957 to 3,648 and rose slightly during the following two years; it increased in 1960 to 14,420 and climbed steeply to a peak of 90,210 in 1965, falling again to 25,058 in 1967 and 42,176 in 1968. The number of days lost by strikes during the period varied from a low point of 31,328 in 1959 to a peak of 242,699 in 1962, going down to 58,286 and 73,153 in 1967 and 1968 respectively. A more significant index, that of the number of days lost per thousand wage earners, showed no consistent trend. The figure was 281.0 in 1949 and 235.1 in 1966, going down to 68.7 in 1959 and rising to 392.7 in 1957 and 447.3 in 1962. In 1967, the index fell to 99.5, rising slightly to 112.6 in 1968. In 1969 there was a slight increase in the number of strikers (44,500) and a considerable one in days lost (102,000). The year 1970 was a particularly bad one, with repeated disputes in the ports (especially in the new port of Ashdod) and prolonged strikes by nurses and secondary school teachers: 114,900 persons struck, and 390,000 days' work were lost. The figures for 1971 were still serious: 80,000 strikers and 154,000 days lost.

The proportion of authorized to unauthorized strikes fluctuated considerably—reliable statistics are available only from 1960. Between 1961 and 1966, most of the working days lost were due to strikes not approved by the Histadrut: the percentage was as high as 93.7% (in 1961) and not lower than 62% (in 1961). From 1967, however, the position was reversed. Not more than 46% of the days lost (in 1972) were due to unauthorized strikes, and in 1970, the percentage was as low as 20%. In 1972, however, there seemed to be a reversal of this trend.

In most of the years 1965–1971, more than half the strikes were in the public sector, 1967 was an exception with 39.5%, but the percentage rose to 62.8% in 1971. The number of strikes in the private sector fluctuated around one-third of the total.

Social Services. While the total population increased about fourfold in the 23 years 1948–71, the number of persons insured in Kuppat Ḥolim grew more than sixfold: from 307,623 to 2,087,000, including members of the religious labor federations and certain other categories outside the Histadrut. The main increase took place in the years of mass immigration, as the great majority of the newcomers joined. In 1948 35.3% of the total population and 43% of the Jewish population were insured with Kuppat Ḥolim; by 1971 these percentages stood at 68% and 80% respectively. It played an important part in providing remedial and preventive medical treatment for the new immigrants, established hundreds of clinics in new towns and rural centers, and taught the elements of hygiene to newcomers from backward countries.

In the early years of statehood there were a large number of small provident funds, reaching 328 in 1953, with 60,000 members, through which workers saved a regular percentage of their wages, with parallel contributions from the employers. The funds provided small loans and other services from time to time, with a lump sum payable upon 133

Histadrut rest home in Nazareth. Courtesy Rechter, Zarhy, architects, and Peri, engineer, Tel Aviv.

retirement. This system was found to be unsatisfactory, and measures were taken to amalgamate small funds into large ones, which would provide pensions instead of lump sum payments. The first of these funds was that for Histadrut employees, founded in 1954. The largest is Mivtaḥim, which provides pension, holiday, and other payments for a large variety of workers, including casual laborers. There are also funds for clerks and officials, employees of Histadrut industries, members of cooperatives, agricultural workers, and building workers. Mivtaḥim and the last two funds also cover payments for holidays, work accidents, rehabilitation, where necessary, and so forth. Pension rates are raised in accordance with the rise in the cost-of-living and keep pace with wage increases. At the end of 1971 the total membership of the funds was some 400,000, together with their families about half the population of the country, and their accumulated capital amounted to more than IL2,345 million. The funds are under treasury supervision and 80% of their capital must be invested in government-recognized securities. Most

of the remainder is invested in securities issued by Gemul,

the Histadrut investment company. Of the remaining 20%, about half is used for cheap loans to members for housing and so forth. The operations of the funds not only constitute a valuable local service but are of considerable economic importance as a method of saving and a source of capital investment.

International Affiliations. When the World Federation of Trade Unions was founded after World War II, the Histadrut cooperated fully with it, but when Communist influence grew in the WFTU and it was left by many Western trade union federations, who formed the International Confederation of Free Trade Unions, the Histadrut, after heated debate, joined the latter in May 1950. The Histadrut maintains close ties with the member federations of the ICFTU and sends experienced trade unionists to advise on labor organization, particularly in Asia and Africa. Its representatives also play an important role in the 15 international federations representing specific trades. Many delegations and groups of students, particularly from developing countries, have come to Israel to study the Histadrut's methods and achievements. The trade unions in these countries are interested in the Histadrut's unitary structure, its success in integrating members with varied cultural and educational backgrounds, and its prominent role in national life. Its Afro-Asian Institute has become an important international center for labor studies.

The Histadrut also belongs to the International Cooperative Alliance, which represents cooperative movements in both Western and Communist countries, and Israel's cooperative economy has aroused widespread interest. Despite Israel's small size, Histadrut representatives play a prominent part in the work of the International Labor Office and are regularly elected to its governing body. The Histadrut's influence in all branches of the international labor movement is an asset of considerable political importance for Israel.

Educational and Cultural Activity. The Compulsory

Education Law, 1949, maintained the "trend" system under which the Histadrut was responsible for one of the four school networks. The Labor "trend," which was controlled by the Histadrut's Educational Center (Merkaz le-Ḥinnukh), aimed at "molding a self-reliant pioneering Jewish personality, imbued with the Zionist-Socialist ideal" and "imparting to the child the values of the labor movement in the country and a sense of participation in the fate of its people." It established new schools in many immigrant centers and in 1953 had some 900 schools and kindergartens, with over 3,000 teachers and 60,000 pupils, out of 3,210 institutions, 15,304 teaching posts, and 320,361 pupils in the entire Jewish educational system.

In 1953, when the Knesset passed the State Education Law, abolishing the "trends," the labor schools were merged with those of the "general trend" to form the nucleus of the state educational system and ceased to be organized in a separate framework. However, the influence of its principles may be seen in the clause of the State Education Law which prescribes that state education shall be based, *inter alia*, "on training in agricultural labor and handicrafts; on fulfillment of pioneering principles; on the aspiration to a society built on liberty, equality, tolerance, mutual aid and love of fellow-man."

The Histadrut's Cultural Department provides a variety of services for members in town and country. These include: lectures, films, publications and periodicals; organized trips; courses in Hebrew and geography, Bible, music, dancing, and the arts; clubs and libraries; educational books and materials; theater performances for immigrants; libraries for schools in immigrant centers, in cooperation with the Presidential Residence Fund; educational circles for the parents, and schools for trade union leaders. Volunteers were organized during the mass immigration period to help newcomers by teaching Hebrew and other subjects. In addition, the local labor councils engage in similar activities on their own initiative, and there is a wide network of cultural committees in towns and villages.

There are special departments for the kibbutzim and the moshavim.

Arab Workers. In the early years of statehood the Palestine Labor League continued to perform trade union functions on behalf of Arab workers, with the close cooperation of the Histadrut. Labor organization was stepped up in the Arab sector; Arabs could now find employment in the Jewish economy, receiving the same pay and conditions as Jewish workers, and the labor exchanges assured them of participation in the fair division of work. In November 1952 the Histadrut Council decided to open the Trade Union Department at all stages to Arab workers on the basis of complete equality and grant them full rights in provident funds and other Histadrut mutual-aid institutions. At the end of 1953 a special section for Arab workers was established in the Trade Union Department. Trade union branches were established in Arab centers and in mixed places of work joint workers' committees were elected by Arab and Jewish workers.

In February 1959 the Histadrut Council decided on the admission of Arabs and members of other minority communities as full members. With the assistance and advice of the Histadrut, agricultural, industrial, consumers' and housing cooperatives were established in Arab centers. Kuppat Ḥolim opened general and mother-and-child clinics in Arab villages and towns. The Histadrut, especially through its youth and women's movements, maintains clubs and cultural activities in the Arab areas. Arab membership of the Histadrut grew from 6,427 (9,956 including housewives) in 1958 to 31,254 (50,446 including housewives) in 1969. The number of Arab members and dependents increased in the same period from 21,534 to 118,098—29% of the Arab population, compared with 10.1% in 1958.

After the reunification of Jerusalem, the Histadrut started to organize the workers among the 65,000 Arabs in the eastern part of the city. Under Jordanian rule, most of them had been badly paid and exploited, and the few trade unions had little influence. Despite the opposition of some Arab notables, about 8,000 workers joined the Histadrut, which tried to equalize their pay with that of the Jewish workers. Most of the Arab employers resisted the efforts, but compromises were reached with the hoteliers and some others. In 1970, there were 2,000 Jerusalem Arabs working for Jewish employers.

Kuppat Holim opened a branch in East Jerusalem, which, after initial difficulties in finding Arab doctors and nurses and overriding the reluctance of Arab women to go to Jewish doctors, won acceptance. Arab trade unionists in Jerusalem took part in Histadrut courses on labor relations and submitted their candidacy in Histadrut elections. The Histadrut's work in the city was regarded as a significant contribution to understanding between Jews and Arabs.

The Women's Labor Movement. All women members—including housewives—are entitled to vote in the elections to Mo'ezet ha-Po'alot, the Women Workers' Council, which thus has a membership of almost half a million—46% of the total. Housewives are organized in Irgun Immahot Ovedot, the Working Mothers' Organization, with branches all over the country. The women's movement has made an important contribution to the integration of the immigrants by teaching the women Hebrew, introducing them to the life of the country, and helping to look after the children. It has also done much to improve the status and conditions of Arab women. Its projects in Israel are assisted by the sister movement abroad, Pioneer Women.

Youth and Sport. In 1959 Ha-No'ar ha-Oved combined with the school youth movement, Ha-Tenu'ah ha-Me'uhedet, to form a single organization of working and student youth. It has over 100,000 members: some 40,000 of them, aged 14–18, in trade sections, which function as a kind of junior Histadrut, and the rest, aged 10–18, in groups for recreational and educational activities. The Ha-Shomer ha-Za'ir youth movement (with 13,000 members) and Dror-Mahanot ha-Olim (5,000), affiliated to Ha-Kibbutz Ha-Me'uhad, are within the framework of the Histadrut.

Table 14. Histadrut Unions

Union	Estimated membership
National Union of Actors, Variety Artists and Musicians	1,300
National Union of Agricultural Education Workers	3,000
National Union of Hired Agricultural Workers	60,000
National Union of Aeronautical Industry Workers	—
Union of Civilian Workers for the Army	—
National Union of Bakery Workers	4,500
National Federation of Building and Building Material Workers	50,000
National Federation of Clerical Workers	120,000
National Union of Clothing and Footwear Workers	2,000
National Union of Diamond Workers	10,000
Electrical Company Employees' Union	5,000
National Federation of Engineers, Architects, and Surveyors	8,000
National Union of Fuel Workers	5,000
National Union of Food Workers	30,000
National Union of Government Employees	53,000
Union of Workers in Histadrut	30,000
Employed Lawyers' Association	3,000
National Union of Medical Practitioners	4,000
National Union of Metal Workers	50,000
National Union of Nurses	8,000
National Union of Physiotherapists and X-Ray Technicians	3,200
Union of Pharmacists	1,000
Union of Microbiologists and Medical Chemists	1,000
National Union of Graduates in Humanities and Social Sciences	8,000
National Union of Printing, Paper, and Cartonage Workers	7,000
National Union of Restaurant and Hotel Workers	5,000
National Union of Rubber, Tire, and Plastics Workers	9,000
Israel Seamen's Union	3,200
National Union of Social Workers	1,500
National Union of Teachers	30,000
National Union of Technicians	8,000
National Union of Textile Workers	20,000
Road Transport Services Union	17,500
Harbor and Warehouse Workers' Union	6,500
National Union of Watchmen	3,500
National Union of Woodworkers	20,000

Ha-Po'el, with 85,000 members in 600 branches all over the country, is the largest sports organization in Israel, engaging in 17 types of sport. Its representatives play a prominent part in the governing bodies of the various sports, such as the Football Association. The Histadrut youth and sports movements have done much to bring new immigrants and their children into the mainstream of Israel life.

Histadrut ha-Ovedim ha-Leummit. This organization was founded in Jerusalem in 1934 as a result of a basic clash of outlooks between Revisionist workers and the Histadrut.

Revisionism criticized the Histadrut for being socialist and a class organ, demanded that it confine itself to trade union organization, and charged it with discriminating in the allocation of employment against members of the Revisionist Labor Bloc, which emphasized the national rather than the class interests of the workers.

In 1930, the convention of the Revisionist Labor Bloc decided to leave the Histadrut and founded Irgun Ovedei ha-Zohar u-Vetar (the Organization of Revisionists and Betar Workers) in Palestine, which, in 1934, became the Histadrut ha-Ovedim ha-Le'ummit. Its purpose, according to its constitution, was to "unite all national workers in Palestine loyal to the principle of the establishment of the Jewish state in all of Palestine." It advocated compulsory national arbitration in all labor disputes, the establishment of neutral labor exchanges, the entrenchment of Jewish labor, fair conditions for the worker, and the development of good relations between workers and employers. Its symbol was the blue and white flag (in contradistinction to the red flag used by the Histadrut); its anthem was *"Ha-Tikvah,"* not the "Internationale"; and it chose the anniversary of Herzl's death, the 20th of Tammuz, rather than the First of May, as its annual workers' holiday.

Later the National Labor Federation became unaffiliated with any political party. In 1971 it had about 85,000 members. It stressed the need for a complete separation between the functions of the employer and those of the trade union, and opposed the combination of the two functions in the Histadrut, whose economic arm, Ḥevrat ha-Ovedim, owns many enterprises employing workers whose interests are represented by the Histadrut's trade union department. Histadrut ha-Ovedim ha-Le'ummit advocates the establishment of a national institution for compulsory arbitration in labor disputes and of nationwide trade unions whose elected organs will decide their policies independently of political party decisions. It is in favor of the provision of basic social services, such as medical care, by the state and the enactment of pension and unemployment insurance laws.

The trades union department of the federation has negotiated labor contracts with more than a hundred concerns employing some 10,000 workers. It has insurance and pension funds, a labor-disputes fund, an unemployment fund, a members' credit fund, a mutual loan fund, and a disablement fund. The National Workers' Sick Fund, Kuppat Ḥolim le-Ovedim Le'ummiyyim, provides medical care for some 240,000 persons in over 110 clinics, including some in Druze villages, and maintains laboratories.

Sela, the federation's housing company, has constructed thousands of apartments for newcomers and veterans, shopping centers, synagogues, and public buildings, some as part of government housing projects. The federation runs a guesthouse and holiday company, Beri'on, which owns guesthouses and convalescent homes. It also owns two cooperative building companies, Merkaz ha-Avodah and Ha-Massad. Its youth wing, Ha-No'ar ha-Oved ve-ha-Lomed ha-Le'ummi (the National Working and Student Youth Association), runs youth clubs in cities, suburbs, and immigrant centers. The supreme body of the federation is the National Conference, which meets once in every four years, delegates being elected directly on a personal basis by secret ballot. Workers' councils in each locality are elected in the same way. The conference elects a national committee, executive committee, and control committee.

9 IDEOLOGY OF LABOR

The Jewish Labor problem was one of the central themes, both ideologically and organizationally, which occupied the attention of the Jews at the beginning of their resettlement in the 1880s. Its ideology was developed by a number of leaders and thinkers, such as Ber Borochov, Nachman Syrkin, A. D. Gordon, Joseph Hayyim Brenner, Joseph Trumpeldor, Berl Katznelson, and David Ben-Gurion, on the basis of Zionist-Socialist analyses of the Jewish problem and the experience gained in the process of resettlement. For specific historical, religious, and social reasons, the occupations of the Jews in the Diaspora had been limited, for the most part, to finance, commerce, teaching, medicine, and law. Few were to be found in the basic sectors of the economy, such as agriculture, industry, transportation, and mining. The desire to renew the political life of the Jewish people in its historic homeland through the creation of a society in which Jews themselves would carry out all the organizational and economic functions required for its maintenance was thus combined with the concept of *kibbush ha-avodah* ("the conquest of labor"). This meant the establishment of a national economy with a varied and all-embracing productive and organizational framework, and the spiritual, vocational and educational preparation of Jews to engage in all the occupations required in such an economy. *Kibbush ha-avodah* was linked with the ideal of *halutziyyut* ("pioneering"), which inspired the individual not only to advocate and support the national revival, but to be ready himself to settle in the homeland as a *halutz*, or pioneer, prepared to do any kind of work, however arduous, unaccustomed, or dangerous, that might be required at the time, to build this new national society.

At first, organized attempts were made to develop the basic, productive branches: agriculture, construction, and handicrafts. Settlement on the land, which was intended to create the agricultural base for the Jewish community in Palestine, was the central sphere of activity in the "conquest of labor" in the first 50 years of renewed national life. Later, in the 1920s and 1930s, construction and handicrafts developed, and so, to a certain extent, did administration, public services, and light industry, which were further expanded by the large wave of Jewish immigration from Germany that followed the Nazi assumption of power in 1933.

The advent of World War II and the increased demand of the Allies for industrial products led to the development of heavy industry, including metals, textiles, and food processing. There was also a considerable technical advance in construction and road building, as a result of army orders, both in Palestine and in other places. At the same time there were significant changes in labor relations and the beginnings of labor legislation.

This process received a great impetus by the establishment of Israel in 1948. Large investments in the development of agriculture, services, administration, industry and mining, construction, sea, air, and land transportation, and all the occupations connected with national defense, widened the productive framework and increased the variety of work available. Labor relations, social conditions, and labor codes were partially transferred from the voluntary to the governmental level.

These events determined the stages of development and affected the status of labor. In the first stage, that of settlement on the land, there was a close identity between ownership and work. Jewish immigrants established villages and cultivated the land on their own farms. At this stage there was no substantial body of hired Jewish laborers and the wage labor needed in agriculture came from the neighboring Arab villages. This division between Jewish 143 employers and Arab proletarians aroused the ideological opposition of young immigrants who came from Eastern Europe in the wake of the abortive revolution and the pogroms in 1905–06, especially in the Russian-ruled areas of Poland and Rumania. Belonging to a class whose social and economic foundations were crumbling, influenced by revolutionary workers' movements, as well as the Zionist ideal, and having absorbed socialist principles on the role of labor in production and of the workers in society, these pioneers fought for the right to work on the Jewish farms. They regarded their own transformation into manual workers as a part of the social and national revolution of the Jewish people and a precondition for the creation of a self-sustaining Jewish society and economy.

At this stage, which continued until the beginning of the 1920s, this Jewish working class was only a small part of the small Jewish community of about 60,000. It lacked vocational training and practical experience, but it had a highly developed working-class consciousness and struggled to develop a modern labor policy, achieve as high a wage level as possible, and establish labor relations similar to those accepted in Western countries. In fact, the theory of an ideological and trade union struggle preceded the development of the means of production in the Jewish community. The Jewish workers who came to the Land of Israel after the failure of the Russian Revolution in 1905, the immigrants of the Second Aliyah, regarded it as their mission to achieve a Zionist solution to the Jewish problem through immigration to the Land of Israel, building up a Jewish economy, and establishing progressive social patterns, and they saw the organization of labor as a basic part of that mission.

With the establishment at the beginning of the Second Aliyah of workers' political parties that carried out some trade union functions, as well as political activity, and the establishment, in December 1920, of the Histadrut (see above), which combined trade-union functions with social-welfare services and independent cooperative and workers' enterprises, a new stage was reached both from an organizational point of view and from the angle of labor's influence in the Jewish community. In many respects the political and trade-union organization of the workers ran ahead of national, social, and economic development. In fact, the established standards and practices in labor relations, wages, and social conditions inside the *yishuv*, although based on voluntary agreements, largely determined the conditions of production.

The organizational structure, practices, and ideology of the Jewish labor movement were, therefore, from the very beginning on a standard characteristic of the advanced industrial countries. The Histadrut, which absorbed the bulk of the immigrants and represented the vast majority of the organized workers, even went beyond that stage by assuming many functions not normally accepted by trade-union organizations in other countries. It saw as its task the practical implementation of social and economic programs that other labor movements regarded as long-term political and social goals. These programs included setting up new villages (moshavim and kibbutzim), industrial and service undertakings, workers' cooperative and contracting enterprises, and public services whose guiding principle was the idea of *avodah azmit* ("self-labor" or "personal labor," i.e., that a man must live by the fruits of his own labor without exploiting the labor of others). This concept was the guiding principle in the determination and implementation of the Histadrut's labor policies.

The ideological principles, trade union policy, and organizational patterns of Israel labor were laid down and assumed the force of binding customs in the life of the *yishuv* during the British Mandatory regime (1920–48), when the level of governmental services was largely determined by the condition and needs of the backward Arab population. In the course of that period they reached a standard that was high even in comparison with those achieved by workers' movements and trade unions in

10 LABOR RELATIONS

LABOR LEGISLATION IN THE MANDATORY PERIOD (1920–1948).
Due to established custom in British colonial territories and because of the possible effects on the Arab
and governmental economies, the British Mandatory
authorities were in no hurry to enact labor laws. For many
years, in fact, they left almost unchanged the situation
which they had inherited from the Ottoman Empire, in
which relations between employer and employee were
regulated by a section of the Mejelle which dealt with leases.
In the first 20 years of the Mandate, only a handful of labor
laws were enacted: the Mining Ordinance (1925), which
regulated safety conditions and prohibited, *inter alia*, the
employment underground of women or children under 14,
and ordinances prohibiting the use of matches made with
white phosphorus (1925) and a law enjoining the fencing
of machinery (1928). Article 21 of the Criminal Code, concerning intimidation in labor disputes, the Defense (Trade
Disputes) Order (1942), and the Defense (War Service Occupations) Regulations (1942) were concerned solely with
meeting emergency needs.

An important, if belated, step was the establishment of a
Department for Labor Affairs in 1943, largely under
pressure of economic developments during World War II.
As if to make up for the backwardness in this field that had
marked the period of British rule, the department set to
work with dispatch in the few years left before the end of
the Mandate, paying more attention to the advanced needs
of the Jewish economy. The Accidents and Occupational
Diseases Ordinance (1945), which provided for compulsory
notification of accidents at work or occupational diseases

which caused more than three days' absence, marked a considerable advance, as did two other ordinances issued in the same year concerned with employment of women and children, which greatly improved health conditions at work. The Factories Ordinance (1946), which established standards of safety and hygiene, was a very important and progressive addition to Mandatory labor legislation. Three other ordinances that would also have improved the Mandatory labor code were issued in 1947, but never came into effect. They were the Trade Boards Ordinance, which was to set up machinery for establishing minimum wages and working conditions in backward industries; the Industrial Courts Ordinance, for the settlement of labor disputes through conciliation and arbitration; and the Trade Union Ordinance, to regulate the legal status of workers' and employers' organizations.

VOLUNTARY AGREEMENTS DURING THE MANDATORY PERIOD. While the Mandatory government concentrated most of its attention on safety conditions, the Jewish community had a large measure of internal autonomy in its labor relations. In the absence of adequate legislation, it established practices and customs which, though voluntary, were firmly adhered to, as attempts to violate them were frustrated by the pressure of the organized community, which was led by the labor movement. This autonomy was reinforced by a High Court ruling to the effect that accepted custom in labor relations was legally binding. An eight-hour work day, annual vacations, severance pay, allocation of work through labor exchanges according to agreed priorities, rest on the Jewish Sabbath and festivals, recognition of the trade unions, collective bargaining, and collective agreements became established practice.

In the early years, labor relations in the Jewish community were concerned mainly not with wages and working conditions, but with the employment of Jewish labor in the citrus groves, which was the main source of employment. Wages and working conditions were practically stable, with slight variations, from the beginning of the

Mandate until the outbreak of World War II, so far as Jewish workers organized in the Histadrut were concerned, and were not, therefore, a serious cause of labor disputes. Tension in the labor sphere was due mainly to unemployment and charges of unfair distribution of the available jobs.

The Histadrut, the General Federation of Jewish Labor, was the largest and most influential workers' organization, but there were also two others, organized along political and ideological lines. The demonstratively secular character of the Histadrut at the time, both in outlook and in practical programs, led to the formation of a religious workers' organization, Ha-Po'el ha-Mizrachi, which later joined the Histadrut's medical-insurance fund and trade union department, while maintaining its separate framework for other affairs. There was also the National Labor Federation (Histadrut ha-Ovedim ha-Le'ummit), organized in 1934 under the aegis of the Revisionist Party, which opposed the Histadrut's socialist outlook and some of its trade union principles—especially the use of the strike weapon. From the beginning it had its own trade union department and medical-insurance fund.

In 1925 the Zionist Executive in Jerusalem intervened in a dispute between Ha-Po'el ha-Mizrachi and the Histadrut, when the contracting company of the former engaged workers without using the Histadrut's labor exchange. This intervention, which was intended to avoid direct interference by the Mandatory government, created a precedent. In the early 1930s the number of labor disputes increased as a result of the growth in the numbers of wage earners and of plants. In the course of a full-scale debate on the problem at the Zionist General Council in 1934, there was a demand for the conclusion of labor contracts which should assure fair labor conditions for the workers "within the economic possibilities of the economy" and, on the other hand, "a reasonable level of output, especially from the agricultural laborer." The meeting decided that the agreements should be based on (1) reasonable working conditions for the employees and adequate productivity; (2) obligatory resort to arbitration; (3) the establishment of labor exchanges on a basis of parity between workers and employers, the chairman and secretary being agreed upon by both sides; (4) the establishment of a labor exchange center under the Va'ad Le'ummi to supervise the local exchanges and appoint the chairman and secretary wherever the two sides failed to agree.

At the same time, the Labor Department of the Jewish Agency began to concern itself actively in labor disputes. This department, which was headed by Yiẓḥak Gruenbaum, with representatives of the Histadrut and Ha-Po'el ha-Mizrachi, was the highest authority in all such matters from its foundation in 1935 until the establishment of the state. During this period it dealt with more than 2,500 disputes, for the most part concerning collective agreements, and through its decisions it set the seal of approval on working conditions and practices worked out by collective agreements. Among other things, it developed a system for the resolution of labor disputes by arbitration or the good offices of the department, which was also recognized as a court of appeal.

LABOR LEGISLATION IN THE STATE OF ISRAEL. The emergence of Israel as an independent state in 1948 marked a turning point in the approach to labor relations. The Mandatory government had not had time to put the Industrial Courts Ordinance (1947) into effect; nor did the Provisional Government of Israel in its early days find time to breathe life into this stillborn enactment. In practice, the procedures and customs which had been accepted amongst the Jews of Palestine remained in force. The government set up a Labor Relations Department in the Ministry of the Interior, which inherited the functions of the Labor Department of the Jewish Agency and after the elections to the First Knesset was transferred to the Ministry of Labor.

Before long the government submitted to the Knesset the first labor law: the Ex-soldiers (Reinstatement in Employment) Law (1949), which was aimed at alleviating the difficulties caused by conscription for the War of Independence. It was followed by a lengthy series of labor laws, many of which gave legal force to procedures already established by custom and agreement within the Jewish community. They dealt, *inter alia*, with hours of work and rest (1951), annual leave (1951), employment of youth (1953), apprenticeship (1953), employment of women (1954), enforcement of collective agreements (1957), settlement of trade disputes (1957), penalties for excessive delays in payment of wages (1958), labor exchanges (1959), severance pay (1963), equal pay for men and women (1964), and labor tribunals (1969).

LABOR EXCHANGES. Under the employment Services Law (1959), employers must engage employees, and employees must accept employment, through the state labor exchange. There are exceptions for the civil service above a certain grade, managerial staff, posts requiring higher education or special training, and persons employing a spouse, parent, child, grandchild, brother, sister, or cousin. The manner in which applicants are referred to jobs is laid down in special regulations which generally take into account the nature of the occupation, the type of work, social condition, disablement, recent demobilization from the armed services, etc. The law prohibits any discrimination on the basis of sex, age, race, religion, nationality, party allegiance, etc. This law legalized the situation which was achieved in the pre-state period by a long struggle on the part of the workers, who established their own labor exchanges in order to prevent unorganized labor and protect new immigrants against closed-shop tendencies that might develop in particular occupations or localities.

Anyone seeking employment is registered at the labor exchange nearest his home. His trade or profession and grading are registered on the production of recognized certificates or on the basis of an examination by a qualified authority. He (or she) must reregister daily or at longer intervals according to his trade or profession. The labor exchange receives requests for staff, allocates them among the registered job seekers, and provides vocational counseling for those who lack skills or wish to change their occupation. Its services are given free of charge. There are 15 regional exchanges, divided into 164 branches and sections, as well as 41 branches in Arab areas and 68 branches for young people aged 14–18. Professional men and women are served by a special exchange with branches in Jerusalem, Tel Aviv, Haifa, and Beersheba. There is also an exchange for seamen in Haifa and special provisions for domestic servants, with seven branches in the large cities.

COLLECTIVE AGREEMENTS. Labor relations in Israel are based upon a system of collective agreements, or labor contracts, which is recognized in the Collective Agreements Law (1957). These agreements, which are signed by an employer or employers' association on the one hand and the representative of the trade union on the other, lay down conditions of work, including wages, social benefits, working hours, shifts, and labor relations, as well as rules of conduct and discipline, engagement of staff and the termination of employment, negotiation procedures, the settlement of disputes, and the rights and obligations of the parties. Collective agreements may be "special," applying to a particular enterprise or employer, or "general," applying to the whole or part of the country or to a specific type of work.

Collective agreements were to be registered by the chief labor relations officer at the Ministry of Labor. The representative organizations conclude skeleton agreements, which are adapted to conditions in each industry by subsidiary agreements negotiated between the trade union or labor council concerned in each case and the appropriate section of the employers' organization. The minister of labor is empowered to issue an order extending the application of the general collective agreement to employees or employers who are not organized in a trade union or employers' organization. In general, collective agreements are negotiated every two years by the Histadrut and the Manufacturers' Association, which was established in 1924.

In 1964, a roof organization called the Coordinating Committee of Economic Organizations was set up to represent the various employers' organizations in agriculture, industry, commerce, etc.

The Trade Union Department of the Histadrut speaks for about 90% of the workers, including, by agreement, members of Ha-Po'el ha-Mizrachi and Po'alei Agudat Israel, the labor wing of Agudat Israel. It consists of representatives of the national trade unions, but in determining its policies it is guided not only by the immediate needs of the workers but also by the long-term interests of the national economy. Histadrut ha-Ovedim ha-Le'ummit, which is in favor of compulsory arbitration in labor disputes, has its own trade unions and does not cooperate with the department. In each town there is a directly elected labor council (mo'ezet po'alim), which deals with local matters.

THE WORKERS' COMMITTEE AND THE LOCAL LABOR COUNCIL. The basic unit of trade union representation is the workers' committee (va'ad ha-ovedim), which is elected by all the workers (whether they belong to the Histadrut or one of the smaller federations) in each factory, office, shop, etc. It consists of three to nine members, depending on the size of the enterprise, elected every two to three years. Theoretically, voting is on an individual basis, but in practice the workers usually support the candidates nominated by their own parties. Labor councils are elected in each town by proportional representation in the same way and at the same time as the national convention of the Histadrut, lists of candidates being submitted by the political parties. The workers' committee, together with the local labor council, represents the workers in all matters connected with the labor contract and protects the rights specified in the contract or the regulations founded on it, as well as rights laid down by law. It discusses with the management any questions of labor conditions or discipline that may arise from time to time and has equal representation on productivity commit- 153 tees. It also organizes mutual aid projects and serves as a channel for information from the management on the position of the enterprise, production plans, technological changes, and so forth. A representative of the local labor council may be invited in advance to join in the discussion of particularly important matters; in any case, he is called in when the workers' committee fails to reach agreement with the management. The committee reports regularly to general meetings of the workers, to which it may submit matters of special importance for a decision by majority. Any decision involving a strike must, according to the regulations, be taken by secret ballot and be approved by the labor council.

WAGES. Wage rates and payments for social benefits in the various branches of the economy are fixed in the annual or biennial labor contracts, in accordance with the wages policy laid down biennially by the Trades Union Department of the Histadrut through negotiation between the trade unions and the employers' organizations. Changes generally take the form of wage increases and higher cost-of-living allowances.

During the British Mandatory regime, the agricultural laborer's wage was generally taken as a basis, the Jewish worker's earnings usually being some 25% higher than the Arab's. In many Jewish public services, such as the Zionist Organization, the Histadrut, the schools, and the health services, the "family-wage" system was in force. Under this system, all employees earned more or less equal wages (with differentials of 20–50% for various professional standards) supplemented by allowances for dependents. During World War II there was a sharp rise in prices, due to the decline in the exchange rate and increased demand for consumer goods and services, coupled with an increased demand for labor for the developing industries and services for the British army. There was a growing need to adjust wage rates to the changing price level. The solution was found in the system of cost-of-living allowances, under which the nominal wage was raised at fixed intervals.

After the establishment of the State of Israel the system at first remained in force in the main branches, but the development of the economy, which called for more skill and managerial responsibility, led to the abolition of the "family" system and demands for higher differentials. Up to the economic recession which started in 1964/65, the system of cost-of-living allowances, adjusted annually, had a great influence on wage levels. From 1965 onward, however, both wage rates and differentials began to rise, largely as a result of regrading in the civil service and the pressure of professional men's organizations.

In the biennial negotiations between labor and employers, on which the government exercises an indirect but powerful influence, general wage increases are based on the average rate of increase in output, with adjustments according to the situation in different industries and the state of the labor market. In many enterprises workers receive premiums in return for output in excess of the accepted norm. This system is encouraged by the trade unions, the employers' associations, and the government. There is a growing use of scientifically measured norms, the contribution of technological progress to productivity being taken into account in order to encourage the introduction of automation.

SOCIAL BENEFITS AND DEDUCTIONS FROM WAGES. The net wage received by the worker consists of the gross wage paid by the employer minus income tax and other deductions. The gross wage includes: basic salary in accordance with accepted wage rates; cost-of-living allowance, fixed by agreement between the Histadrut and the employers in accordance with the annual fluctuations in the consumer's price index, which is determined by the government's Central Bureau of Statistics; seniority increment for each year of employment in a given enterprise—ranging from IL5 to IL15 per annum up to a fixed "ceiling" of years of service or total increment; allowance for a wife, laid down in the labor agreement; children's allowances for the first three children, paid out of an 155 equalization fund financed by the employers collectively through the National Insurance Institute (allowances for the fourth and subsequent children come directly from national insurance).

The following deductions are made from the salary: income tax, national insurance, and pension fund: in many concerns, by custom or agreement, deductions are also made at the source for Histadrut membership fees (covering trade union and Kuppat Holim), municipal rates, and contributions to national institutions. The employer's contribution for social benefits includes: basic pension—11% of gross wage, excluding overtime and bonuses (with 5% more paid by the employee); comprehensive pension—11% of gross wage (with a further 5% from the employee); parallel fee—2.7% of wages, paid by the employers to the medical insurance fund; vacation pay—4% of wage to cover paid holidays for those employed less than 75 consecutive days (workers with permanent status receive their wages without interruption throughout the vacation period); vacation expenses—cost of accommodation in a recreation home for a certain number of consecutive days at an agreed rate per day, as fixed in the labor contract; sick leave, up to one month per year—the right being cumulative within limits laid down in the labor contract. Salary for a "13th month" is paid in some undertakings and offices. In some offices or institutions, generally in the academic professions, there is a special payment, up to an agreed maximum, for professional literature. Some employers make a monthly deposit to meet the cost of severance pay. In certain posts, mainly managerial, the employer provides a car and pays for upkeep and fuel up to a fixed number of kilometers. He may pay the cost of a home telephone, the employee making a fixed contribution to cover the cost of his private calls.

Permanent status may be granted under the terms of the labor contract after a trial period of six months, which may be extended by prior notice for a further six months. An

156 employee with permanent status may not be dismissed

without the agreement of the workers' committee and only in accordance with an agreed order of priority. In some academic posts senior employees are given a sabbatical year with pay. In case of bankruptcy, employees are guaranteed priority over other creditors for the payment of their wages up to a sum of IL2,100 as well as severance pay up to IL1,050 per employee.

INSPECTION, SAFETY, AND HYGIENE. Many factors increased the danger of work accidents after the establishment of the state: the rapid development of industry, construction, and transportation; the expansion of the electricity network; automation and the use of more sophisticated equipment; and the employment of new immigrants and untrained workers. To meet the situation a considerable body of safety legislation, along the lines of international conventions, was enacted in a short time to comply with local needs. The powers and scope of the factory inspectorate were extended in the Labor Inspection (Organization) Law of 1954, which also established the Safety and Hygiene Institute, jointly run by the Ministry of Labor, the employees, and the employers' organization, for the prevention of industrial accidents by research, guidance, and publicity. Regulations have been issued specifying safety measures required in various occupations. Industrial injuries compensation is provided through national insurance.

HOURS OF WORK AND REST. The standard working day in Israel consists of eight hours and the working week of 47 hours. If more than eight hours are worked, whether for unforeseen reasons or under an official overtime permit, each of the first two hours in excess of eight is regarded for wage purposes as an hour and a quarter, and every additional hour as one and a half hours. Every employee is entitled to 36 hours rest per week. The weekly holiday day is Saturday for Jews, Friday for Muslims, and Sunday for Christians. Religious holidays recognized by the government are rest days for workers of the religion concerned, and national holidays are rest days for all workers. Work on the weekly rest day is allowed by special permission of 157 the Ministry of Labor if it is essential for the defense of the state, the safety of the person or of property, the prevention of serious injury to the economy, the maintenance of a continuous work process, or the supply of the essential needs of the public or part of it. A general permit of this kind may be granted by a committee composed of the prime minister, the minister of religious affairs, and the minister of labor. For wage purposes, each hour worked on the day of rest is regarded as not less than one and a half hours.

ANNUAL VACATION. Under the Annual Leave Law (1951), every employee is entitled to an annual vacation with pay totaling at least 12 days not including weekly rest days and national and religious holidays. Shift workers receive four additional days. Every employee must be given an annual vacation of at least seven consecutive days; in certain occupations, specified in the regulations, a longer period is obligatory. Collective agreements also provide for longer vacations for workers in certain posts, whether at higher levels of responsibility or in certain occupational grades. Day laborers who are constantly changing their place of work receive a cash payment in lieu of vacation. This is paid through a special fund to which the employer contributes 4–5% of wages.

An employee is entitled to accumulate vacation periods, with employer's consent, up to a stipulated maximum (65 days for civil servants) and during a stipulated period in accordance with the labor contract. By mutual agreement an employee may receive a cash payment in lieu of vacation in excess of the seven obligatory days. The dates of the vacation for each employee are fixed by the management in consultation with the workers' committee, taking the wishes of the employee and the needs of the enterprise into account. The following are not included in the vacation period, but are stipulated in collective agreements: sickness during the vacation, if the employee informs the employer within 24 hours; periods of reserve duty or military service; days of mourning, i.e., seven days from the death of a member of the family, in accordance with religious custom;

special leave of one day for a son's or daughter's wedding or the birth of a child, and three days for the employee's own wedding. Jewish religious holidays are New Year (Rosh Ha-Shanah) two days, Day of Atonement one day, Sukkot two days, Passover two days, and Shavuot one day, as well as Independence Day and two optional days. For civil servants, the latter may be chosen from the eve of the Day of Atonement, Hoshana Rabba (7th day of Sukkot), the Tenth of Tevet, Purim, the eve of Passover, Martyrs' and Heroes' Remembrance Day, Israel Defense Forces Remembrance Day, Lag ba-Omer, the first of May, 17th Tammuz, and the Ninth of Av.

Under most labor contracts employees are entitled to an annual allowance sufficient to pay for seven days' accommodation in a recreation home or inexpensive hotel on condition that he takes at least ten consecutive days' vacation during the same year. This right is acquired after three years' service to the same employer (two years for employees under 18). Day workers are entitled to allowances for four to ten days, depending on seniority and other factors, in return for a contribution of 0.5% of wages to a special fund, matched by a similar contribution from the employer. Permanent employees are entitled to paid sick leave usually up to 30 days per year, which may be accumulated on terms laid down in the labor contract. Employees are insured through the insurance funds and are entitled to up to seven months' sick leave per year.

EMPLOYMENT OF WOMEN. Women have the right to work, without discrimination, at equal pay for equal value of work in the same jobs as men so long as they can do the job in accordance with their physical capacity without impairing their health. Jewish women played a prominent part in the work of the pioneers, in settlement on the land and the "conquest of labor," in the Jewish underground defense forces, and in political effort. The government makes special efforts to increase the share of women in the labor force. The role of women is particularly important in the liberal professions and primary, secondary, and higher **159** education, in administration, in retail distribution, in industries like food processing, textiles, and electronics, and in various agricultural jobs. Women are constantly penetrating into vocations once regarded as male preserves.

In 1971 women constituted 31% of the labor force, which is lower than in most developed industrial countries. The reason is that a large portion of the Jewish population came from Muslim countries, where it was not customary for women to work outside the home. Among the second generation there is a growing tendency to go out to work, which is more marked where the educational level is higher. The fact that girls aged 18–20 (with the exception of those excused on religious grounds) serve in the armed forces increases their readiness to seek work on the completion of their service. The minister of labor is empowered by law to prohibit or restrict the employment of women in a particular job or industrial process which may seriously impair their health. Women may not be employed on night shift, with the exception, under certain conditions and subject to the minister of labor's approval, of work in managerial posts, the customs, telephone exchanges, the police, airline stewardesses, hospitals, newspapers, hotels and restaurants, places of entertainment, etc. By law, a working mother is assured 12 weeks' maternity leave, beginning six weeks before the birth, if the mother chooses, as well as to a maternity grant from the National Insurance Institute. She is also entitled to be absent from work during pregnancy and breast-feeding or up to one hour's leave per working day for the purpose of breast-feeding.

EMPLOYMENT OF JUVENILES. The employment of, or peddling by, children under 14 is forbidden, but they may be employed in art or entertainment with the approval of the minister of labor. The employment of young persons (aged 14–18) is forbidden in any place which is likely to have an undesirable effect on their physical, emotional, or moral development, such as hotels, cafés, dance halls, mental institutions, mines, abattoirs, various types of 160 manufacture, and so forth, as specified in a list of occupations published by the ministry. Young workers must undergo medical examination before starting work and at six-month intervals, depending on the nature of the job, up to the age of 21. They may be employed for no more than eight hours per day and no more than 40 hours per week, and those under the age of 17 must not be employed at night without the approval of the minister of labor.

According to the law, every young person aged 14–18 in employment must be enabled by his employer to learn a trade, and the employer must not make deductions from his earnings for absence for the purpose of attending recognized lessons. Guidance in the choice of a trade by a qualified vocational counselor must be provided. The Apprenticeship Law (1953) empowers the minister of labor to define certain trades as apprenticeship trades, in which the employment of young persons is prohibited unless they are learning the trade through an approved program of study. During his training, the apprentice is paid in accordance with the collective agreement for the trade. For $1-1\frac{1}{2}$ days per week he is required to attend a special school for apprentices, where he studies the theoretical aspects of his trade and continues his general education. After three years' apprenticeship, he generally receives a trade certificate. In 1970 there were 23 such schools, attended by about 15,000 apprentices; a total of some 50,000 apprentices had qualified since the passing of the law.

DISMISSALS. Labor contracts usually obligate the employer to consult the workers' committee and receive its consent before dismissals are carried out. Grounds for dismissal may be low output, infractions of discipline, sabotage, unjustifiable absence, or unpunctuality. Most labor contracts call for at least two weeks' notice of dismissal. When staff has to be reduced, it is generally stipulated that the last-in-first-out rule be observed, with certain exceptions: for instance, relative levels of skill and social circumstances, such as size of family, are also taken into account. A dismissed employee is entitled to severance pay if he has worked for the same employer for at least one year without interruption, or in two consecutive years in the case of seasonal employees. An employee who resigns is not entitled by law to severance pay, but in many cases he receives it by agreement with the employer. Resignation due to impaired health, change of residence due to marriage, a move to an agricultural settlement, or the resignation of a mother within nine months of the birth of a child for the purpose of looking after the child, or when she has adopted a child, are regarded as equivalent to dismissal for the purpose of severance pay. Severance pay is also awarded in case of resignation due to proven and substantial worsening of working conditions or special circumstances connected with labor relations. The rate of severance pay laid down by law is one month's wages for every year of employment on monthly salary by the same employer, and two weeks' wages for every year during which a worker has been employed on a daily basis. In general, a month's salary, for the purpose of calculating severance pay, is the salary of the last month, but with regard to the years before 1964 there is a special basis for calculation which is specified by law.

VOCATIONAL TRAINING. From the early days of Zionist pioneering, when Jewish traders, shopkeepers, and students tried to turn themselves into farmers, vocational training in the widest sense of the term (then called in German *Umschichtung*) was a fundamental part of the national goal. During the period of independent Israel the vocational training system was built on the foundations established by the Jewish Agency and other voluntary bodies. It started by extending the apprenticeship system and setting up various courses for adults. Later, adult vocational centers were established throughout the country and furnished with up-to-date equipment. The network of vocational schools grew with the help of ORT (Organization for Rehabilitation and Training), which established well-equipped vocational high schools and also engaged in the training of apprentices.

Vocational high schools are owned and run by public bodies and supervised by the Ministry of Education and **163**

Culture. In 1970 there were 278 such schools with 51,000 pupils, run by: ORT-Israel—84 schools with 13,000 pupils; the Amal network of the Histadrut—25 schools and 5,250 pupils; local authorities—94 schools with 15,000 pupils; Youth Aliyah—22 schools and 32,000 pupils; Agudat Israel—24 schools with 2,000 pupils; the Working Women's Council (Mo'eẓet ha-Po'alot)—25 schools and 1,000 pupils; Mizrachi Women's Federation—four schools and 1,540 pupils; WIZO—three schools and 1,250 pupils; the Hadassah Organization—two schools with 900 pupils; and other bodies with 30 schools and 5,600 pupils, most of them learning clerical skills. Students receive both vocational and general education for three or four years, leading to a recognized trade certificate. There are also vocational schools attached to specific industries, the curriculum including practical work on the factory floor. Courses are held for adolescent drop-outs (aged 14-18) from the high schools, the curriculum being devised to enable them to serve in the army in their trades, thus extending their period of training.

For adults, the Ministry of Labor runs specially equipped training centers, some established with outside assistance (e.g., technical aid from the U.S. government, the U.N., and the International Labor Office), giving 3-18-month courses depending on the trade. In 1970 there were 22 of these, with about 12,000 trainees. In addition, on-the-job training has been used to deal with the huge number of unskilled adults among the immigrants. The trainee is taught by a skilled tradesman until he is fit for normal employment and the employer receives a subvention from the government in return for the training. Special attention is devoted to the training of tradesmen to the levels of practical engineer, instructor technician, and foreman, which provide a link between the graduate engineer and the artisan. The shortage of staff at these intermediate levels is one of the more serious defects in Israel's labor force. To fill this gap, the Government

Institute for Technical Training has been set up jointly by

the Ministries of Labor and Education and Culture, with the technical aid of the International Labor Organization. The institute runs day and evening courses, directly and through the Technion, the universities, and the ORT network. About 6,000 tradesmen attend courses each year. The aptitudes and inclinations of young workers are examined in special vocational guidance centers. There are also diagnosis and observation centers to guide handicapped persons in the choice of a vocation.

ARBITRATION AND MEDIATION. Labor contracts contain provisions for settling differences, generally by agreed arbitration. Sometimes the parties agree on a single arbitrator and sometimes an arbitration court, consisting of one representative each of employees and the employer and a third person agreed upon by both sides, is set up. This procedure is normally used in disputes over the interpretation of clauses in the labor contract, but not where a new demand is made. Where agreed arbitration is not used, or where the issue is not dealt with in the labor contract, the good offices of the chief labor relations officer at the Ministry of Labor, whose powers are derived from the Settlement of Trade Disputes Law (1957), are invoked. His authority applies to disputes between employers and employees, between an employer and a trade union, or between one trade union and another, but not to disputes between individuals. Either party to a dispute may notify the chief labor relations officer, but in the event of a threat to strike, or to impose a lockout, the party which makes the threat must make the notification.

The officer may mediate in person or appoint a mediator; in general, he prefers the two parties to settle the dispute themselves. Each party must give reasoned replies to the claims of the other side and appear before the mediator at his demand. The parties are not compelled to accept the mediator's proposals, but any signed settlement, whether reached by the parties themselves or in response to the mediator's proposals, has contractual force. The same applies to the ruling of an arbitrator or arbitration **165** commission nominated by the chief labor relations officer when the labor contract provides for agreed arbitration.

There is no compulsory arbitration law in Israel. Attempts to introduce such a law have never secured a majority in the Knesset. Opponents of compulsory arbitration argue that it restricts the freedom of the workers to fight for their interests, that in a democratic country there cannot be control of wages without parallel control of profits, and that, in any case, compulsory arbitration cannot be effectively enforced. Proposals to introduce compulsory arbitration in essential services have also been rejected for the same reasons, as well as because of the difficulty of defining essential services.

STRIKES AND LOCKOUTS. The right to strike is recognized in Israel: strikers and employers imposing a lockout enjoy immunity under the Collective Agreement Law (1957) and the Civil Damages Ordinance. According to the Histadrut's rules, strikes must have the approval of its competent authorities, but wild-cat strikes are not infrequent.

Most strikes are over claims for pay rises and break out before the signature of a new labor contract. The number of strikes over dismissals, the transfer of enterprises, or non-recognition of labor unions is relatively small; such issues are usually settled through the arbitration machinery specified in the labor contracts. About 60% of the strikes which took place in the decade ending in 1969 were over pay and related issues, 20% over delays in the payment of wages, 10% over dismissals, and 10% over the signing of agreements and the recognition of trade unions; very few were over classification, transfer of factories, and other matters. Strikes are not more frequent in Israel than in other industrialized countries, but in view of the military and economic pressures to which Israel has been subject for a long time, they constitute a grave economic and social burden.

According to an amendment to the Settlement of Trades Disputes Law, passed in 1969, employees or employers must give 15 days' notice to the chief labor relations officer at the Ministry of Labor and to the other party of their intention to declare a strike or a lockout as the case may be, in order to enable the two parties to settle the dispute through direct contact or the chief labor relations officer to attempt to settle it by mediation. Labor contracts include provisions for the settlement of disputes through accepted forms of arbitration. In the great majority of cases, agreements for the settlement of disputes also settle the issue of strike pay. The Histadrut has a strike fund from which grants or loans are made to workers who are on a recognized strike. Neither strikes nor lockouts are regarded in law as a breach of contract, and those responsible are not, therefore, liable for damages—except in cases of sabotage.

UNEMPLOYMENT AND UNEMPLOYMENT INSURANCE. Fluctuations in the dimensions of immigration and the rate of economic growth, as well as the changing security situation, have led to a varying incidence of unemployment from time to time. A further cause of periodic unemployment has been the dependence of a large part of the Israel economy on construction, which is affected by fluctuations in supply and demand. To alleviate unemployment, the government initiated public works financed from the public purse, such as afforestation, land reclamation, drainage, archaeological excavations, and road construction and maintenance. Relief work of this kind was allocated to the unemployed, each applicant receiving 12–24 days' work per month depending on the number of persons he had to support. Wages were linked with those of agricultural laborers. Special programs, with five hours' work a day five times per week, were instituted for those with limited ability to work.

Total unemployment figures include both those actually unemployed and those employed on relief work. Two sets of data are published: (a) manpower surveys, covering a statistical sample of those who make up the civilian labor force aged 14 and over, which define as unemployed those who did not work at all during the week to which the survey related (see p. 161); and (b) the daily average of unemployed, which is calculated by dividing the total number of unemployment days during the month among those who registered as work seekers at the labor exchanges at least once a week, by the number of working days in the month. The first set of data includes those who do not normally work; the second covers only those registered at the labor exchanges. Table 16 gives the figures according to the daily average of registered unemployment, on the basis of which employment policy and programs were framed, with the numbers **actively seeking** work. In addition, a daily average of 12–17,000 persons with limited working capacity, who seldom figure on the labor exchange registers as work seekers, were employed on special projects. Relief work, which could be adapted to seasonal fluctuations and regional variations in the employment situation, served in place of unemployment insurance.

In 1965 it was decided that unemployment grants should be made from the public purse to those unemployed who, for one reason or another, could not be employed even on relief work. The grants were made to persons registered at the labor exchange who had been unemployed for at least 34 days in accordance with the applicant's marital status and number of children. Under an amendment to the National Insurance Law passed in 1972, the payment of unemployment insurance allowances, based on the relation between the applicant's wage when working and the average wage in the economy, was due to begin on Jan. 1, 1973.

LABOR COURTS. The Labor Courts Act, establishing a separate judicial network for matters related to labor, came into force in 1969. These matters include labor laws, social conditions, and national insurance questions. The labor courts are empowered to adjudicate claims between employer and employee, disputes arising out of a special collective agreement, touching on the maintenance, applicability, implementation or infraction of the agreement, claims of an employee against a trade union, and any matter related to the National Insurance Law. The claims

168

may relate to trade disputes, employment services, reinstatement of demobilized soldiers, compensation to employees on reserve duty, severance pay, delayed payment of wages, etc.

There is a national labor court, which is also a court of appeal, and four regional labor courts. Each regional labor court is composed of one judge and two lay members, one representing the employees and the other the employers. The national labor court is composed of three judges and one or two representatives each of labor and employers, depending on the case. The labor courts are not bound by the rules of evidence, except in special cases, and are empowered to use the procedure which they regard as best suited to serve the ends of justice. Parties may be represented by appointees of employers' organizations or trade unions, who need not be lawyers.

PENSIONS. There are three types of retirement-insurance schemes:

(a) The national insurance old-age pension (see Social Security and Welfare, pp.218ff).

(b) Budgetary insurance entitles the employee to a pension on reaching retirement age (and in certain circumstances at a lower age) equal to 2% of his salary for every year worked, after not less than ten years' service. When an employee has started work after reaching the age of 40, the competent authority may increase his pension in accordance with customary or agreed rules. In this type of scheme, which is in force in the civil service, the employee makes no contribution to the cost of the pension.

(c) There are two types of insurance through pension funds. "Basic insurance" covers pension for the insured person, partial pension and a lump sum for his heirs, mutual life insurance for pensioners and active members of the fund, withdrawal grants, and loans to members. "Comprehensive" pension insurance provides, in addition, full pension for survivors and a full or partial disablement pension.

Contributions vary from 7.5–10% of wages for basic pension, 4–5% coming from the employee and the rest from the employer, and 13.5–16% for the comprehensive pension, the employee paying 4–5% and the employer the rest. Retirement age is 65 for a man and 60 for a woman, or earlier in certain occupations. If an employee continues to work beyond the retirement age, he receives a higher pension on retirement, up to 70% of his salary. The qualifying period of membership is ten years. Accumulated rights may be transferred from one pension fund to another under special conditions laid down in the regulations. An employee who stops working before reaching retirement age is entitled to a severance grant, which includes the accumulated total of his contributions and those of the employer, plus accumulated interest and linkage increments (related to changes in the rate of exchange or the cost of living). Alternatively, if he has at least ten years' contributions to his credit, he may opt to receive the grant on reaching retirement age or continue to pay his contributions in order to receive a full pension. Surviving dependents are entitled to payments ranging from 20% of the deceased's pension for an orphan who has lost one parent to 60% for a widow. Surviving relatives of a member of the fund who dies before acquiring pension rights receive a bereavement grant. A person holding comprehensive insurance for not less than three years is entitled to a disability pension, provided he began to work before the age of 55 (50 for a woman). The pension for a totally disabled person who is unable to work two hours per day is 50% of wages, plus 5% for every dependent (up to a maximum of 20%), plus 1% for every year of service. A partially disabled person receives a pension calculated on the basis of the percentage of disablement.

The Histadrut maintains seven pension funds: for employees of Histadrut institutions, industrial workers, building workers, workers in Histadrut enterprises, agricultural workers, office workers, and workers in cooperatives, excluding transport. There are also company insurance funds in banks, private companies, etc. The pension ranges from 35–40% of the last salary, on the completion of ten years' insurance, up to a maximum of 70% on the completion of 32–35 years.

11 EMPLOYMENT

The successive waves of Jewish immigration generally brought with them periods of considerable unemployment and a legacy of underemployment, from which, even in the changed circumstances of the 1960s, it was difficult to escape. Stress was laid on the need to build up the goods-producing sectors—agriculture, industry, and building. In the early days, the development of agriculture was the central Zionist theme, although it is doubtful whether employment in agriculture ever reached 20% of the Jewish labor force. Industrial development began on a serious scale only during World War II, and received special attention after 1955. Because of the lack of previous agricultural and industrial training of most of the immigrants, and the limited growth of the goods-producing sectors, Israel always had a service-based economy.

As late as 1955, 46% of the Jewish labor force was employed in the goods-producing sectors (a proportion slightly higher than that in the United States, the most service-oriented economy in the world, and much lower than in Western Europe). Within the service sectors, the proportion of Jews employed in public and government services was 22%, by far the highest in the world. Whereas in most countries underemployment tended to be concentrated in agriculture, in Israel it tended to be concentrated in public and government services. The unemployment rate, traditionally high in Israel because of unrestricted immigration, reached a peak of about 10% in 1953, but dropped to 7% in 1955 (see Table 18).

Between 1955 and 1965, while the Israel gross national product expanded at a real annual rate of 10%, the structure

Table 17. Employment in Israel by Economic Sector (1955–1971)

Year	Percentage distribution by economic branch									Total employment
	Agriculture	Industry and mining	Construction	Utilities	Commerce	Transportation	Public services	Finance and business services[1]	Personal services	
1955	17.6	21.5	9.3	2.0	13.5	6.6	21.2		8.3	585,700
1960	17.3	23.2	9.3	2.2	12.3	6.2	22.0		7.5	701,800
1965	13.0	25.4	10.5	1.8	12.6	6.9	22.6		7.2	879,200
1969[1]	9.7	24.0	8.1	1.1	13.3	7.9	22.7	5.1	8.1	945,800
1970[1]	—	24.3	8.3	1.2	13.0	7.5	24.0	5.2	7.7	963,200
1971[1]	8.5	25.2	8.9	1.1	12.7	7.4	25.3	5.4	7.3	997,100

[1] New classification introduced in 1968.

Source: Labor Force Surveys, Central Bureau of Statistics.

Table 18. Employment and Unemployment in Israel (1955–1971)

Year	Population of working age	Total labor force	Percent of population in labor force	Employed	Unemployed	Percent unemployed
1955	1,178,500	631,200	53.6	585,700	45,500	7.2
1960	1,391,900	735,800	52.7	656,100	34,000	4.6
1965	1,727,400	912,400	52.8	815,000	33,200	3.6
1969	1,977,800	990,100	50.1	945,800	44,300	4.5
1970	2,032,200	1,001,400	49.3	963,200	38,300	3.8
1971	2,097,200	1,032,400	49.2	997,100	35,700	3.5

Source: Labor Force Surveys, Central Bureau of Statistics.

of employment in Israel underwent radical changes. The proportion in the goods-producing sectors actually advanced slightly, from 48.4 to 48.9% (this includes the Israel Arabs). Employment in agriculture, following world trends, declined over the decade, but relative gains in industrial and construction employment more than offset this. Small relative declines in commerce and private services were only partially offset by a relative expansion in public services. The slight rise of employment in goods-producing sectors was contrary to world trends: in Western Europe the proportion employed in the goods-producing sector fell to 50–55%. As Israel living standards neared European levels during this decade, the broad distribution of the labor force between economic sectors began to resemble that of Western Europe. By 1965 the distribution of the labor force by economic sectors had begun to approach normalcy, though some sharp differences were still evident. The proportion of the labor force in industry, despite the rapid absolute and relative rise, was still low compared to Western Europe, as was the proportion in commerce. On the other hand, comparatively large proportions were still engaged in construction and in public services.

The picture of total employment had also changed over the decade (see Table 18). From 1955 to 1960 unemployment fell steadily, from 45,500 to 34,000, or from 7.2 to 4.6% of the labor force. Thereafter, the number of unemployed tended to remain stable, though because of increased employment the percentage dropped. The unemployment rate fluctuated only between 3.3 and 3.7% from 1961 through 1965. This rate was considerably lower than that prevailing elsewhere. During the early 1960s, Israel enjoyed its first sustained period of full employment. The residual unemployment was essentially of a frictional character. Indeed, in 1964, a peak year, there were large numbers of unfilled jobs.

The proportion of the total population of working age in the labor force declined slightly over the 1955–1965 decade, **175** but this decline was purely demographic. The number of people in the 14–17 age group and over 55 years of age expanded significantly over the period. This offset increased labor force participation by specific age groups, though differently for men and women. Between 1955 and 1965, labor force participation of male youths aged 14–17 grew: it grew substantially for those over 55 years of age. Thus, while in 1955 it could be argued that male labor force participation was low by West European or American standards, by 1965 it was quite normal.

The labor force participation rates of women also advanced rapidly during the same decade. Despite the unfavorable demographic development, the participation rate grew from 26.5% in 1955 to 30.3% in 1965. But, despite this increased rate, the overall level was generally below that in the United States or Western Europe. The 1965 employment rate for women up to the birth of their first child was comparable to that in other countries. Thereafter, particularly after the age of 35, the rate was much lower, i.e., fewer married women with children tended to return to the labor force as compared to other advanced countries. This is due to the extremely low labor force participation of Jewish women originating from Islamic countries. These women had many children, lived in traditional style, and had few labor market skills. Daughters of these immigrant women are, however, adapting more to Western work and childbearing patterns, and the problem appears to be simply generational.

The economic and employment growth patterns were abruptly halted by the recession of 1966–67. During this period, employment declined, especially in industry and building, and unemployment soared briefly over the 10% mark. After the Six-Day War a very rapid recovery set in with a trend to return to full employment. There was, however, a further relative shift to services and a further decline in agricultural employment.

In the 1970s, Israel's capacity for economic growth
tends to be limited largely by manpower shortage, mitigated

by Arab labor from the administered areas. The important tasks are to reduce frictional unemployment and to utilize underemployed manpower by increased training in needed skills.

Part Four
THE ARAB POPULATION
12 DURING THE YEARS OF BRITISH RULE, 1917-1948

GENERAL SURVEY. In 1917, with the British conquest of Palestine during World War I, the country's Arabic-speaking population numbered less than 600,000 persons; in 1947 it was estimated at 1,200,000. This enormous increase, by more than double in 30 years, was accompanied by steady progress in health, education, and standard of living. These achievements were partly due to the more efficient administration introduced by the Mandatory government, which improved security, consolidated land tenure and lessened the power of local autocrats, paid more attention to the needs of the villagers, expanded health and educational services, fostered agriculture, and abolished conscription. In the main, however, Arab progress—far superior to that registered in the neighboring countries, where Britain and France had introduced similar administrations—was connected with the growth of the Jewish community and its efforts to develop the country. This is shown by the comparative vital statistics, percentage of school attendance, and number of doctors, nurses, teachers, and so forth. Tax revenue received from the Jews by the Mandatory government enabled it to improve its health and education services for the Arabs. The Jews introduced better transportation and more modern banking and production methods; they provided an expanding market for Arab agricultural produce, as well as a convenient labor outlet. Their public services, which were partially at the disposal of the Arabs, stimulated them and the government to create similar facilities for the Arab population. Thousands of Arab immigrants, mostly illegal, entered the country throughout the period.

In the Countryside. About 67% of Palestinian Arabs worked on the land, the majority living in about 900 villages. Their agricultural methods were primitive: much of the plowing was done with the wooden "nail," unchanged since ancient times: there was little systematic fertilization (natural manure was used for fuel, and chemical fertilizer was rare); no attempt was made to tap water for irrigation; modern methods of marketing, cooperative purchasing, and credit did not take root, while loan sharks held sway over thousands of families. Large stretches of land—according to various estimates 25–30%—were under collective village ownership *(mushāʿ)*, and since they were periodically redistributed the farmers were not interested in improvements, land amelioration, etc. The ownership of land by the *waqf* (religious trusts) was also regarded as a hindrance to its rational utilization. Nevertheless, the Arab fellahin or peasants were progressing from a natural economy, working only for its own needs without technological and social development, to a more modern economy. Not only landowners, but thousands of fellahin undertook intensive fruit and vegetable growing, using fairly modern methods, as well as poultry and livestock raising. Not only were substantial sums of money pumped into the Arab village—at least part of which was invested in the improvement of economic, housing, and other conditions—but thousands of youths were attracted to the cities and the Jewish settlements, some of them returning to their villages equipped with new ideas and ways.

Although these developments led to the growing disintegration of the rural social structure, the old patriarchal framework still wielded great power. The patriarchal family or group of interrelated families *(ḥamūla)* was still the dominant social unit. It was not the individual who determined his relationship to society, to his neighbors and the government, to organizations and political parties, but the family or *ḥamūla,* the head of which still held absolute sway not only in business, marriage and family affairs, but even over the lives of its members. Nomadic customs, such as blood feuds and collective family responsibility, survived. The killing of girls or married women by their brothers, husbands, or other relatives for deviation from accepted village morality was a common occurrence.

For the most part, the village *ḥamūla* was bound by a kind of alliance—sometimes through consanguinity or common origin—with others in neighboring villages. Thus, networks of clans arose, connected, in semi-feudal fashion, with urban families or with regional or urban notables. In exchange for protecting the interests of the villagers against rival families, the authorities, the police, and the courts and "arranging" their economic, financial, employment, and public affairs, the village notables and the leading urban families enjoyed the villagers' political loyalty. This was the basis of political life among the Palestinian Arabs. Although the political attitudes and party affiliations of the urban leaders frequently changed, their relationship with the village families remained almost fixed. Hence the "parties" formed in the cities, with the recurrent formation and disintegration of factions, were the concern of limited groups of urban intellectuals and politicians, and their influence on the village masses was negligible.

In the Cities. Of the 30–35% of Palestinian Arabs who lived in the cities, 30–35% were engaged in manual labor, industry, and construction; 15–17% in haulage and transportation; 20–23% in business; 5–8% in the free professions; 5–7% in public services; 6–9% in domestic services and the like; and the rest in miscellaneous occupations. The traditional manufactures of the urban Arabs, including home industry (such as the production of soap, oils, flour, and textiles), were increasingly displaced by new local industries and cheap foreign products. However, side by side with the traditional manufactures, and in great measure deriving from them, a modern Arab industry was developing, especially in textiles and cigarette manufacture. At the end of the period, the number of urban Arabs in steady employment in industry, crafts, public works, construction, and international and Jewish projects was estimated at 25,000–30,000, in addition to a few thousand in home industries. Many were semi-rural transients who later returned to their villages.

A similar development took place in commerce, where, side by side with the traditional small concern, modern Arab wholesale commerce evolved, especially in food marketing. Arabs also played an important role in the import and export trade, as well as in banking. In addition to the international and British banks—which employed many Arab managers and senior officials—and the Jewish banks, there were two Arab ones: the Arab Bank (established 1930) and the Arab People's Bank (established 1940). Although the characteristic features of the urban economy in Arab countries—preference for commerce over industry and the investment of surplus capital in real estate—existed in Palestine, they gradually became less clear and prominent there, doubtless because of the Jewish example. The middle class, including an intellectual stratum, was also more developed among the Palestinians than in other Arab societies. There were three or four dailies (one founded in 1911) during the period, as well as several weeklies and other periodicals, and textbooks and essays were published in Arabic; there was no significant literary work, however. The bulk of their cultural nourishment came from Egypt and, second hand, via Lebanon. Likewise, the Palestinian Arabs scarcely evinced any artistic capacity in theater, music, etc.; here, too, Egypt was the main source of supply.

Demography and Vital Statistics. The first official census in 1922 counted some 752,000 inhabitants, of whom 83,790 were Jews. Of the 668,258 non-Jews, 78%—589,177—were Muslims; there were 71,464 Christians and 7,617 Druze and others. In March 1947 the non-Jewish population was given as 1,319,434: 1,157,423 Muslims, 146,162 Christians, and 15,849 others. (The figures for Arabs in 1947 were, apparently, inflated because of the institution of rationing in 1942 and the consequent reluctance to report deaths.) Most of the Christians were also Arabs, but their total **181** included a substantial number of English, other Europeans, and Armenians as well (see Table 19).

Most of the Arab growth was a result of the extraordinary natural increase, due to the fall in the death rate and the rise in fertility, while the birthrate remained stable. Natural increase rose from 23.3 per thousand in 1922–25 to 30.7 in 1941–44 (see Table 20). Fertility, as measured by the average number of children born to a Muslim mother, rose from 6.1 in 1927–29 to 8.1 in 1942–43. In Egypt, on the other hand, the death rate was 33.7 per thousand in 1924–26 and 30.3 in 1939–41, while the fertility rate in 1940 was 6.4. As the British Mandatory government's *Survey of Palestine* (1946) put it: "The Arabs of Palestine have, during the last two decades, been in an almost unique demographic position. This improvement is particularly noticeable in those sub-districts of the coastal plain which have been the main Jewish immigration areas" (p. 714).

Improvements in health conditions by the drainage of swamps, better sanitation, and modern medical methods were largely responsible for almost halving the infant mortality rate among Muslim children and raising the average life-span by more than ten years (see Table 21). In 1921 there were 304 government hospital beds in the country, 402 Jewish, and 782 Christian. By 1944 there were 1,377 beds in government and 1,410 in Jewish hospitals. The percentage of malaria patients dropped from 7.17 in 1922 to 0.7 in 1944. In Egypt, by comparison, there was no decline in infant mortality during the period; life expectancy for males rose from 31 to 34.2 between 1917–27 and 1927–37, while for females it actually fell from 36 to 31.5.

Part of the increase in Arab population, however, was due to migration. In the 20 years between 1922 and 1942 20,015 Muslims, 15,645 Christians and 336 others (excluding Jews) were officially registered as immigrants to Palestine. Since there was considerable unrecorded movement of laborers across the borders, especially from Syria the actual number of immigrants was undoubtedly much larger; it has been estimated as high as 100,000.

Table 19. Population of Palestine, 1922–47

Year	Muslims	Christians	Druze & Other	Jews	Total
1922	589,177	71,464	7,617	83,790	752,048
1931	759,700	88,907	10,101	174,606	1,033,314
1936	862,730	108,506	11,378	384,708	1,366,692
1942	995,292	127,184	13,121	484,408	1,620,005
1947	1,157,423	146,162	15,849	614,239	1,933,673

Table 20. Muslim Births, Deaths, and Natural Increase

Years	Births	Deaths	Natural Increase
1922/25	50.2	26.9	23.3
1931/35	50.3	25.3	25.0
1941/44	50.1	19.4	30.7

Table 21. Muslim Infant Mortality and Life Expectancy

Years	Child Mortality* (per 1,000 births)	Life Expectancy	
		Male	Female
1926/30	412	37.1	37.9
1936/40	289	46.4	47.7
1941/44	251	49.4	50.4

* Deaths per 1,000 in the first five years of life.

Education. There was also a significant improvement in education. In July 1920 the 171 government schools in the country had 408 teachers and 10,662 pupils, almost half of whom were Arab. In July 1944, as a result of the British drive to improve the system, there were 64,790 Arab pupils in government schools (59,045 Muslims and 5,745 Christians), as well as 39,828 in private schools (17,815 Muslims and 22,013 Christians). To a large extent the increase was due to the construction of new schools in the villages. Education did not reach all the Arabs, however. According to the 1931 census, 85.6% of the Muslims, 76.7% of the Druze, and 42.3% of the Christians over seven years old were illiterate. In 1944 only 34% of the total school-age population was in school. The most deprived were the village girls. While 85% of the Muslim boys and 52% of the girls in the urban areas received some schooling, in the villages the percentages were only 65% for boys and 5% for girls.

The demarcation lines laid down in the armistice agreements with Egypt and Jordan split the Arabs of Western Palestine between three territorial units: the State of Israel; the central hill region of Judea and Samaria, annexed to Transjordan as the "West Bank" of the Jordan kingdom; and the Gaza Strip, under Egyptian occupation.

13 IN THE STATE OF ISRAEL

With the flight of thousands of Arabs immediately before and during the War of Independence some 156,000 were left in Israel in November 1948, out of an estimated 750,000 who lived in the area at the end of 1947. The succeeding two decades saw a sharp increase in their number: it trebled by the end of 1971, when there were some 458,000. From 1951 to 1966 they accounted for about 11% of the population; in 1967 with the reunification of Jerusalem, the percentage jumped to over 14%: Table 22 shows the Arab and Druze population at the end of each year, in thousands.

The major reason for this growth was the unusually high rate of natural increase, one of the highest in the world, which rose in Israel from 33.7 per thousand in 1950 to 42.8 in 1960 and 43.4 in 1966, falling to 37.3 in 1971. There was a drop in the death rate from 9.48 per thousand in 1950 to 7.5 in 1960 and 6.1 in 1971 and a high birthrate: 56 per 1,000 in 1950, 50.3 in 1960 and 45.5 in 1971. The average number of children born to an Arab woman in 1971 was 7.15, while the average Arab family in 1971 consisted of 6.6 persons. The rate of natural increase, per thousand, for Israel non-Jews is illustrated by Table 23. A breakdown of these figures by religious groups shows that the Muslims are mainly responsible for this high rate (see Table 24).

As a result of this unusual rate of natural increase, the Arab population is very young. The median age, which was 17 years in 1955, dropped to 16.3 in 1961 and to 15.1 in 1971. In 1955, 45% of the Arab population was under 15 years old. By 1971 that age group accounted for almost half of the population (49.8%), and almost threequarters of all the Arabs (74.2%) were younger than 30. Just over half the Israel Arabs are males: in 1971, 51.3% of the Mus-

Table 22. Non-Jewish Population, 1949–71 (in thousands)

Year	Muslims	Christians	Druzes & Others	Total	% of Population
1949	111.5	34.0	14.5	160.0	14.9
1950	116.1	36.0	15.0	167.1	12.9
1951	118.9	39.0	15.5	173.4	11.4
1952	122.8	40.4	16.1	179.3	11.0
1953	127.6	41.4	16.8	185.8	11.0
1954	131.8	42.0	18.0	191.8	11.2
1955	136.3	43.3	19.0	198.6	11.1
1956	141.4	43.7	19.8	204.9	11.0
1957	146.9	45.8	20.5	213.2	10.8
1958	152.8	47.3	21.4	221.5	10.9
1959	159.3	48.3	22.3	229.9	11.0
1960	166.3	49.6	23.3	239.1	11.1
1961	174.9	51.3	26.3	252.5	11.3
1962	183.0	52.6	27.3	262.9	11.3
1963	192.2	53.9	28.5	274.5	11.3
1964	202.3	55.5	28.6	284.6	11.3
1965	212.4	57.1	29.8	299.3	11.5
1966	223.0	58.5	31.0	312.5	11.8
1967*	286.6	70.6	33.1	392.7	14.1
1968	300.8	72.1	33.3	406.3	14.3
1969	317.0	73.0	34.0	424.0	14.5
1970	328.6	75.5	35.9	440.0	14.7
1971	343.9	77.3	37.3	458.5	14.8

* Including 55,000 Muslims and 12,000 Christians added as a result of the reunification of Jerusalem.

Table 23. Live Births, Deaths, and Natural Increase per thousand —Non-Jews in Selected Years—1951–71

Year	Births	Deaths	Natural Increase
1951	46.5	8.8	37.8
1955	46.0	8.6	37.4
1961	49.3	7.3	42.0
1966	49.5	6.1	43.4
1969	46.7	5.9	40.8
1971	45.5	6.2	37.7

lims, 50% of the Christians, and 51.4% of the Druze were males.

Other factors also helped to augment the number of Arabs in Israel. While emigration was negligible (about 6,000 Arabs left Israel between 1949 and 1971), there was a substantial immigration, some 40,000 returning under the "reunion of families" scheme. Border adjustments by the 1949 Armistice Agreements also added some 30,000 Arabs in the "Little Triangle" area, a narrow strip from the Jezreel Valley to Kafr Qāsim.

In the Villages. The majority of Israel Arabs live in villages, as they have throughout the centuries, but the percentage of rural inhabitants has steadily decreased: from about 78% of the Arab population at the end of 1949 to 57% —some 263,000 souls—in 1971. Most of the Arab villages are in the northern section of Israel (Northern and Haifa districts), where four-fifths of the rural Arab population lived in 1971, making up two-thirds of its rural population. Of the 100 Arab villages, 43 held 2,000 or more inhabitants each, and 57 less than 2,000. More than a third (38%) of the Arabs lived in the large villages and 10% in the small ones; almost 9% were Bedouin. Table 25 shows the division of the Arab population, by districts and subdistricts.

While agriculture is still the main occupation, there has been a noticeable drop in the percentage of Arabs working on the land. In 1954 58% of Israel Arabs were engaged in agriculture; by 1964 this figure had decreased to 39% and in 1971 (after the addition of over 70,000 East Jerusalem Arabs to the urban population) it was only 22.4%. On the other hand, the area cultivated by Arabs in Israel increased from 340,000 dunams (85,000 acres) in 1948/49 to 795,000 dunams (199,000 acres) in 1971/72 and the area under irrigation went up from 8,000 dunams (2,000 acres) in 1948/49 to 56,000 dunams (14,000 acres). Of the cultivated area about half (400,000 dunams) is cultivated by the Bedouin. Almost 90% of the area (apart from that cultivated by the Bedouin) is privately owned.

The government has done much to aid the development of the Arab villages. An IL85,000,000 five-year plan for the purpose was completed in 1967 and a second, to cost **187**

Table 24. Live Births, Deaths, and Natural Increase—Non-Jews, by Religion, in 1971—rates per 1,000

	Muslims	Christians	Druze and others
Live Births	50.4	25.6	42.3
Deaths	6.1	7.0	5.5
Natural Increase	44.3	18.6	36.7
Infant Deaths	38.7	33.8	31.7

Table 26. Employment by Economic Branch, 1971

Economic Branch	Number	Percentage
Agriculture, forestry, and fishing	21,200	22.4
Industry	12,300	13.1
Construction	22,000	23.3
Electricity, water, and sanitation	200	0.3
Commerce, restaurants, and hotels	13,100	13.9
Transport, storage and communications	6,100	6.4
Public and community services	13,800	14.6
Personal and other services	5,000	5.3
Finance and business services, including 200 unclassified	700	0.7
Total	94,400	100.0

District and Sub-District	Population (Thousands)			Percentages		
	Nov. 8 1948	May 22 1961	Dec. 31 1971²	Nov. 8 1948	May 22 1961	Dec. 31 1971²
Jerusalem district	2.9	4.2	81.6	1.8	1.7	17.8
Northern district	90.6	142.8	219.5	58.1	57.7	47.8
Safed sub-district	1.9	3.0	4.3	1.2	1.2	0.9
Kinneret sub-district	5.1	7.9	11.8	3.3	3.2	2.6
Jezreel sub-district	34.9	53.5	81.3	22.4	21.6	17.7
Acre sub-district	48.7	78.4	122.1	31.2	31.7	26.6
Haifa district	27.4	48.0	74.6	17.6	19.4	16.3
Central district	16.1	26.9	43.3	10.3	10.9	9.5
Sharon sub-district	10.4	17.4	27.0	6.6	7.0	5.9
Petah Tikvah sub-district	3.0	4.7	8.0	1.9	1.9	1.8
Ramleh sub-district	2.6	4.4	7.7	1.7	1.8	1.7
Rehovot sub-district	0.1	0.4	0.5	0.1	0.2	9.1
Tel Aviv district	3.6	6.7	8.8	2.3	2.8	1.9
Southern district	15.4	18.6	30.7	9.9	7.5	6.7
Ashkelon sub-district	2.4	0.3	0.5	1.6	0.1	0.1
Beersheba sub-district	13.0	18.3	30.2	8.3	7.4	6.6
Total	156.0	247.2	458.5	100.0	100.0	100.0

¹ According to present boundaries of the sub-districts.   ² Including East Jerusalem.

IL115,000,000, was launched. The three main goals have been the intensification of cultivation, diversification of crops, and the extension of land area. The first aim was implemented through a program of increased irrigation, mechanization, fertilization, and disease control; the second through the introduction of industrial crops, such as cotton, ground nuts, and sugar beet; and the third by reclaiming unused land and protecting the soil from erosion and overuse. In addition, access and internal roads were built, loans and technical assistance provided, and electricity and piped water supplied. As a result of these efforts and of the general rise in the country's standard of living, life in the villages improved markedly. At the end of the British Mandate there were only five farm machines in the entire Arab sector: by 1971 there were 700 tractors in the Arab

Escorting the bridegroom at a wedding in the village of Ṭayyiba. 1970. Courtesy J.N.F., Jerusalem. Photo Dafnai.

villages and 220 among the Bedouin. Before Israel was established hardly a single Arab village had either electricity or running water; by 1972 virtually every village was connected to the national electric grid and every home had running water.

These changes have altered many of the traditional aspects of the Arab village. About half the members of the Arab labor force now work outside their regular place of residence, as many of the villagers have found employment in the cities, while continuing to live in their villages. Modernization and democratization have weakened the hold of traditional institutions, such as the *ḥamūla*, or extended family, which depended upon its economic power, ownership of the land, and influence with the government to maintain control of the village. Now, with outside employment available, compulsory education, and the election of local councils, a leadership more responsive to the wishes of the villagers has been created and strengthened.

Olive-oil press in Ṭayyiba, 1960s. Courtesy Government Press Office, Tel Aviv.

Acre fishermen mending their nets. Courtesy Government Press Office, Tel Aviv.

In the Cities. The major urban centers inhabited by the Israel Arabs include the six "mixed cities" of Acre, Haifa, Jerusalem, Lydda, Ramleh, and Tel Aviv-Jaffa, as well as the two wholly Arab towns of Nazareth and Shepharam. The percentage of Arabs living in cities and towns has steadily increased since the end of the Mandate. In 1947 some 25% of all Palestinian Arabs were urban; by 1971 the figure had grown to 43%, totaling 196,000 persons. The population rise in the two wholly Arab towns between 1950 and 1972 is indicative of the general trend. Nazareth's population grew during the period by almost two-thirds: from 20,000 to 33,300, while Shepharam grew three times in size, from 3,900 to 11,800. Of the total non-Jewish population in Israel in 1971, aged 14 and over, 42% belonged to the labor force. Of these 97% were employed—the largest percentages in construction and agriculture. The division is given in Table 26.

192   In 1959, the Histadrut began to accept Israel Arabs

individually as full members (prior to that date they were only admitted to its medical insurance fund and to the trade unions). As a result, the number of Arab members increased from approximately 6,000 in 1955 to 46,000 in 1972 and accounted for about half the Arab working population.

Histadrut membership, together with labor legislation that prescribes equality between Arab and Jewish workers, improved the conditions of the Arab laborer. Efforts were made to reduce pockets of unorganized and unskilled Arab labor, which did not yet benefit from wage protection and other social benefits.

HEALTH, EDUCATION, AND CULTURE. The sharp decrease in the death rate among Israel Arabs is basically a result of improved health services (see Health Services, pp. 199 ff.). While the general death rate fell from some 9.48 per thousand in 1948 to 6.2 in 1971, the infant death rate dropped from 48.8 per thousand in 1951 to 37.7.

The Compulsory Education Act of 1949, providing for free and compulsory education between the ages of 5 and 14, and the construction of a school in almost every Arab village completely changed the picture of education for Israel Arabs.

While the Arab population has roughly tripled since 1949, the number of schools has grown (by the school year 1971/72) from 56 to 333, of teaching posts from 186 to 4,826 and of pupils from 11,129 to 123,470—increases by ratios of six, 26 and 11 respectively. In the latter year there were over 600 Arab students enrolled at the institutes of higher learning.

Regular publications in Arabic include three dailies, four weeklies, many monthlies and quarterlies. Some of these periodicals are affiliated with political parties and some with religious groups, while others are independent. Books in Arabic are widely available, many of them published in Israel by public or private concerns. Some are written by Israel Arabs or translated from other languages, including Hebrew. Works by Arabs in other countries are **193**

School nurse teaching a hygiene class in an Arab school. Courtesy Government Press Office, Tel Aviv.

also available. There is a large central library in Jaffa, with almost 100,000 volumes. Arabic theater performances are held, mainly by amateur companies. Arabic movies and musical performances attract large audiences. Regular Arabic radio programs put out by the Israel Broadcasting Authority for 14 hours a day include readings from the Koran and church services, as well as news, literary features, music, and items of human interest. Nightly television programs are broadcast in Arabic.

Local Government. The Ministry of the Interior has strongly encouraged the formation of local councils in order to raise the level of Arab local government to that of the Jews, to serve as a link between the villages and the government, and to act as a vehicle for economic progress, as part of the program for rural development. In 1948 only three Arab localities under Israel rule were governed by local councils. The municipal council of Nazareth was established in 1935 and that of Shepharam in 1934, while the village council of Kafr Yasīf dates back to 1925. By 1971 there were two Arab municipalities, 46 villages with local councils, and another 27 within larger regional councils. These covered some 80% of Israel's Arabs. Participation in local elections, which has been larger than that of either Jews or Arabs in national elections, bears witness to the close relationship between the council and the villagers. Generally the national parties only vie for council seats in the larger localities, such as Nazareth; in the smaller villages the candidates generally represent rival families, clans, or religious communities. The major part of the councils' budgets is raised by local taxes, calculated according to the area of land or number of rooms owned, but the government makes substantial contributions, especially for development projects, like the installation of electricity and water lines, or the construction of roads and schools, to which it usually contributes about 50% of the total expenditure.

National Politics. The Arab community plays a full and active role in national politics. Except for the first Knesset election in 1949, the proportion of Arab voters has been higher than that among the Jews. Table 27 shows the comparison. After the first Knesset, which had only three Arab members, there have been at least seven and sometimes eight (Second, Third, and Fifth Knessets). Most of these—two in the First Knesset, five in the Second, Third, and Fourth, four in the Fifth and Sixth, and five in the Seventh—have been members of lists associated with, or affiliated to, Mapai (since 1968 the Israel Labor Party) or its alliances with other parties. These lists, which have names like Cooperation and Fraternity or Progress and Development, are generally divided along religious, geographical, and family lines. While the percentage voting for Mapai (Labor) or its affiliated lists dropped from more than 60% in 1949 to 50% in 1965, it nevertheless remained greater than that of any other party and rose to 57% in 1969 for the **195**

Labor-Mapam alliance (Ma'arakh). Arabs have served as deputy speaker of the Knesset and as deputy minister in the government.

The Israel Communist Party tried to attract Arab votes by making an Arab nationalist appeal, and provided a legal way of opposing the regime. This was particularly true of Rakaḥ (New Communist List), the larger of the two factions into which the party split in 1965—the smaller, Maki, being mainly Jewish. Rakaḥ succeeded, together with Mapam, in gaining control of the Nazareth municipal council for a short period, from December 1965 to March 1966 and thereafter remained a strong opposition. The strength of the Communists in the Knesset elections has been irregular; winning 22% of the Arab vote in 1949 they dropped to 10% by 1959 but went up again to 22.6% in 1965, when they secured 38,800 votes (of which 38,000 went to Rakaḥ), as compared with the labor affiliated lists' total of 48,000. In 1969 Rakaḥ obtained 34,000 votes to 67,000 for the Ma'arakh and its affiliated lists.

Mapam, the third of the national parties to appeal to the Arabs on a sustained basis, always included an Arab candidate in a prominent place on its list. Its strength gradually increased to 12.5% of the Arab vote in 1959 and fell slightly to 9.2% in 1965.

Table 28 shows how the Arab vote has been divided between the main parties. There have been a number of attempts to organize wholly independent Arab parties —the first began immediately after the establishment of Israel—but all have proven unsuccessful. An extremist group, known as al-Ard was declared illegal by the Supreme Court for opposing the existence of the State of Israel.

The two major national issues which have agitated the Israel Arabs have been those of military government and absentee property. Military government was established immediately after the 1948 war to control areas bordering on the Arab states and other sections of the country which the government considered strategically important. These areas included those in which most Israel Arabs lived, with **197** the exception of the mixed cities. Movement was restricted within the areas and passes had to be obtained from the military government for travel to other parts of the country, whether on business, for work or study, or for short visits. Military government was gradually curtailed as security improved and opposition to it grew among Jews as well as Arabs. On Dec. 1, 1966 it was completely abolished. The problem of absentee property arose from the flight of the Arab refugees. In 1950 the government appointed a custodian to handle the property abandoned by those who left the country. Some of the land was used for the settlement of Jewish refugees and the establishment of new towns. However, many Arabs protested against inequities in defining an absentee owner and, in 1953, a Land Acquisition Law was passed. By 1965 the government had restored, exchanged, or paid compensation under this law to two-thirds of the claimants requesting redress.

Part Five
HEALTH, WELFARE, AND SOCIAL SECURITY

14 HEALTH SERVICES

IN THE PRE-STATE OF ISRAEL PERIOD. At the beginning of the 19th century, the Land of Israel was ridden with disease. Wide areas were infested with malaria; enteric fever, dysentery, and trachoma took a heavy toll; and infant mortality was very high. There was an improvement under the British Mandatory administration, but, due to budgetary restrictions, its earlier efforts were concentrated almost exclusively on malaria and smallpox control. Its elementary preventive and curative health services, moreover, were mainly intended for the Arab population, and the Jews had

The original Bikkur Ḥolim Hospital in the Old City of Jerusalem. The cornerstone was laid in 1854 by Sir Moses Montefiore; the building was partially destroyed by the Arabs in 1947. Courtesy Bikkur Ḥolim, Jerusalem.

199

to build up their own. Their efforts were spearheaded by two voluntary organizations: Hadassah, the Women's Zionist Organization of America, and Kuppat Holim, the medical insurance fund of the Histadrut.

In 1913 Hadassah sent two American-trained nurses to do pioneer work in the Old City of Jerusalem; they were followed in 1918 by the American Zionist Medical Unit. From these modest beginnings grew a country-wide network of diagnostic, preventive, and public health services and teaching and research institutions. In 1918–19 modern hospitals were opened in Tiberias, Safed, Jaffa, Haifa, and Jerusalem. The first Jewish nursing school was opened in Jerusalem by Hadassah in 1918. A network of mother-and-child care stations was established in many parts of the country, while school hygiene and luncheon programs were initiated in Jerusalem. Most of these were handed over, at different stages, to the municipalities or to the Jewish authorities and, later, to the government of Israel. This also applied to the hospitals, except the one in Jerusalem, which in 1939, in partnership with the Hebrew University, became the country's first university hospital.

Whereas Hadassah began its services in a town, the initial aim of Kuppat Holim was to bring medical care to the villages. However, its curative services—clinics and hospitals—soon spread to the towns as well, playing a vital role in the development of Jewish medical care. It set up an organizational pattern that still prevails, assuring that medical services are available to every member, no matter where he lives. Today its membership includes 90% of the country's workers.

By the time the State of Israel was proclaimed in 1948, health standards among both Jews and Arabs had risen enormously. Malaria had been wiped out; all children were inoculated against smallpox and typhoid; and infant mortality was low, even by international standards. The Mandatory government's Department of Health was succeeded by a ministry, but existing health services had to be taken over as they stood and gradually adapted to the changing needs. Due to the conditions prevailing at the time, more radical planning for the future had to be postponed.

IMMIGRATION PROBLEMS. On the whole, there was a serious deterioration in the health of the population after 1948. Among the hundreds of thousands of immigrants were many whose health standards were low, and a high proportion suffered from contagious diseases, some of which, like trachoma, had been eliminated in Erez Israel. For example, thousands of Yemenite Jews were stricken by tuberculosis within months of their arrival, and tens of thousands more, who hailed from other Eastern countries, lacked the most elementary knowledge of hygiene. Problems were enormous, and immediate solutions had to be found. The new Ministry of Health had to begin *de novo*, recruiting medical personnel previously employed by various Jewish public institutions and voluntary organizations. The ministry was faced with the dual task of detecting and treating all cases of infectious diseases among the newcomers, while protecting the health of the existing population. Since there had been neither time nor opportunity to examine the immigrants in their countries of origin, this had to be done thoroughly on their arrival. Arrangements for such examinations were set up in the transit camps. Serious cases were immediately hospitalized, putting considerable pressure on the country's limited hospital resources, while milder cases were treated on the spot. Health services, such as mother-and-child care stations and general clinics, were set up in the immigrant camps and *ma'barot*, and women's voluntary organizations, like WIZO (the Women's International Zionist Organization) opened crèches and kindergartens in them.

The slowdown in immigration between 1952 and 1954 gave the Ministry of Health a breathing space and enabled it to organize on a more permanent basis. By the time large-scale immigration was resumed in 1954, the reception of the newcomers had undergone a radical change. Health examinations took place before their departure for Israel, **201** and healthy arrivals were taken immediately to permanent accommodation. A small number of would-be settlers had their entry deferred if their health fell far below the required standard.

HEALTH OF THE POPULATION. The state of health of the people compares favorably with Western standards. Life expectancy at birth in 1969 was 69.5 for males and 73.3 for females among Jews, and 68.6 and 71.2, respectively, among non-Jews, as against 66.6 and 73.4 in the United States (in 1963). The crude birth rate in 1969 was 23.4 per 1,000 among Jews and 46.4 among non-Jews, compared with 19.4 in the United States, 18.4 in Britain, and 41.6 in Egypt. The crude death rate was 7.2 for Jews and 5.9 among non-Jews, as against 9.4 in the U.S., 11.5 in Great Britain, and 14.8 in Egypt. The infant mortality rate, which rose to 51.7 per 1,000 live births among Jews in 1949 with the arrival of large numbers of immigrants, has fallen steadily to 19.0 among Jews and 40.3 among non-Jews (1969).

The principal causes of death are: diseases of the heart and circulatory system, malignant neoplasms, diseases of early infancy (including malformations), external causes, and pneumonia. Mortality from tuberculosis is receding, malaria has been eradicated, and venereal diseases are a comparatively minor problem, although there has been some increase in recent years. There was a mild outbreak of cholera in 1970, mainly in Jerusalem and, later, in the Gaza Strip, which was brought under control by intensifying sanitary precautions and stopping the manuring of vegetable plots with sewage water.

THE MINISTRY OF HEALTH. In addition to being the supreme authority in all medical matters, the Ministry of Health operates as the licensing body for the medical, dental, pharmaceutical, nursing, and paramedical professions and is responsible for carrying out all health legislation passed by the Knesset. It is the policy of the ministry to step in where no services are furnished by nongovernmental institutions in order to assure the provision of adequate medical care throughout the country. It is, in addition, Israel's principal public health agency. It has two main divisions: curative services and preventive and promotive public health services. The former is responsible for the licensing and supervising of nongovernmental medical institutions and operates all government hospitals (general, mental, tuberculosis, and other long-term illnesses). The division for public health services coordinates the six district and 14 sub-district health offices. It maintains its own public and preventive services and supervises those of nongovernmental institutions, operates mother-and-child care centers and school health services, and is responsible for industrial hygiene, water purity, milk and food supplies, and prevention of air pollution by industry, motor vehicle exhausts, and radiation.

VOLUNTARY ORGANIZATIONS. There are organizations dealing with the aged, first aid, crippled children, etc. that maintain services and clinics for their special purposes, working closely with the larger hospitals. They include the following:

MALBEN, from the initials of Mosedot le-Tippul be-Olim Neḥshalim—Institutions for the Care of Handicapped Immigrants, which is financed chiefly by the American Jewish Joint Distribution Committee. From its inception until 1969, it spent over $150,000,000, providing individual care for more than 75,000 people. Its program includes care for the aged, chronically ill, mental patients, and handicapped adults and children.

Magen David Adom (Red Shield of David), which corresponds to the Red Cross in other countries, provides a public ambulance service, runs blood banks, operates a first-aid service, and organizes practical first-aid training. It functions primarily with the help of 6,000 volunteers, organized in 63 branches. It also acts as an auxiliary service to the Medical Corps of the Israel Defense Forces and as the medical service of the civil defense organization.

The Hadassah Medical Organization has devoted its main efforts since 1961 to the development of the Hadassah-Hebrew University Medical Center at Ein Ker-

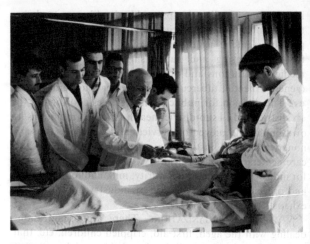

Professor Moshe Rachmilewitz and his students examine a patient in one of the internal medicine wards at the Hadassah Hospital, Jerusalem. Courtesy Hadassah Medical Organization, Jerusalem. Photo David Harris, Jerusalem.

em, Jerusalem. Its Family and Community Health Center in the Jerusalem suburb of Kiryat ha-Yovel is used for instruction in social and community medicine. After the reunification of Jerusalem in 1967, the Ein Kerem center helped to raise the standards of the institutions in the east of the city itself and provided greatly improved services for the Arab population.

The Israel Anti-Tuberculosis League, founded in 1924, operates three clinics and shares with the Ministry of Health the financing and administration of others. The clinics also function as consultation centers for chest diseases. Among the league's foremost tasks is the education of the public. It provides economic support for tuberculosis patients and their families while they receive rehabilitative care.

204 The Israel Cancer Association began to function in 1952.

Its activities include the promotion and subsidization of centers for the early detection of the disease; home-care programs; the provision of research grants, and education of the public. It has 41 branches.

ILAN, Israel Foundation for Handicapped Children, resulted from the amalgamation in 1964 of three organizations: Ilanshil-Polio, Shatlem (for the care of children with cerebral palsy), and the Alyn hospital for crippled children. It serves more than 10,000 children in cooperation with the Ministry of Health.

Women's organizations, like WIZO and Mo'ezet ha-Po'alot, run baby homes, nurseries, mothercraft training centers, and the like.

The Israel Diabetes Association has five branches, which organize lectures by doctors, provide answers to patients' questions, and run summer camps for diabetic children.

MUTUAL HEALTH INSURANCE. Over 90 percent of Israel's population are covered by mutual health insurance, which is operated by *kuppot holim* (sick funds). The insured are entitled to free treatment in clinics, at home, or at the physician's residence, free hospitalization, dental and optical care at reduced rates, medicines, facilities for convalescence, and so forth. The largest is run by the Histadrut for its members and three associated organizations; it provides treatment mainly in clinics and mother-and-child care stations. In the smaller funds, the members are generally treated by individual doctors, chosen from a set list, in their own surgeries. In 1970 the government announced its intention to introduce legislation for general health insurance mainly through the existing sick funds.

The following are the principal health insurance funds:

Kuppat Holim, the first health insurance institution in Israel, was founded in 1911 by a small group of agricultural workers and taken over in 1920 by the Histadrut. It is the largest countrywide fund of its kind, with its own medical institutions and a staff of almost 19,000 in 1972, including about 3,200 doctors and 6,000 nurses. Sixty-eight percent of the population is insured with Kuppat Holim, which covers workers in town and country, manual laborers and professional men, salaried and self-employed, Israel-born, veterans, and new immigrants, on a basis of mutual aid.

Its countrywide organization enables it to extend its services to the most outlying areas. It provides medical care in its own clinics, and has its own laboratories, pharmacies, and convalescent homes. Hospitalization, the largest item, is provided in its own hospitals, situated in rural and development districts, as well as in urban areas, or at its expense in other hospitals. They have outpatient clinics for consultation and the follow-up of discharged patients, as well as nurses' training schools, and some of them have centers for postgraduate medical training and research.

Every Histadrut member is automatically a member of Kuppat Holim and his insurance dues are included in his membership fee, which is graded according to income. Members of certain other workers' organizations, such as Ha-Po'el ha-Mizrachi and Po'alei Agudat Israel, are also insured with Kuppat Holim. Between 1948 and 1971, its membership, including dependents, increased sixfold: from 328,000 to 2,087,000.

Kuppat Holim grants medical care to insured breadwinners and their families (covering industrial injuries and chronic illness), as well as convalescence and sick pay. It provides the services of general practioners, specialists, and nurses in clinics and at the patient's home, hospitalization in its own and other hospitals, X-ray treatment, physiotherapy and medical rehabilitation, and laboratory tests; medicaments and medical appliances come from its own pharmacies. Preventive medical services include mother-and-child care, industrial medicine, and health education. Eye glasses and dental treatment are provided at moderate charges. Dependents may be covered by: (1) family insurance, in return for an additional 80% of the membership dues, entitling all dependents (including parents) to medical treatment, including hospitalization, free of charge; or (2) limited insurance, without any addition to the membership dues, entitling dependents to medical care in

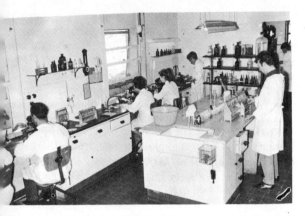

Laboratory at a Kuppat Ḥolim clinic in Jerusalem. Courtesy General Kuppat Ḥolim of the Histadrut, Jerusalem Branch. Photo Sport, Jerusalem.

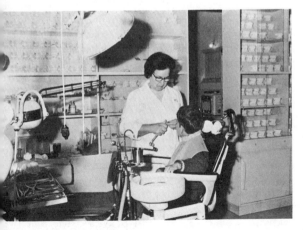

A Kuppat Ḥolim orthodontic clinic in Jerusalem. Courtesy Kuppat Ḥolim of the Histadrut, Jerusalem.

return for partial payment of the cost of certain treatments. Some 97% of members' families are covered by family insurance. Kuppat Ḥolim provides medical services for new immigrants from the day of their arrival, with no qualifying period. During the period of mass immigration, newcomers ignorant of the elementary rules of health and hygiene were instructed in its clinics and mother-and-child centers.

Kuppat Ḥolim le-Ovedim Le'ummiyyim (Sick Fund for National Workers) was founded in 1933. Its services in 1971 encompassed a total of 237,000 persons in 110 localities. Although it is linked to the National Labor Federation (Histadrut ha-Ovedim ha-Le'ummit), members of the sick fund are not obliged to belong to the federation. Its main feature is the free choice of a doctor by the patient, in addition to the maintenance of dispensaries and arrangements for hospitalization for the insured in government and other hospitals.

Kuppat Ḥolim Amamit ("Popular Sick Fund") was founded in 1931 on the initiative of Hadassah, mainly for farmers in villages not affiliated to the Histadrut. Later it also became active in cities and towns in the non-Histadrut sector. It serves 82,000 persons. In the larger centers members are free to choose their doctor; in smaller places the fund employs doctors for the insured. It has arrangements for the hospitalization of its members in government and other public hospitals.

Kuppat Ḥolim Maccabi (Maccabi Sick Fund), which was founded in 1941, serves more than 208,000 persons in 88 localities (1971). Most of its members live in the Tel Aviv area, smaller towns, and rural localities. They are free to choose their doctors; hospitalization is arranged with government and other hospitals.

In addition there are Kupat Ḥolim Merkazit (serving 76,000) and Iggud Kupat Ḥolim Asaph (37,000).

MOTHER-AND-CHILD HEALTH SERVICES. The objective of these services is to provide for prenatal, natal, and postnatal care for every mother and full preparation for he birth of every child: protection and promotion of health for child from birth to adolescence; and the detection and rehabilitation of handicapped children. Health protection includes routine immunization. Every child is vaccinated against smallpox, and a triple vaccination against diphtheria (mortality from which has virtually vanished), tetanus, and whooping cough is automatically given to over 80% of children from age three months upward, as is immunization against measles. Following a serious polio epidemic that started in 1950, the Salk vaccine was administered to all children between six months and four years from 1956 and the Sabin vaccine has been in use since 1961. As a result, cases of the disease in Israel are very rare, though the public

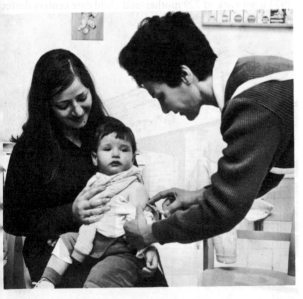

Immunization against measles at the Rishon le-Zion Mother-and-Child Welfare Clinic. Courtesy Government Press Office, Tel Aviv.

health problem of rehabilitating patients from previous years remains.

One of the characteristics of Israel's mother-and-child care services has been their flexibility, in response to the demands of a constantly developing society. The scope of the services also aims at promoting the healthy growth and development of the family as a unit, and, since the family is bound up with the neighborhood in which it lives, the centers have undertaken to serve the surrounding community. In addition to coordination between preventive and curative services, several family health centers assume full responsibility for promotive, preventive, and curative services for all members of the family. In two Arab villages (Ṭayyiba and Ṭīra) they also provide lying-in facilities. In 1971 a network of 729 mother-and-child care centers dotted

The government medical center in the Arab village of Ṭīra near Kefar Sava. Courtesy Government Press Office, Tel Aviv

he country (in contrast to 120 in 1948). Of these, 482 were run by the Ministry of Health and 201 by Kuppat Ḥolim, he remainder being the responsibility of the Jerusalem and Tel Aviv municipalities. Three were still retained by the Hadassah Medical Organization in Jerusalem (including a family and community health center) as part of its teaching framework.

SCHOOL HEALTH SERVICES. Health services for children of school age, originally started by Hadassah in the early 1920s, are provided by the Ministry of Health for 66% of the pupils who benefit, and local authorities for 20%, while Kuppat Ḥolim looks after the remainder. The work is done by school health teams, consisting of a physician and a public health nurse, special attention being given to the requirements of handicapped children. The control of infectious diseases through immunization is continued in this older age group, with the addition of the BCG vaccination in the seventh grade. There is also considerable activity in the field of health education.

School dental health services were established in Mandatory times in Jerusalem, Haifa, and Tel Aviv; by 1971 they covered some 75% of the elementary school population, as well as, to a lesser extent, secondary school pupils and children of preschool age. The service includes dental examination of every child in elementary school, comprehensive and emergency treatment, and reexamination of each child at regular intervals.

HOSPITALIZATION. Though Kuppat Ḥolim is responsible for two-thirds of the population, it provides only 25% of the country's hospital beds, which are available primarily for its own members, and it pays for the treatment of members in other hospitals. Government, Hadassah, municipal, private, and mission hospitals accept all fee-paying patients and take turns in admitting emergency cases immediately (on days set by the Ministry of Health), financial adjustments being made afterward. Between 1948 and 1971 the number of beds increased from 4,626 to 24,213, currently spread over 159 hospitals. Of these, 10,069 beds are in 211 general hospitals, 7,382 are for mental diseases, 3,166 for mental retardation, 2,933 for chronic diseases, 521 for rehabilitation, and 12 for tuberculosis patients.

A reduction in the average period spent in the hospital has led to better utilization of beds. This has been due to the combination of up-to-date medical skills, the establishment of more special departments, and the development of laboratory facilities. Nevertheless, the availability of beds still falls far short of the country's requirements, particularly in relation to chronic patients. In order to remedy the situation, a master plan for the construction of hospitals was worked out by the Hospital Planning Unit of the Ministry of Health.

All Jewish births and 93% of non-Jewish births take place in hospitals. Jewish women in Israel have always preferred hospital to home confinements, but Arab women, as well as many of the new immigrants, were not accustomed to this. To induce them to avail themselves of the advantages of

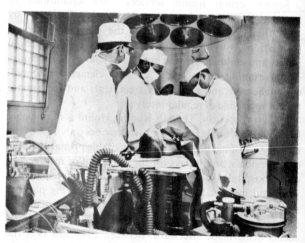

Operating theater at Jerusalem's Sha'arei Zedek Hospital.
Courtesy Sha'arei Zedek, Jerusalem.

delivery under safe conditions, the National Insurance Law of 1953 stipulated that the maternity grant is payable only to mothers confined in the hospital.

MEDICAL PERSONNEL. There were 7,723 licensed doctors in Israel at the end of 1971: one for every 401 persons (and the supply of specialists in Israel does not lag behind that of other progressive countries). This is the highest ratio in the world, but many of the doctors are in the higher age groups. Over 1,000 of Israel's doctors graduated from the Hadassah-Hebrew University Medical School, and the remainder studied abroad. It was therefore necessary to equalize the various levels of training gained in different countries by additional training for the immigrant physicians. In partnership with Kuppat Ḥolim, the Medical School established in 1962 the Institute for Postgraduate Training, which specializes in short-term refresher courses. A second medical school was opened at Tel Aviv University in 1965 and a third in Haifa in 1969.

Most doctors are salaried full-time staff in hospitals and other institutions; few are in private practice. All are members of the Israel Medical Association, which has adapted Hebrew terminology to the needs of contemporary medicine, set up libraries and information services, and, through its Scientific Council, laid down qualifications for specialization. There are 14 nursing schools in Israel. The diploma of registered nurse is awarded after a three-year course, according to standards set by the Nursing Department of the Ministry of Health. In 1968 a University School of Nursing affiliated to the Faculty for Advanced Studies in Medicine of Tel Aviv University was inaugurated, leading to a B.A. degree. Schools of occupational therapy, physiotherapy, and X-ray and laboratory techniques function in different parts of the country. The Hebrew University's course for the M.A. in Public Health provides training in administration. There is a dental school at the Ein Kerem Medical Center.

HOSPITAL EMERGENCY SERVICES. Israel's security situation demands a well-planned emergency system that can be 213 speedily put into operation. The effectiveness of this advanced planning was put to the test during the Six-Day War (1967) when the main hospitals—Beersheba, Tel ha-Shomer, Beilinson, and Hadassah—were ready to receive the wounded immediately after hostilities broke out. Beds, operating and laboratory facilities, and equipment were available underground, and casualty teams worked around the clock. The use of helicopters to facilitate the speedy transport of the wounded to the hospitals and the remarkably high standards of preparedness and treatment saved many lives. During the succeeding years of almost continuous border warfare, the hospitals continued to maintain this degree of preparedness.

MEDICAL RESEARCH. The first steps toward establishing

Arrival of a wounded soldier by helicopter at the Hadassah Hospital, Jerusalem, during the Six-Day War. Photo Werner Braun, Jerusalem.

medical research institutions in Palestine were taken before World War I, with the erection in Jerusalem of the Nathan Straus Health Center and Dr. Beham's Pasteur Institute. The Institute of Microbiology (Parasitology), founded in 1924 at the Hebrew University, with its departments of biochemistry and bacteriology and hygiene, founded two years later, served as the basis for the first Medical Center on Mount Scopus. In 1927 I. J. Kligler opened the Malaria Research Station at Rosh Pinnah, which initiated research, control, and supervision of anti-malarial projects in all areas of Jewish settlement and in the adjacent Arab villages. Hadassah and the Hebrew University still carry out most of the research in the medical field; their doctors and scientists publish an average of 150 papers a year in leading scientific journals.

Some noteworthy recent achievements in Israel's medical research were the diagnosis of leprosy; the diagnosis of heart disease with the use of radioactive isotopes; prenatal determination of sex; a vaccine for undulant fever; a vaccine against trachoma (in an advanced experimental stage), and a method for early diagnosis of cancer. Israel's many ethnic groups make the country an ideal field for comparative medical studies, some of which have elicited worldwide interest. It has been found, for example, that some of the oriental and Yemenite Jews, as well as the Bedouin, seem freer of such plagues of modern society as coronary thrombosis, lung cancer, and diabetes than Jews from Western lands. In 1962 a ten-year nationwide research program on the incidence of heart disease was initiated by researchers from Hadassah, the Ministry of Health, and the National Institutes of Health in the United States, 10,000 civil servants acting as a "population sample" for the project. Similar joint research efforts with other countries were a study of oncocerciasis with England, of detached retina with Tanzania, Liberia, and the United States, and of the prevention of oral pathology with the U.S. National Institution of Dental Research.

MEDICAL CONTRIBUTION TO DEVELOPING COUNTRIES. 215

As many of Israel's health problems were similar to those encountered by the newly emerging states of Asia and Africa, its doctors and health experts had been invited to cooperate with these countries in applying their experience and the methods used to tackle the problems. Through the World Health Organization and the Division of International Cooperation of the Ministry for Foreign Affairs, 61 students from 20 different lands took the full six-year course in medicine at the Hadassah-Hebrew University Medical School and a number of doctors from Thailand, Burma, Tanzania, and Korea received postgraduate training in eye and skin diseases, physiology, hematology, and nutrition. Israel specialists established Liberia's first eye hospital in Monrovia, while Liberian doctors and nurses received special ophthalmology training in Jerusalem and then took over from the Israel staff. Similar programs were launched in Tanzania and Malawi. Girls from Malawi completed a three-year nursing course in English at the Hadassah nursing school, while nurses from Africa received postgraduate training at the Beilinson and Tel ha-Shomer hospitals.

SERVICES FOR THE ARAB POPULATION. When the Ministry of Health was established, a special division was set up to serve the Arab and Druze communities. In 1952, however, with their progressive integration into the structure of the state, the division was abolished. The ministry set up clinics and mother-and-child health centers in Arab areas. An Arab officer is attached to the Regional Services Administration of the ministry to act as a liaison between the head office and the field units. Many Arabs and Druze have joined Kuppat Ḥolim, which has set up clinics in many villages. Integrated preventive and curative services are available at six health centers, in addition to 79 general clinics and 75 mother-and-child centers, covering more than 80% of Israel's Arabs. Case-finding activities are conducted among the Bedouin tribes in the Negev to combat tuberculosis, trachoma, and ringworm. The incidence of these once-prevalent diseases has decreased considerably,

216

Mobile medical unit in the Gaza strip, operated by a medical team from the Tel ha-Shomer Hospital, 1969. Courtesy Government Press Office, Tel Aviv.

thanks largely to a mobile unit that regularly visits Arab villages and Bedouin encampments examining children and others. This service facilitates the early diagnosis and treatment of these diseases where they still exist. Eighty-four percent of Arab women now have their babies in hospitals, and the supervision of the mother-and-child centers is highly valued.

15 SOCIAL SECURITY AND WELFARE

Social security and welfare services are important for Israel's efforts to build a welfare state based on the community's obligation to care for all its members. The services steadily developed from the solely "curative" approach to social welfare, the ministry, local authorities, and voluntary organizations dealing with various forms of social distress and disability, to include the "preventive" institution of national insurance and social security benefits.

GOVERNMENT WELFARE SERVICES. The Ministry of Social Welfare, which began to operate in June 1948, was a natural development from the Social Welfare Department established in 1931 by the Va'ad Le'ummi and the Mandatory government's Welfare Department, established in 1944. Certain aspects are regulated by legislation. Thus, the Social Welfare Service Law (1958) obliged local authorities to provide social welfare services under the supervision of the ministry and gave claimants the right to appeal against dismissal of their claims to benefits.

A network of social service bureaus, established and maintained by the local authorities and staffed by trained social workers, covers the country. They deal with family welfare, including social assistance, youth welfare, and community welfare. The last is a relatively new branch of social welfare, directed mainly toward social and cultural integration of new immigrants. The bureaus also maintain clubs for young people, women, and the aged, and undertake rehabilitation of the handicapped, especially the blind. The ministry provides probation services for juveniles and adults, and, under a law of 1960, maintains institutions for children in need of care and supervision as well as for the mentally retarded. Under a 1965 law, the ministry also supervises homes for children and the aged. Consultation with social workers has been made obligatory in cases of adoption (under a 1960 law) and the marriage of minors (under the Marriage Age Law of 1950). The ministry trains staff for social educational institutions, as well as social workers, the latter usually in schools affiliated with the universities.

VOLUNTARY AGENCIES. In spite of the ever-growing influence of the state on social welfare work and its increasing share of the costs, voluntary agencies still play an important role in all fields of social welfare. These include the Jewish Agency, Malben, financed by the American Joint Distribution Committee, which cares for the aged, the welfare branches of the Histadrut, and women's organizations, like Mo'ezet ha-Po'alot and WIZO, which are particularly active in child welfare and vocational training for girls and women. The Jewish Agency, Malben, and the women's organizations are financed mainly by donations from abroad.

SOCIAL INSURANCE. Compulsory social insurance was introduced six years after the establishment of the state. The vast experience gained in the voluntary insurance schemes developed by the Histadrut paved the way for the National Insurance Act of 1953, which became effective on April 1, 1954. The act established a National Insurance Institute which administers old-age and survivors' pensions, work injury compensation, maternity benefits, family allowances, and unemployment insurance (see pp. 168 ff.).

Old-Age and Survivors' Pension. Men and working women born after Nov. 18, 1886, and unmarried women are eligible for old age pensions. Housewives may join voluntarily. The minimum qualifying period is generally five years of insurance with full payment of contributions. The retirement age is 70 for men and 65 for women, but persons who retire from work are eligible for old age pensions at 65 (men) or 60 (women) even if they continue working part time, provided their income from such work does not exceed fixed limits. Pension rates are not affected by previous income; they depend on marital status, number of dependents, and the cost-of-living index. Pensions are increased, after at least ten years of insurance, by 2% a year for each additional year of insurance, up to a maximum of 50%, and by a further 5% a year, with a limit of 25%, for those who postpone retirement. In 1972 the basic monthly rates were IL111 (about $26) for single persons and IL123.75 ($35) for couples. Pensioners dependent mainly on their pension are entitled to an increment of about 40%. Special pensions are payable to new immigrants, persons with scanty resources, and certain other groups, even if they do not qualify under the regulations.

The scope of survivors' insurance is the same as that of old age pensions, but the qualifying period is only one year, and in some cases even less. Benefits consist of funeral grants and widows' and orphans' pensions.

Work Injury Compensation. Insurance against work injury (for work accidents and defined occupational diseases) covers employed persons, working members of cooperatives, persons in vocational training or under rehabilitation, and self-employed persons. The benefits awarded for work injuries are: medical treatment, medical and vocational rehabilitation; work injury allowance at the rate of 75% of the last wages, up to a fixed maximum; and temporary or permanent invalid pensions, according to the degree of invalidism and former wages. In case of death, pensions for dependents are paid at the rate of 60% of the full invalid pension for a dependent wife or husband, and up to 100% for a wife with three or more children.

Maternity Insurance. Maternity insurance provides for both a birth grant and maternity allowance. A woman is entitled to a maternity grant if she is insured in her own right or a housewife whose husband is insured, and if her confinement takes place in a hospital. The grant in 1972 was IL510 (about $120) to cover hospital expenses and IL150 in cash. For twins the grant was IL1170 and for triplets IL1,680. A maternity allowance is paid during 12 weeks to employed and self-employed women, the rate being 75% of the average income during the last three months prior to interruption of work, up to a fixed maximum.

Allowances for Large Families. Allowances for each additional child after the second under the age of 18 are paid to all insured persons, including the self-employed and the non-employed. In 1972 the allowance was paid at the rate of IL30 (about $7) for the third child; IL45 for the fourth; IL47 for the fifth; and IL40 for every subsequent child. Self-employed persons receive allowances from the third child. Employed persons receive allowances for the first three children under a different part of the scheme

Table 29. Monthly National Insurance Contributions as Percentages of Wages or Incomes

	Employers	Employees	Self-employed
Old age and survivors'	4.5	1.6	4.5
Maternity	0.6	0.3	0.6
Large Families	1.0	—	1.5
Employed persons' children	1.8	—	—
Unemployment	3.0	1.0	—
Invalidity	0.5	—	0.5
Work injury	0.7–4.0*	—	0.8
Equalization fund	3.2	0.6	1.2
Total	15.3–18.6*	3.5	9.1

* Depending on the degree of risk involved in the work.

(see below). If a member of the family has served, or is serving, in the armed forces, an additional allowance of IL15 per month is paid for the fourth and subsequent children as compensation for the family's loss of his earnings.

Allowance for Children of Employed Persons. Employed

Part Six
THE ROLE OF WOMEN

16 WOMEN IN MODERN ISRAEL

Women began to take part in public and communal life early in
the 20th century. In the summer of 1914 a handful of young women
from the Second Aliyah met in Merḥavyah and established
Mo'eẓet ha-Po'alot (Council of Working Women), the first
women's organization in the country. The Council provided
agricultural training for women to prepare them for working on the
land alongside the men. They joined in debates on public issues and
left no doubt about their desire and ability for responsible
citizenship. Significantly, there was no opposition from the men; in
Ha-Shomer, in the Teachers' Association, and in the kibbutzim
women enjoyed full equality from the very beginning. They
participated in the *yishuv's* public bodies since the 1920 elections to
its "parliament," Asefat ha-Nivḥarim, when they were given the
vote despite objections from extreme religious groups.

Since educational opportunities are the same for girls and boys,
except in yeshivot, women are to be found in all institutes of higher
learning, as both students and teachers. The number of women in
the Knesset has fluctuated between eight and ten. Golda Meir as
prime minister is Israel's best known woman but others have been
prominent in all fields of culture and artistic endeavors. Women's
organizations representing every shade of opinion, as well as
non-party bodies, do important work in social service, running
creches, kindergartens, clubs, etc.; examples are Mo'eẓet ha-Po'-
alot, WIZO, and associations affiliated to the Mizrachi (NRP),
the Liberal Party, and others.

Women have played their role in the defense of the country.
Three thousand volunteers served during World War II with the
British army ATS and WAAF. Hannah Szenes and two other
women were parachuted into occupied Europe. Girls served in considerable numbers in the Palmaḥ and the Israel Defense Forces.
There is a difference, however, in the Israel army's recognition of
women's special characteristics: they do not fight. Most perform
clerical, medical, housekeeping, and communications duties. Some

223

pack parachutes, teach, or do cultural work in development areas. Unmarried women from 18 to 26 are conscripted for 20 months. Orthodox girls with scruples about army service are exempt.

17 LEGAL STATUS OF WOMEN

Israel's Declaration of Independence clearly and emphatically ensures complete equality of social and political rights to all its inhabitants, irrespective of religion, race, or sex. A natural consequence of this declaration was the universal suffrage clause inserted in the first law regulating elections—the Constituent Assembly Elections Ordinance—and perpetuated in the Knesset Law. This clause naturally applied equally to the women of the Muslim and Christian communities of Israel, who, in consequence, voted for the first time in their lives.

The Nationality Law (1952) also takes it for granted that women have exactly the same rights and duties as men. It provides neither for the acquisition of Israel nationality, nor the loss thereof, by marriage. In addition, it vests a child, born either of a mother or father who is an Israel national, with Israel nationality from birth.

The real Magna Carta of the Israeli woman is the Women's Equal Rights Law of 1951, giving women equal legal status with men. It vests married women with the right to own and deal with property and gives them equality with men in respect of guardianship of children. It is incumbent upon every religious tribunal to respect the provisions of this law, even though they may be repugnant to Jewish, Muslim, or Canon Church law, unless all the parties are 18 years of age or over and consent of their own free will to having their cases tried according to their religious law.

The Women's Equal Rights Law makes unilateral divorce against the will of the wife a criminal offense. This is in accordance with existing Jewish religious law but is a great boon to the Muslim women of Israel. Muslim law allows a man to divorce his wife by merely repeating three times before witnesses: "I hereby divorce you." Another provision of this law forbids polygamy. Before it was enacted, Muslims of Israel could—and did—have as many as four wives at a time; while bigamy was legitimately, if rarely, practiced by the Jews of the oriental communities, on the basis of biblical law.

The Equal Pay for Equal Work Law, 1964, was another important contribution to women's equality. It applied equally to private and government employment. It must be noted that all the professions are open to women and there are actually very few prejudices against their employment. The only legal restrictions are in the case of such work, as, for example, night work or heavy, physical labor, which might prove prejudicial to their health. These restrictions are contained in the Employment of Women Law, 1954, which also ensures women security of employment during pregnancy and a year's leave of absence without pay after birth, at the option of the woman. Women are also entitled to three months' maternity leave with pay under the national insurance scheme.

The only field of law in which there remains a degree of selective discrimination against women is that of personal status. Matters of marriage and divorce come within the exclusive jurisdiction of the religious courts, as there is no civil marriage or divorce in Israel. Thus, in accordance with Jewish law, a divorce has to be given by the husband to the wife. Cases of hardship can occur if the husband obdurately refuses to grant a divorce and in the case of his insanity. Attempts have been made by the rabbinical authorities to alleviate this unfortunate position, and an increasingly liberal interpretation is given to the laws of presumption of death of a missing husband to enable his wife to marry. On the other hand, should the husband eventually prove to be alive, the consequences for the woman and her children are dire. She is obliged by Jewish law to be divorced from both her second and her first husbands, and her children from the second husband are *mamzerim*. Another cause of discrimination is the need for *ḥaliẓah* by the deceased husband's brother when the husband has died childless. There is a wide feeling that whatever the reasons may have been in the past to justify this law, it is not in keeping with the modern woman's status in society and could well be dispensed with without in any way undermining the fundamental structure of Jewish family law. Orthodox circles, who administer the law, however, regard it as immutable.

In one respect Jewish law discriminates against men and vests women with an advantage: children take the national identity (*le'om*) of their mother and not of their father, with the result that the children of a mixed marriage will be Jewish if the wife is Jewish, and non-Jewish if she is non-Jewish, even if the husband is a Jew.

While the emancipation of the women of Israel is a legal reality, its observance in the spirit is still dependent largely upon the traditions and customs of the different communities. The women of the oriental and of the ultra-Orthodox communities may not, therefore, as yet enjoy the equality and freedom which the women of the occidental and less observant communities take for granted.

Part Seven
HUMAN GEOGRAPHY[*]

In respect of human as well as of physical geography, it is convenient to divide the Land of Israel into five major units: (1) the Mediterranean Coastal Plain; (2) the hill regions of northern and central Cisjordan (west of the Jordan); (3) the Rift Valley of the Jordan River and the Dead Sea; (4) the desert regions of the Negev and the Arabah Valley (which are similar to parts of the Sinai Peninsula); and (5) the Transjordanian Plateau. The great variety in natural features entails profound differences in historical evolution, demography, and economic development.

In the light of present-day economic considerations, the Coastal Plain has clear advantages and the deserts of the south come last for human settlement. Throughout most of history, however, security considerations were paramount in determining population density. In most periods, therefore, the hills were preferred to the lowlands. On the hilltops or the upper slopes, even small villages could hope to defend themselves against superior enemy forces; they used the poorest and rockiest ground, while retaining the better soils in the valleys for farming. Their economy being basically autarkic, they depended little on lines of communication. Settlers were repelled from the Coastal Plain and the large valleys of the interior (the Jezreel, Beth-Shean, and Upper Jordan valleys), on the other hand, because the international thoroughfare, the Via Maris, ran through this area and provided foreign armies, which would plunder the

[*] All figures, unless otherwise stated, are for the end of 1971; 1972 figures are given according to the census of May 1972

inhabitants of any territory through which they passed, with access to this region. Moreover, the assiduous hill farmer could build his terraces with primitive tools, make cisterns in which to collect his drinking water in winter and store it all year round, and thus draw a livelihood—albeit meager—from the soil. In many parts of the lowlands, on the other hand, which were covered with dense brush or malarial swamps, superior skill and knowledge were required to prepare the ground for habitation and agriculture and develop sources of fresh water. Consequently, successive generations of conquerors and rulers shifted the center of population and administration alternately between the Cisjordanian hills (west of the Jordan River) and the Coastal Plain. Peoples coming from the land side (i.e., mainly from the east), whose achievements in material civilization were inferior (e.g., Israelites, Arabs, Mamluks, and Turks), generally preferred the hills, while those crossing the sea from the west, possessing technical know-how and a talent for international commerce, like Phoenicians, Philistines, Hellenes, Romans, Crusaders, or Jews in modern times, preferred the coast.

Only in periods of peak density and cultural achievement did the sedentary population spill over into the poorest areas—the northern and central Negev, the Lower Jordan Valley, the Arabah Valley, and southern Transjordan. As soon as the regime showed signs of weakness and decline, these regions again became the exclusive domain of the Bedouin nomad. The border between the desert and the arable land, though basically determined by climatic data, oscillated considerably with the interplay of human factors. Border peasants, protected by a strong central power, could extend their holdings over marginal lands in the transition zone, and governments sometimes settled active or demobilized soldiers to farm desert outposts. The nomads, on the other hand—dependent on the same transition zone for grazing in the dry season—awaited every opportunity to harass the farmers, tear down the fences and destroy homes, and cut trees for firewood or burn them **229** down to use the ground for pasture. If they met no effective resistance, they penetrated ever deeper into the settled area. It happened repeatedly, however (as in the case of the Israelites), that intruding nomads or semi-nomads gradually became tillers of the soil themselves and later found it necessary to repel fresh Bedouin onslaughts.

As the country lies on the crossroads of three continents and two oceans, its population was in constant flux. Multitudes came and went, not only in the wake of historical events (e.g., the entry of the Israelites, the Muslim-Arab conquest, the Crusaders, or modern Jewish immigration), but even in periods when large-scale movements were hardly in evidence. Thus, for example, Egyptians may be supposed to have settled in considerable numbers during the first half of the 19th century, under the rule of Muhammad Ali. Under the British Mandate, there was again a substantial, though unrecorded and uncontrolled, immigration of Arabs overland from Transjordan, the Hauran, Egypt, etc.

Fundamental changes in the country's population were brought about not only by migration but, perhaps on an even larger scale, by the assumption of new national, religious, or linguistic identities on the part of entire sections of the population. Most of the Philistines, for example, seem to have been gradually absorbed into the Canaanite population, which, in turn, was largely Hellenized after the conquest of Alexander the Great. In both the First and Second Temple periods, a considerable part of the pagan population may be assumed to have adopted Judaism. The nascent Christian faith attracted followers among both pagans and Jews, and the process of conversion was accelerated when Christianity became the Roman, and then the Byzantine, state religion. A solid rural Jewish population existed for centuries, however, during the Roman and Byzantine periods, particularly in Galilee and Judea. While the early Arab rulers did little to promote the adoption of Islam by the indigenous population, Islamization spread before and after the Crusades, which led not so much to conversion to Christianity as to a fierce competition between the various Christian denominations. The group most strongly affected by developments from the early Middle Ages was the Samaritans; once prominent in the central areas, they dwindled to some 400 by the middle of the 20th century. Conversion to Islam, which seems to have engulfed the bulk of the remaining autochthonous Jews from the seventh century, continued among both Samaritans and Christians into the 19th century and later. Of the present Christian population, the majority speak Arabic and regard themselves as Arabs.

Distribution of the Population. After Israel's War of Independence (1948) and the signing of armistice agreements with its neighbors, the State of Israel measured 7,993 sq. mi. (20,700 sq. km.), of which 7,821 sq. mi. (20,255 sq. km.) constituted land surface. East Jerusalem, with an area of 24 sq. mi. (70 sq. km.), was reunited with the rest of the city after the Six-Day War (1967).

The areas that came under Israel administration in June 1967 total 26,476 sq. mi. (68,589 sq. km.): the Golan Heights 444 sq. mi. (1,150 sq. km.); Judea-Samaria (the "West Bank"), with the districts of Jenin, Nablus, Tulkarm, Ramallah, Jordan Valley, Bethlehem, and Hebron, 2,270 sq. mi. (5,878 sq. km.); the Gaza Strip 140 sq. mi. (363 sq. km.), and Sinai 23,622 sq. mi. (61,198 sq. km.), with the districts of north Sinai, central Sinai, and Merḥav Shelomoh (the Sharm el-Sheikh region). The entire area governed by Israel from June 1967 thus totaled 34,493 sq. mi. (89,359 sq. km.).

The emergence of the State of Israel led to far-reaching changes in the geographical distribution of the Arabs. With few exceptions, they left those parts of the Coastal Plain, the Foothills and Hills of Judea, the Manasseh Hills, the Ḥuleh and Beth-Shean valleys, etc. that were occupied by Israel forces in 1948–49, and most of the Negev Bedouin left the region when it finally came into Israel hands. In Galilee, however, a considerable part of the non-Jewish population, particularly Druze and Christians, remained, while 231 a larger number of Muslims left. In the small areas added to Israel territory in 1949 in accordance with the Armistice Agreement with Jordan—notably the east rim of the Sharon Plain and the Iron Valley and Hills—the entire Muslim population remained. Thus, Upper and Lower Galilee, the Iron Valley and Hills, and the eastern rim of the Sharon Plain constitue the main centers of Arab and Druze population inside the pre-1967 armistice lines: to these, East Jerusalem was added after the Six-Day War. Of the 38,400 Bedouin in Israel, most live in the Arad region east and northeast of Beersheba.

At the end of 1971, the overall population density was 401.4 per sq. mi. (152.2 per sq. km.), as compared with 111.6 per sq. mi. (43.1 per sq. km.) in 1948. As in most countries in the 20th century, rapid urbanization has taken place. Of Israel's population, 82.6% (89.5% of its Jews) were inhabitants of 29 towns and 49 other urban communities; of the 2,555,500 town dwellers, 2,366,200 were Jews and 189,300 non-Jews. The categories termed "large" and "small" villages, totaling 154, included 99 Arab villages and 55 Jewish moshavot or villages of similar form; the former had 220,400 and the latter 44,400 inhabitants. The 347 moshavim, with 123,600 inhabitants, constituted the largest Jewish rural group, followed by the 229 kibbutzim, with 86,300. There were 27 moshavim shittufiyvim, with 5,700, and 50 farms, institutions and schools with 13,700. There is a preponderance of moshavim in comprehensive regional settlement areas (e.g.,Lachish, Taanach, Merḥavim, etc.) and a concentration of kibbutzim in the Jordan-Yarmuk (Kinneret), Ḥuleh, Beth-Shean, and Harod valleys and in areas near the pre-1967 borders. Of the 29 cities and towns, 21 were exclusively Jewish, two (Nazareth and Shepharam) exclusively non-Jewish, and six others (Jerusalem, Tel Aviv-Jaffa, Haifa, Acre, Ramleh, Lydda) were mainly Jewish but had non-Jewish minorities. Inside the pre-1967 armistice lines, Israel had a total of 885 settled places, 78 urban and 807 rural.

Although the geographer's "law of the primate city"

(the tendency of the largest city in a country or region to overdevelop at the expense of the more remote) is at work in Israel, as in other modern countries, planning and development have succeeded to some extent in counteracting the overriding attraction of the metropolis and influencing the distribution of the Jewish population. In 1936, 78% of Palestine's Jewish population lived in the central part of the Coastal Plain, between Haifa in the north and Gederah in the south; 12% in Jerusalem and the Judean Hills; 9.6% in Galilee and the interior valleys; and only 0.4% in the Negev. This compares with an estimated 62% for the central Coastal Plain in 1971; 9.6% in Jerusalem and the Judean Hills; 12.1% in the South and the Negev (Ashkelon and Beersheba sub-districts); 10% in the northern district; and an estimated 6.3% in those parts of the Haifa, Haderah, Ramleh, and Rehovot sub-districts lying outside the Coastal Plain or south of Gederah.

The Coastal Plain. The lowland strip along the Mediterranean shore is geologically the youngest part of the country. The shoreline is mainly straight with a few promontories and indentations, notably Jaffa Hill; a stretch of the Carmel coast between Dor and Athlit, with diminutive bays and headlands; the slightly protruding Carmel cape; and Haifa Bay further north. The straight course of the shoreline is unfavorable to the construction of anchorages and ports and has, through most of the country's history, given little encouragement to the development of seafaring and fisheries. The Coastal Plain narrows gradually from 25 mi. (40 km.) wide in the south (at the latitude of Gaza) to 9–12 mi. (15–20 km.) in the Sharon, a few hundred meters in the northern Carmel coast, and 2.5–3 mi. (4–5 km.) in the Acre Plain south of Rosh ha-Nikrah. It is crossed by numerous watercourses, of which the majority are ephemeral. Of the few perennial ones, the Yarkon River carries the most water. Sands thrown up by the sea form a belt of coastal dunes obstructing the outlet of watercourses and contributing to the forming of swamps, principally in the Sharon and

Zebulun valleys, which finally disappeared in the 20th century with intensive Jewish settlement and drainage work. The most characteristic soil of the central Coastal Plain is the "red sand," which combines a coarse, porous texture, easily drained and aerated, with adequate mineral content; it is best suited to the cultivation of the local "Jaffa" orange. Toward the south and Negev, it has an admixture of loess, which is concealed over certain stretches beneath a cover—generally thin—of arid dune sand. The eastern Sharon, the Carmel Coast, and the Acre Plain have mostly heavier soils, and parts of the Zebulun Valley are characterized by black swamp soil.

The climate of the Coastal Plain is influenced by the sea, which reduces temperature spans between day and night and summer and winter. Relative humidity is generally high; in built-up areas, like Tel Aviv, it is an irritant on hot summer days. Annual precipitation increases in general from south to north: rainfall ranges from 4–6 in. (100–150 mm.) at the southern end of the Gaza Strip to 20–24 in. (500–600 mm.) in the Sharon, the Carmel Coast, and the Zebulun Valley, and somewhat more in the Acre Plain. With the exception of its Negev and Sinai sections, the Coastal Plain forms part of the lowland type of the Mediterranean vegetation zone.

The Coastal Plain, which was prosperous during the period of the Crusades, was laid waste by the Mamluk ruler Baybars to prevent any further Crusader invasions. Of the seaports, all but Jaffa and Acre ceased to exist, and even these retained only a fraction of their former importance. Paradoxically, the destruction was worst in those parts enjoying a relatively humid climate, where impenetrable brush and malarial swamp spread quickly, providing hideouts for highway robbers. At the end of the 18th century, conditions reached their nadir.

From the beginning of the 19th century, villages situated near the western rim of the hills began to cultivate lands in the adjoining plain, and even hill peasants from more remote villages ventured out into the lowlands, at first staying only during the sowing and harvesting seasons but later transforming their temporary huts into permanent dwellings. These became daughter settlements of hill villages and often bore the same names, with the Arabic words *nazla* ("descent"—from the hills) or *khirba* ("ruined place" or "outpost") attached. At approximately the same time, new villages, which supposedly drew many of their inhabitants from Egypt, came into being in the southern Coastal Plain. Jaffa, too, began to expand again, serving as the country's only port for, *inter alia*, renewed Christian and Jewish pilgrimages. Orange and other fruit groves were planted in the town's immediate neighborhood; Sir Moses Montefiore's[5] aid to the Jewish community included the planting of a citrus grove near Jaffa (today Tel Aviv's Montefiore quarter). In the second half of the 19th and the beginning of the 20th century, the German Templer colonies were founded, mostly in the Coastal Plain (Sarona near Jaffa, Wilhelma near Lydda, and Neuhardthof and the German Colony near Haifa).

A new era in the history of the area opened with the establishment of the Mikveh Israel farming school in 1870. Then came the attempt by "old *yishuv*" families from Jerusalem to set up Petaḥ Tikvah in 1878 and, finally, from 1882 onward, the founding of the first modern settlements by Jewish pioneers from abroad: Rishon le-Zion, Nes Ziyyonah, Gederah and Mazkeret Batyah south and southeast of Jaffa; the new site of Petaḥ Tikvah northeast of the town; and Zikhron Ya'akov on Mt. Carmel north of the Sharon. In the 1890s followed the establishment of Reḥovot and Ḥaderah, and the tentative erection of two settlements further south (Be'er Toviyyah and Ruḥamah). The transition from grain to fruit farming and the larger openings for hired labor entailed therein increased the capacity of the Coastal Plain moshavot to absorb Jewish newcomers, but also stimulated a large-scale migration of Arabs from the

---

[5] British philanthropist, active in promoting Jewish settlement in Ereẓ Israel (1784–1885)

hills—and even from beyond the country's borders—and the quick expansion of Arab villages in the area.

In the first decade of the 20th century, citrus groves were planted in the veteran moshavot of the Coastal Plain and Jewish workers' quarters, some of them with auxiliary farm holdings, were established to absorb immigrants from Yemen and elsewhere (Nahalat Yehudah near Rishon le-Zion; Tirat Shalom, Sha'arayim, and others near Rehovot; Mahaneh Yehudah near Petah Tikvah; Nahali'el near Haderah). The network of villages began to spread in the southern Sharon (Kefar Sava, Kefar Malal, and others). Parallel with this was the accelerated growth of Jaffa, where a sizable Jewish community took root. The Palestine Office of the Zionist Organization opened there under Arthur Ruppin in 1908, and Tel Aviv was founded as a suburb of Jaffa in 1909. On a more modest scale, Haifa took on an urban character: the Hadar ha-Karmel quarter was founded, and the Jewish community of the city began to grow.

In the years following World War I, the settlement network became closer in the southern Sharon (renewal of Kefar Sava, founding of Herzliyyah, Ra'anannah, etc.), the citrus groves expanded, and Tel Aviv became a town on its own. In the beginning of the 1930s a continuous chain of Jewish villages was already in existence in the Sharon, thanks to the acquisition (in 1927/28) of the Hefer Plain by the Jewish National Fund (J.N.F.), which had also purchased parts of the Zebulun Valley (Haifa Bay area) and prepared their development according to a master plan, dividing them into industrial, residential, and agricultural zones.

This was followed by the establishment of numerous kibbutzim and moshavim in the Sharon and the Rishon le-Zion–Gederah area, as well as the first Jewish foothold in the Acre Plain (Nahariyyah, 1934; Shavei Zion, 1938). The Petah Tikvah–Haderah road, completed in 1936, was the first fairly long communications line running through an area inhabited exclusively by Jews. Tel Aviv and Haifa became the country's largest cities. The port of Haifa was

Tel Aviv, viewed from the northeast, with the Shalom Tower building dominating the horizon, 1969. Courtesy Government Press Office, Tel Aviv.

opened in 1934, and Tel Aviv was permitted to construct an anchorage when the Arab riots paralyzed Jaffa port in 1936. At the same time, the Arab villages in the Coastal Plain, particularly those in the Jaffa-Lydda area, expanded further, thanks to the prosperity brought by Jewish settlement activity. Tulkarm and Qalqılya, on the eastern border of the Sharon, as well as Majdal (Ashkelon) in the south, became small towns.

The founding of Negbah in 1939 heralded settlement in the southern Coastal Plain and the northern Negev, which was pursued throughout World War II and the 1946/47 struggle with the British authorities; Dorot, Nir Am, Gevaram, Yad Mordekhai and other outposts came into being, and another kibbutz, Beror Ḥayil, was set up in May 1948 during a War of Independence battle on the site. With few exceptions (e.g., Fureidis near Zikhron Ya'akov and al-Mazra'a near Nahariyyah), the Arab villages in the Coastal Plain were abandoned in the 1948 war, generally   237 even before Israel forces occupied them. On the other hand, the population stayed on in the Arab villages of the eastern Sharon (al-Ṭīra, Ṭayyiba, Jiljiliya, Qalansawa, etc.), which became Israel territory in 1949, following the Armistice Agreement with Jordan. At the end of the War of Independence, few Arabs remained in former Arab towns (Acre, Ramleh, Lydda, Majdal) and mixed towns (Jaffa, Haifa), where Jewish immigrants were housed from the end of 1948.

After 1949, several veteran moshavot in the Coastal Plain (Rishon le-Zion, Reḥovot, Petaḥ Tikvah, Netanyah, Ḥaderah, Nahariyyah) acquired city status. New villages, mostly moshavim, were set up in all parts of the area, especially in the Acre Plain, the eastern rim of the Sharon, the Lydda Plain, and the Southern Plain. Settlement in the latter region expanded further, mainly eastward, with the implementation of the Lachish regional development project from 1954. From the middle 1950s, a number of development towns were erected, particularly in the south (Kiryat Gat, Kiryat Malakhi, Sederot, etc.). Simultaneously, the Tel Aviv region became Israel's major conurbation.

In the 1960s Ashdod, Israel's second Mediterranean port, was founded and quickly expanded on the sand dunes near the mouth of Naḥal Lachish. Similarly, other Coastal Plain cities and towns progressed, some reaching populations of 50,000 and over. The population of the Tel Aviv conurbation, together with the "outer ring," exceeded 1,300,000 in 1971.

After 1967 industry and services expanded still further in the Coastal Plain. Haifa and Ashdod ports and Lydda Airport attained record turnovers. All these entailed a further concentration of population and a further steep increase in population density. At the end of 1971, the inhabitants of the districts lying within the Coastal Plain (including also parts of Haifa on Mt. Carmel) numbered 2,130,200, amounting to 68.8% of the total population within the pre-1967 borders. The Tel Aviv conurbation and, to a lesser degree, the Haifa conurbation have naturally formed the major attraction for immigration and internal migration. At the same time, however, there has been a slight but constant displacement of the population center toward the south since the early 1950s. This is due not only to the speedy growth of Beersheba (see below), but also to the successful planning and development of Ashdod, Ashkelon, and smaller urban centers in the southern Coastal Plain and to the sound foundations laid for farming villages.

THE SOUTHERN PLAIN (NEGEV COASTAL PLAIN AND PHILISTINE PLAIN). The Southern Plain extends from the mouth of Naḥal Lachish to the south and southwest to merge, almost imperceptibly, with the Sinai coastal area. In the east, it borders on the southern Judean foothills and, in the southeast, on the Beersheba depression, where again, the transition is hardly noticeable. The parts lying within the pre-1967 borders cover an area of some 560 sq. mi. (1,450 sq. km.), whereas the Gaza Strip measures 140 sq. mi. (363 sq. km.). Of all sections of the Coastal Plain, this has experienced the most thorough transformation since 1948.

The population of the Gaza Strip at least tripled when it was flooded by refugees late in 1948. At the end of 1971, the Gaza Strip, together with northeastern Sinai (El-Arish sub-district), had 381,800 inhabitants; thereby it approached again (after a temporary decrease between 1967 and 1969) the peak figure of the 1967 census (389,700). The population density lies therefore in the Gaza Strip proper (Gaza and Khan Yunis sub-districts) very near 2,590 per sq. mi. (1,000 per sq. km.). The Ashkelon sub-district, evacuated by practically all its Arab inhabitants in the wake of the same events, has been covered by a network of 94 Jewish villages, towns, and cities; it has grown faster in population and density than any other area in Israel, with the exception of the northwestern part of the Beersheba sub-district. Its population rose from 7,200 (4,800 Jews and 2,400 non-Jews) in November 1948 to 149,500 (149,000 239

Jews and 500 non-Jews) at the end of 1971 and the population density of the sub-district increased from 14.0 per sq. mi. (5.8 per sq. km.) to 304.5 per sq. mi. (117.6 per sq. km.).

Concurrently, land use underwent profound changes in the Gaza Strip and the rest of the South, as irrigated fruit orchards and garden and field crops replaced dry farming. While in the Gaza Strip this entailed the drilling of numerous, mostly shallow wells and the over-exploitation of the groundwater table, in the Ashkelon sub-district and the northwestern Negev it was the regional Yarkon–Negev pipeline and, later, the National Water Carrier that made intensification of agriculture possible. In the Gaza Strip and the western part of the Ashkelon district, which have lighter soils, citrus groves took the lead. On the heavier soils further inland, particularly in the central and eastern parts of the Lachish region, preference is given to irrigated field crops (cotton, sugar beets, fodder plants, etc.). In the southernmost reaches (Sha'ar ha-Negev and the Eshkol development region), out-of-season export vegetables and flowers, which are favored by mild winters, have become important since the late 1960s. There are 24 Jewish villages in the northwestern part of the Beersheba district (the Besor region, part of which belongs geographically to the Coastal Plain) and 90 in the Ashkelon district. Most are moshavim, although kibbutzim are preponderant in the zone next to the Gaza Strip. Comprehensive regional planning, facilitated in the Southern Plain by the extensive areas abandoned in 1948, is characterized by clusters of villages around regional centers, which in turn depend on regional towns (Sederot, Kiryat Gat, Kiryat Malakhi). These towns also introduced industry based generally on farm produce. The oil wells of the Ḥeleẓ-Beror Ḥayil area introduced an additional feature. Ashkelon (founded 1948) and Ashdod (founded 1955) became the sites of industrial plants. The economic pivot of Ashdod is its port. Ashkelon has also developed recreation and tourism. The erection of the terminal of the large oil pipeline at Ashkelon and the refineries, whose construction began in 1970 at Ashdod, herald a quickened urbanization process in the South.

JUDEAN PLAIN. The term Judean Plain may be applied to the section lying between a line running east from the mouth of Naḥal Lachish and the bed of the Yarkon River. Together with those parts of the Tel Aviv district and Petaḥ Tikvah sub-district, which, lying north of the Yarkon River, belong geographically to the Sharon area, it measures 310 sq. mi. (about 800 sq. km.). It includes the Tel Aviv district, the Reḥovot and Petaḥ Tikvah sub-districts, and most of the Ramleh sub-district. This region was the scene of the earliest modern Jewish settlement (Mikveh Israel, Petaḥ Tikvah, Rishon le-Zion, etc.). Today most of it is occupied by the Tel Aviv conurbation (Tel Aviv-Jaffa, Ramat Gan, Holon, Bat Yam, Bene Berak, Givatayim) and its outer ring (Rishon le-Zion, Reḥovot, Ramleh, Lydda, Petaḥ Tikvah, etc.). In 1971 there were 125 settled places in the Judean Plain. Thanks to a rich groundwater table and the light "red sands" which are prevalent in the southern and southwestern parts, the plain is one of the main centers of Israel's citriculture. On the heavier soils between Lydda and Petaḥ Tikvah there are citrus groves and other intensive crops, largely of the truck-farming type. The Judean Plain contains over half of Israel's industrial enterprises, as well as the country's most dense communications network. Planning efforts in this area aim largely at preventing it from becoming one shapeless "megalopolis" and preserving a neat separation between residential, commercial, industrial, agricultural, and recreational zones, permitting the cities within the conurbation to merge, with time, into one single social and economic unit, but guarding the independence of the towns in the "outer ring." It is thus intended to keep commuting within reasonable limits and not to complicate the grave traffic problems even further.

SHARON. The Sharon, extending from the Yarkon River north to Naḥal Tanninim, is Israel's foremost farming area. Administratively, it includes the Sharon sub-district and most of the Ḥaderah sub-district, as well as the northern 241 part of the Petaḥ Tikvah sub-district. The Sharon measures about 269 sq. mi. (696 sq. km.). It has 140 settled places and 275,800 inhabitants (including 11 Arab towns and villages with 43,900 inhabitants) and the population density is 1021.6 per sq. mi. (396 per sq. km.). The western halves of all three sub-districts are characterized by light "red sands," particularly favorable to citriculture, while in the east heavier soils prevail. Water supply is ample throughout the region. The southernmost reaches are included in the Tel Aviv conurbation (Herzliyyah, Ramat ha-Sharon, North Tel Aviv) and its outer ring (Ra'anannah, Kefar Sava, etc.). Netanyah is the urban center for the central Sharon and Ḥaderah for the north. A dense network of Jewish rural agglomerations—mostly moshavim and moshavot, with a smaller number of kibbutzim—covers most of the Sharon. The eastern rim, however, on both sides of the pre-1967 armistice lines, has a mainly Arab population. Ṭayyiba is the largest community within the former borders, while the towns of Tulkarm and Qalqīlya lie beyond them. Besides farming enterprises based exclusively on citrus and villages combining citrus with truck farming (vegetables, dairy cattle, poultry), there are also farms geared to special export crops, such as flowers. There are industrial plants in the major towns and moshavot, as well as in the kibbutzim. Tourism and recreation are catered to by towns and villages near the coast.

CARMEL COAST REGION. Administratively, most of this narrow, elongated area belongs to the Ḥaderah sub-district. With an area of 29 sq. mi. (76 sq. km.), it has 15 settled places (13 Jewish and two Arab) with 9,900 inhabitants (including 3,400 non-Jews), and a population density of 341 per sq. mi. (130 per sq. km.). The region has the advantages of fertile, mostly heavy, alluvial soil and an abundant groundwater reserve, not only facilitating fully irrigated farming but also leaving a water surplus, which is diverted to other parts of the country. In addition to citrus groves, vineyards, deciduous fruit, and field, fodder, and garden crops, there are banana plantations, which benefit from the mild winters and, particularly, from the wind shelter provided by the wall-like slope of Mt. Carmel rising in the east. In addition to 13 Jewish and two Arab villages, a number of settlements on Mt. Carmel (e.g., Bet Oren, Ma'yan Ẓevi) cultivate fields in the Carmel Coast region. Athlit is the principal agglomeration. The northernmost part, with Tirat Karmel, belongs to the Haifa conurbation.

HAIFA BAY AREA (ZEBULUN VALLEY). Mt. Carmel in the southwest, the Tivon-Shepharam Hills in the southeast, and the hills of Lower Galilee in the east clearly delineate this valley; in the north, the Acre-Aḥihud highway is a recognizable border. It covers an area of some 90 sq. mi. (230 sq. km.). Administratively, its southern part belongs to the Haifa district and the northern one to the Acre sub-district. This area was the object of the first regional planning effort, undertaken with the aid of the British town planner, Patrick Abercrombie, at the end of the 1920s and the beginning of the 1930s, which determined its present physical and habitational characteristics.

Night view of Haifa with the lights of the "kerayot" suburbs lining the far side of the bay. Courtesy Ministry of Tourism, Jerusalem. Photo Werner Braun, Jerusalem

Arab and Jewish shops in the market of Acre's Old City. **Courtesy** Government Press Office, Tel Aviv.

ACRE PLAIN. The Acre Plain extends from the Acre–Aḥihud highway north to Rosh ha-Nikrah and the Ḥanitah-Adamit ridge. In the east, the limestone hills of Upper Galilee rise in stark contrast to the fertile, intermediate-to-heavy soil cover of the Plain which, measuring about 45 sq. mi. (some 120 sq. km.), is included in the Acre sub-district. In addition to Acre, Nahariyyah exercises administrative and economic functions as a second center of this region. Apart from highly intensive and almost fully irrigated farming, recreation facilities are important in the region's economy. Industry is principally based on the two towns. There are 17 Jewish and nine non-Jewish villages and the development town Shelomi.

The Hills. At least half of Israel's area within the pre-1967 armistice borders, and over 60% of Cisjordan, have a hilly or mountainous topography. Elevations reach 3,380 ft. (1,035 m.) in the Negev (Mt. Ramon), 3,350 ft. (1,020 m.) in Judea (Mt. Ḥalḥul), 3,085 ft. (940 m.) in Samaria (Mt.

Ebal), 3,963 ft. (1,208 m.) in Galilee (Mt. Meron), and, outside Israel-held territory, 9,233 ft. (2,814 m.) at the peak of the Hermon block. Apart from the Negev, the hill region proper includes Judea in the south, Samaria in the center, and Galilee in the north. The transition from Judea to Samaria is gradual, but Galilee is clearly separated from Samaria by the tectonic valleys of Jezreel and Ḥarod. The characteristic soil of limestone areas is the reddish-brown, relatively heavy and fertile "terra rossa." The chalk hills have mostly rendzina soils of paler hues which, although inherently poorer, are friable and easy to till; on valley bottoms, they are often enriched with organic matter. Erosion runoff has always been the central problem of hill farming. The streambeds are dry in summer and even in winter carry water only occasionally after heavy rain.

The hill climate differs, generally, from that of the Coastal Plain in sharper temperature differences between day and night and, mainly on hilltops, in perceptibly cooler winters, although even there the summer heat is equal to that of the lowlands, and the *sharav* (ḥamsin) is even more oppressive. Humidity is generally lower in the hills, except in midwinter, and evaporation stronger, but rainfall on the western side of the hills is superior to that on the Coastal Plain. Snow falls in Jerusalem and Hebron on the average once in two or three years, and in the highest parts of Upper Galilee nearly every year, although, as a rule, it remains on the ground for a few hours only. In contrast, the eastern side of the hills descending to the Jordan rift lies in the rain shadow, but the arid zone in Samaria is much narrower than in Judea, and on Galilee's eastern slopes rainfall is everywhere above 16 in. (400 mm.) per year. Deforestation has left few remnants of the original plant cover, belonging to the hill type of the Mediterranean vegetation zone. The eastern side of Judea (the Judean Desert, Wilderness of Judah) and of Samaria belong partly to the Irano-Turanian dry-steppe zone and partly to the Saharo-Arabian desert zone. Of the hill regions west of the Jordan—Judea, Samaria, and Galilee—the lower parts (Shephelah, northern 245

Samaria, Lower Galilee), with their broader intermontane valleys, deeper soils, and easier thoroughfares, have been better endowed for settlement since antiquity than the higher reaches (Judean Hills, southern Samaria, Upper Galilee).

Since the late 18th century, Christian churches and monasteries erected in the hills have contributed to the progress of farming, at least in their immediate neighborhood (e.g., Ein Kerem near Jerusalem, Bi'r Zayt in southern Samaria, Kafr Kannā in Lower Galilee), as well as to the importance of towns sacred to Christianity (Bethlehem, Nazareth). In the 19th century, earthquakes caused ravages at Safed, Tiberias, and Nablus, but in the long run did not impede a certain amount of growth in these centers, paralleling that of other towns in the hills and on their outskirts (Hebron, Ramallah, Tulkarm). For Jerusalem, a new chapter began when Jews and non-Jews founded new quarters outside the city walls. At the end of the 19th

Nablus (Shechem), the largest urban center in Samaria, occupying the narrow vale between Mts. Ebal and Gerizim. Courtesy J.N.F., Jerusalem. Photo E. Orni, Jerusalem.

Mizpah, a moshavah west of Tiberias, founded in 1908. A basalt defense wall surrounds the closely grouped farmsteads. From *Photographs of the New Working Palestine,* Haifa, 1935.

A byway in Jerusalem's Me'ah She'arim quarter, 1959. Courtesy Government Press Office, Tel Aviv.

century, however, the hills began to cede their dominant position to the Coastal Plain. Although emissaries of early Jewish pioneer groups tried to acquire land for settlement near Hebron and elsewhere in the hills, they were soon discouraged by the high prices of land, the unavailability of sizable holdings, and the restricted possibility of farming on European models. Of the three small Jewish hill settlements established before 1899—Moẓa, Ein Zeitim, and Hartuv— the latter two existed only intermittently.

A new phase opened in the first decade of the 20th century, when the Jewish Colonization Association (ICA) founded grain-farming villages in eastern Lower Galilee (Ilaniyyah, Yavne'el, Kefar Tavor, etc.). A few private villages (Miẓpah, etc.) were established and a training farm opened at Kefar Ḥittim on J.N.F. land. All these villages, like their few predecessors in the hills, did not develop satisfactorily. Kiryat Anavim, a kibbutz founded in 1920 west of Jerusalem, made the first steps toward modernization of hill farming, and two more small villages, Atarot and Neveh Ya'akov, were set up north of Jerusalem. The next hill settlement, Kefar ha-Ḥoresh, was founded only in 1935 west of Nazareth.

Three out of the four traditional "holy cities," all of them in the hills, suffered setbacks in the 1930s. The old Jewish community of Hebron ceased to exist after the 1929 Arab riots; the Safed community gradually dwindled; and that of Tiberias stagnated. Only Jerusalem's Jewish population increased vigorously in that period.

Hill outposts were finally established on a planned basis and on a larger scale as stockade and watchtower settlements: from 1937 in the Manasseh Hills (Ein ha-Shofet, Daliyyah, etc.), with the aim of creating a "settlement bridge" between the Sharon and the Jezreel Valley; in eastern Lower Galilee (Sharonah, Kefar Kisch, etc.), to strengthen the existing network of villages; and, since 1938, near the Lebanese border in western Upper Galilee (Ḥanita, Eilon, etc.). In the Judean Hills, Kiryat Anavim was joined, in 1938, by Ma'aleh ha-Ḥamishah, and, in 1946, by Neveh

Ilan. The Ezyon Bloc was established in the Hebron Hills between 1943 and 1947, but was destroyed in the 1948 War of Independence, when Neveh Ya'akov and Atarot also had to be evacuated. While the 1947 U.N. partition map allocated practically all the hill regions to the proposed Arab state (with the exception of a narrow strip of eastern Galilee, Mt. Carmel, and part of the Manasseh Hills), the 1949 armistice borders added to Israel the rest of Galilee and the Manasseh Hills, the Jerusalem Corridor, and most of the Shephelah, as well as part of the Iron Hills.

Energetic settlement activity started at the end of 1948 in the Jerusalem Corridor and, to a lesser degree, in Galilee. To overcome the particular difficulties of hill settlement, which requires large investments in land reclamation in the initial stage and a long period of waiting until farming becomes remunerative, the J.N.F. established work villages. Afforestation was carried out on a large scale, transforming the landscape and providing initial or supplementary employment to new settlers in the hills. In 1955, the development of the Adullam region, south of the Jerusalem

The Adullam regional settlement plan is explained to a group of surveyors in 1955. Courtesy J.N.F., Jerusalem, Photo Malafsky, Jerusalem.

Corridor, was commenced as an extension of the Lachish region, and in 1963 another development program was launched in central and northern Galilee. Of the relatively few development towns built in the hills, not all expanded as anticipated. In Galilee, Ma'alot struggled hard to overcome its difficulties and attract industry, while the hope of turning Shelomi into a growing urban center was practically given up. Naẓerat Illit (Upper Nazareth) and Migdal ha-Emek, on the other hand, succeeded after initial hardships, and the progress of Karmi'el, slow until 1967, accelerated after the Six-Day War. Similarly, Beth-Shemesh in the Judean Hills, for a long time problematic, made some progress only after sizable industrial plants were established there in the late 1960s. Of the ancient towns in Galilee, Safed and Tiberias regained their original population figures soon after the flight of their Arab inhabitants, but further growth was slow after the early 1950s. Nazareth, which hardly suffered in the War of Independence, greatly improved its economic situation in the State of Israel and became its primary Arab center. There were record increases (averaging 4% and more annually) in the population of the Arab hill villages of Galilee and the Iron Hills, which greatly broadened their economic foundation.

JUDEA. The parts of the region west of the 1949 armistice lines belong to the Jerusalem, Ramleh, Ashkelon, and Petaḥ Tikvah sub-districts. East Jerusalem was reunited with the capital's western parts in 1967. The remaining area of the former Jordanian Jerusalem district was added partly to the Bethlehem and partly to the Ramallah district. The third district of former Jordanian-held Judea is that of Hebron.

Shephelah (Foothills). In this area, which was completely abandoned by Arabs in 1948 and had only a few small Jewish settlements (Ḥuldah, Gezer, Ben Shemen), re-settlement began at the end of that year near the "Highway of Valor" (Kevish ha-Gevurah), built to secure the access to Jerusalem, and in 1949 east of Ramleh and Lydda. The kibbutzim of Netiv ha-Lamed-He and Bet

Kiryat Gat, urban center of the Lachish region, from the west, 1963. In the foreground is new housing, behind it, older dwellings. In the background is the industrial zone. Courtesy Government Press Office, Tel Aviv.

Guvrin were at first solitary outposts further south, but more villages were established as part of the Adullam Project after 1955. At the southern and northern extremity of the area, only isolated villages were founded on the sites of the projected Adoraim and Modi'im regional schemes. While Kiryat Gat, Ramleh, Lydda, and Petaḥ Tikvah, all situated outside the western rim of the Shephelah, have become population centers for the area and exercise economic and other functions, Beth-Shemesh is the only development town in the Shephelah proper. In population density, the Shephelah remains well below the average of central and northern Israel. Farming is mostly of a transition type, with partly intensive field crops located on valley bottoms (Elah, Aijalon, Sorek valleys, etc.) and deciduous fruit orchards and vineyards prominent on higher ground. Afforestation takes up considerable areas.

Jerusalem Corridor. In the part of the Judean Hills 251

Yemenite immigrants at Givat Ye'arim pruning fruit trees on the terraced slopes of their moshav near Jerusalem, 1956.
Courtesy J.N.F., Jerusalem. Photo Werner Braun, Jerusalem.

proper included in Israel in 1948/49, the first new settlements were founded near the Jerusalem highway, and others were added later further south. The easternmost reaches (Mevasseret Zion, Moẓa, Bet Zayit) have since the late 1960s been gradually becoming suburban extensions of Jerusalem. Farming is based principally on poultry and fruit orchards, the latter planted on laboriously terraced hillsides, but there are also some recreation and tourist facilities.

SAMARIA. Most of this region lies in what was, after 1967, the Israel-held territory of Judea–Samaria, comprising the three districts of Nablus, Tulkarm, and Jenin. Only the northwestern extension of the Samaria Hills, composed of the three subregions of the Iron Hills and Valley, the Manasseh Hills, and Mt. Carmel, as well as the northern rim of Mt. Gilboa, were part of pre-1967 Israel.

Iron and Manasseh Hills. Of the Iron and Manasseh Hills, belonging partly to the Ḥaderah and partly to the Jezreel sub-district, the former is predominantly inhabited by Arabs and characterized by partly intensive mixed farming, in which there was considerable progress after 1949. Villages like ʿAra, ʿArʿara, and Umm al-Faḥm much more than doubled their population. Mei Ammi was founded in 1963 as a border kibbutz on the armistice line. Farming in the Manasseh Hills—which contain 11 Jewish villages, mostly kibbutzim, as well as one Arab village—comprises intensive field crops and fruit orchards, milch cows, sheep, poultry, and so on. Most kibbutzim have industrial enterprises to complement their economy. The Manasseh Forest, with over 7,000,000 trees planted by 1971, is the largest in the country.

Mt. Carmel. The northwestern extremity of the Mt. Carmel block is occupied by suburbs of Haifa. Large parts of its central and southeastern sections have been declared nature reserves, and the expanses covered with pine woods form the background for the recreation facilities developed at several sites (Bet Oren, Yaʾarot ha-Karmel, Nir Ezyon, etc.). Villages on or near the mountain's western edge cultivate land in the Carmel coastal plain below. On the top of Keren ha-Karmel, at the mountain's southeast corner, a Catholic monastery stands on the spot traditionally held to be the site of the prophet Elijah's contest with the priests of Baal.

GALILEE. Administratively, the Galilean hill country belongs to the Acre, Kinneret, and Safed sub-districts. The hills proper cover an area of over 700 sq. mi. (approximately 1,820 sq. km.). Their population density amounts to about 370 per sq. mi. (142 per sq. km.). Arabs and Druze are in the majority, with 191,000 out of 258,100 inhabitants.

Lower Galilee. The area south of the Bet ha-Kerem Valley and southwest of the Ammud Gorge falls into two separate parts. The first is western and central Lower Galilee, with the towns of Nazareth and Naẓerat Illit (Upper Nazareth) and a few Jewish rural settlements scattered among many Arab villages, some of which are large. The second part is the exclusively rural southeastern Lower Galilee, characterized by nearly flat basaltic plateaus dissected by deeper gorges, in which Jewish villages constitute the majority. In the west and center, olives, deciduous fruit orchards, and vines are to be found on hillsides, while field crops, primarily wheat, are cultivated in the valleys. The largest intermontane valley, Bikat Bet Netofah, with an open canal of the National Water Carrier running through it, is in some rainy winters partly flooded, and its fertile soil is therefore used mainly for summer crops. Eastern and southeastern Lower Galilee, which before 1948 cultivated grain almost exclusively, have introduced additional crops (e.g., cotton, deciduous fruit, etc.) since Israel's independence.

Upper Galilee. Bordering on the Acre Plain in the west, Lower Galilee in the south, the Ḥuleh Valley in the east and northeast, and Lebanon in the north, Upper Galilee bears a more pronouncedly mountainous character. Its cultivated area therefore constitutes only a small percentage of its total surface, whereas considerable expanses are covered with stunted remnants of natural woods or planted forests. Hill farming, with olives and tobacco prominent in Arab villages and deciduous fruit orchards, vineyards, and poultry in Jewish settlements, is practiced largely on terraced slopes. Among the non-Jewish population, Druze are prominent in the west and center (Yirkā, Jatt, Beit Jann, Ḥurfaysh, etc.), and Christians in the north-center (Mi'ilyā', Fussūṭa, Gush Ḥalav, etc.), while the majority of Jewish settlements lie close to the Lebanese frontier. Urban agglomerations are Safed and Ma'alot.

The Jordan and Dead Sea Rift and Its Jezreel Valley Branch. The outstanding features of the Rift Valley in Israel, which is part of the 4,000 mi. (6,500 km.) Syrian-East African Rift, are its straight north–south course, the precipitous mountain walls hemming it in on both sides, and the thick cover of alluvium, nearly flat on the surface, which conceals the enormous depth of the rift bottom. The rift neatly separates Cisjordan from Transjordan. It falls into five major sections: the upper Jordan Valley, comprising the Huleh Valley and the Rosh Pinnah-Korazim sill; the central Jordan Valley, including Lake Kinneret and its surroundings and the Beth-Shean Valley; the lower Jordan Valley, with the subregions of the Succoth and Peza'el (Phasael) valleys and the Jericho Plain (Ha-Kikkar); the Dead Sea and its region; finally, the Arabah Valley, which, at least in aspects of human geography, is closely related to the Negev. The Huleh Valley measures 15 mi. (25 km.) from north to south and 4–6 mi. (6–8 km.) from west to east. The northern rim of the valley is 525 ft. (170 m.) above sea level and the surface of the former Lake Huleh was 220 ft. (70 m.) above sea level. The surface of Lake Kinneret lies some 696 ft. (213 m.) below sea level, the figure oscillating with the seasons and the rainfall. With a capacity estimated at 3,000,000,000 cubic meters, it serves as the National Water Carrier's principal reservoir. Three river terraces may be distinguished in the Beth-Shean Valley, the Jordan meandering on the lowest and the town of Beth-Shean lying on the highest. South of this valley the Samaria Hills approach the Jordan bed, leaving only a narrow passage on its west bank. Further south, the rift widens into the Succoth Valley. Mt. Sartaba separates the Succoth Valley from the still wider Peza'el Valley, which, in turn, goes over, south of Wadi 'Awjā, into the Jericho Plain, where the west–east distance between the slopes of the Judean Desert and the edge of the Moab Plateau is 20 mi. (32 km.) and where the valley bottom lies between 820 and 11,250 ft. (250–380 m.) below sea level. The Dead Sea is an inland lake covering the deepest continental depression on earth: in 1963 its water surface lay 1,308 ft. (398.5 m.) below sea level. The Lashon (Lisān) Peninsula divides the lake into a larger, northern and a smaller, southern basin. The high temperatures and evaporation, as well as the absence of any outlet, explain the extremely high salt content of the sea—the highest of any body of water on earth, attaining 29–32% in the southern basin—and the specific gravity of these waters exceeding that of any other lake.

A side branch of the Rift, composed of the Harod and Jezreel valleys, leads from the Beth-Shean Valley northwestward. The Harod Valley, 11 mi. (18 km.) long and 3 mi. (5 km.) wide, is a narrow corridor separating the Ẓeva'im Ridge in Lower Galilee from Mt. Gilboa in Samaria. Naḥal Harod runs through it from its source at the foot of Mt. Gilboa toward Beth-Shean and the Jordan River. The Jezreel Valley is triangular in shape, its apex pointing south to the town of Jenin.

Soils in the Jordan Rift Valley change from dark, heavy alluvium (partly swamp and peat soils) in the Ḥuleh Valley and alluvium of partly basaltic origin around the northern shores of Lake Kinneret to pale, marly *lashon* soils,

Digging drainage ditches as a prerequisite to settling the Jezreel Valley, 1921. Courtesy Central Zionist Archives, Jerusalem.

predominant from Lake Kinneret southward through the Beth-Shean and Succoth valleys to the Jericho region.

In the past, extensive swamps and waterlogging excluded human settlement from the larger part of the Ḥuleh Valley. In the Beth-Shean Valley, the success of farming was dependent on the readiness of settlers to prevent flooding of fields by spring waters and watercourses; when this was not done, thorny brush spread and soils became increasingly saline. In the lower Jordan Valley, agriculture is essentially oasis farming, of which Jericho is the most striking example. The heavy, alluvial soils of the Harod and Jezreel valleys resemble those of the northern parts of the Jordan Valley, as did, until the recent past, their swamps and their waterlogging problems. All the swamps are now drained.

Going from north to south, the climate of the Jordan Valley becomes progressively hotter and drier. The Ḥuleh Valley has a mean annual temperature of 68°F (20°C); although summer days are frequently oppressive, winter frosts, caused by temperature inversion, exclude subtropical crops but are beneficial to the extensive apple orchards. The Kinneret region has hot summers and mild winters, and the Beth-Shean Valley is characterized by a continental temperature regime, with peak summer heat but not entirely frost-free winters. On the Dead Sea shore, the mean annual temperature soars to 77°F (25°C), with summer maximums frequently exceeding 104°F (40°C). Differences in rainfall are no less extreme: the Ḥuleh Valley's northern rim receives an annual precipitation average of 24 in. (600 mm.); the Kinneret region between 16 and 20 in. (400–500 mm.); the Beth-Shean Valley between 10 and 16 in. (250–400 mm.); and the Jericho region about 4 in. (100 mm.), while at Sodom only 2 in. (50 mm.) are registered. The lower the averages, the more extreme are the fluctuations between one rain year and the next. Evaporation in the Rift is very strong, particularly from Lake Kinneret southward, having a negative influence on the water balance and promoting salination.

Great variety is found in the Rift's flora and fauna. The   257

Huleh Valley belongs to the Mediterranean vegetation zone's lowland type; in the former Huleh swamps there is a dense vegetation grouped around the papyrus reed, which has been partly preserved in the Huleh Nature Reserve; the Kinneret region is of a transition type between the Mediterranean and Irano-Turanian (dry-steppe) vegetation zones, and the Beth-Shean and Succoth valleys are within the confines of the latter zone. The Jericho and Dead Sea regions belong to the Saharo-Arabian (desert) zone; the flood terrace of the Lower Jordan River and some other stretches have a halophytic (salt-loving) flora, whereas Jericho, En-Gedi, and some other cases constitute enclaves of the Sudanian (moist-tropical) vegetation zone.

Lines of communication crossing the Rift from west to east were through most of history of greater importance than lengthwise north-south roads. The Jordan Valley's role in prehistory is outstanding; finds from the Paleolithic (Ubaydiyya), the Neolithic (Jericho, Sha'ar ha-Golan), and the Chalcolithic periods (Tulaylāt al-Ghusūl, etc.), have been discovered. In most prehistoric and historic periods, however, habitation was discontinuous in time and space; sections of the valley often had more contacts with the adjoining hill regions than with each other. The decline setting in after the Muslim conquest was, in the initial centuries, less pronounced in the Jordan Valley than in other parts of the country; after the Crusades, however, the Rift Valley remained a total waste, as did the Jezreel Valley. In the 19th century, new Arab villages came into being in the Huleh Valley, many of whose settlers presumably hailed from Egypt.

Some of the earlier Jewish settlements in the country (Yesud ha-Ma'alah, Mishmar ha-Yarden, etc.) were founded in or near the Huleh Valley. In the first decade of the 20th century, Jewish settlement gained a foothold in the Jordan-Yarmuk Plain (Kinneret, Deganiyyah). The Jezreel and Harod valleys became the principal object of pioneering efforts in the 1920s, and in the Beth-Shean Valley the first stockade and watchtower settlements were erected in

The Balfour Forest near Kibbutz Ginnegar in 1929, shortly after its planting. Courtesy J.N.F., Jerusalem.

The Balfour Forest after twenty years' growth. Courtesy Zionist Archives, New York.

the 1930s. The Lower Jordan Valley, on the other hand, did not come into the scope of Jewish development (with the exception of the Rabbat Ashlag potash works and Bet ha-Aravah) and remained outside Israel's 1948 armistice borders. Between 1951 and 1958, the great Ḥuleh drainage project was carried out, making the lake and swamp disappear and creating conditions for adding new settlements, particularly the town of Kiryat Shemonah and the development town of Ḥazor. In the Kinneret region, few new villages were founded after 1948. In the Beth-Shean Valley, the town of Beth-Shean became Jewish, and a few more moshavim and kibbutzim were founded. The Jezreel Valley settlement expanded southward with the establishment of the Taanach village bloc. In the Lower Jordan Valley, tens of thousands of 1948 Arab war refugees were housed in camps of mud-brick huts by the Jordanian regime.

Two of the moshavim of the Taanach regional settlement area in the Jezreel Valley. Courtesy Government Press Office, Tel Aviv.

Kiryat Shemonah, a development town in the Ḥuleh Valley at the foot of the Naphtali range, 1955. Courtesy J.N.F., Jerusalem. Photo Malafsky, Jerusalem.

Naḥal Gilgal, an outpost settlement founded in 1970, in the lower Jordan Valley. Courtesy J.N.F., Jerusalem. Photo Strajmayster, Jerusalem. **261**

HULEH VALLEY. The Huleh Valley, measuring 93 sq. mi. (240 sq. km.), forms part of the Safed sub-district. It has 23 settlements and 23,800 inhabitants (nearly all Jewish), 15,400 in Kiryat Shemonah and the rest in kibbutzim and moshavim. The area of the valley, fully and intensively cultivated, is entirely covered with irrigated apple and other deciduous fruit orchards, carp ponds, and field and fodder crops. In addition to the local villages, Galilee hill settlements have been allocated fields in the Huleh Valley. Industry exists in Kiryat Shemonah and in several kibbutzim.

ROSH PINNAH SILL (HAZOR REGION). The Rosh Pinnah Sill has an area of 41 sq. mi. (106 sq. km.). There are nine settled places with 9,500 inhabitants (eight of them are Jewish with 7,900 inhabitants), 5,200 of whom live in Hazor. Farming is partly intensive, but a relatively large area is covered with basalt boulders and can serve, at best, as grazing land.

THE KINNERET REGION. The Kinneret region forms part of the Kinnarot sub-district. With an area of 59 sq. mi. (152 sq. km.). It has 20 settled places (all Jewish) with a population of 33,700, 24,200 of whom live in Tiberias, where their economy is principally based on tourism and recreation. In the rural sector, the 15 kibbutzim are the predominant element, as this was the area where collective settlement came into being and where important ideological and cultural centers of the kibbutz movement (study centers, museums, etc.) are located. Farming, highly intensive and fully irrigated, specializes in tropical and subtropical species (bananas, date palms, etc.); field and fodder crops, vegetables, dairy cattle, and poultry are also important. In addition to carp ponds, fishing in Lake Kinneret is developed. Industrial enterprises are to be found in some of the Jordan-Yarmuk Plain kibbutzim.

THE BETH-SHEAN VALLEY. The Beth-Shean Valley, with an area of 85 sq. mi. (219 sq. km.), numbers 18,800 inhabitants (all Jewish) in 20 settlements. The town of Beth-Shean (with 12,100 inhabitants) contains the majority

The Ginnosar valley in the Kinneret region, with Kibbutz Ginnosar at center. The favorable climate and fertile alluvial soil allow intensive farming with emphasis on subtropical fruits and vegetables. Courtesy Government Press Office, Tel Aviv.

of the population. Among the villages, 14 are kibbutzim and five are moshavim. Farming is based on salt-resistant date palms and pomegranates, cotton, and other intensive field crops, and carp ponds (making use of brackish spring water); bananas are not cultivated because of the danger of frost. A number of kibbutzim have industrial plants.

LOWER JORDAN VALLEY. Since 1968, Jewish outpost settlements have been set up in the region, numbering 12 at the end of 1972 (including two west of the Dead Sea). With more water becoming available from new wells, they expand the cultivated area to new parts of the region.

THE DEAD SEA REGION. In spite of its economic importance and interest for the tourist trade the Dead Sea region has only a few inhabited places: two new settlements, kibbutz En-Gedi, and the young recreation center of Ein Bokek-Rosh Zohar: the employees of the Dead Sea Works do not live at Sodom.

The Negev. Covering an area of over 4,600 sq. mi. (some 12,000 sq. km.), the Negev constitutes a challenge to Israel's constructive efforts because of its relative vastness, the potential of its mineral wealth, and its position as a communications link with the Red Sea and the Indian Ocean. While the desert climate sets it apart from the country's center and north, structurally it continues the division of Cisjordan into the Coastal Plain, the Hill Region, and the Rift Valley to the south. The Beersheba depression, gradually rising eastward from some 300 ft. (less than 100 m.) to 1,650 ft. (500 m.) above sea level, has a thick cover of fine-grained, yellowish-brown loess as its outstanding characteristic, although large stretches in the west and southwest are overlaid by sand dunes. The loess is susceptible to severe gullying by flash floods and to sheet and wind erosion, necessitating special soil conservation measures, e.g., contour plowing and planting of shelterbelts of eucalyptus and tamarisk trees around the fields, to make farming possible. Almost the entire Beersheba region belongs to the drainage basin of Naḥal Besor.

The topography of the Negev Hills is basically determined by parallel folds running from northeast to southwest, the highest elevations lying in the southwest. On the bedrock of the Negev Hills, desert erosion has imposed sharp, angular landscape features, most strikingly exemplified in the three *makhteshim* ("erosional cirques" or "craters"): Makhtesh Ramon, Ha-Makhtesh ha-Gadol (Ḥatirah), and Ha-Makhtesh ha-Katan (Ḥaẓerah). There is hardly any arable soil.

The Eilat Mountains at the Negev's southern extremity, which belongs to the same geological province as southern Sinai, eastern Egypt, Edom, and western Arabia, are fundamentally different from the rest of the Negev. The landscape is of infinite variety, with narrow clefts hemmed in by rock walls rising 1,000 ft. (300 m.) over them, which 264 cut through the granite mountains in various directions.

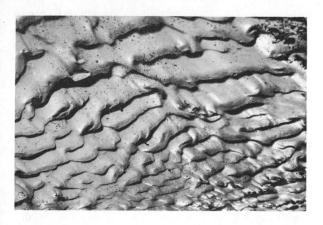

Loess soil in the wadi bed of Naḥal Besor, southwest of Beersheba, after a flood. Courtesy J.N.F., Jerusalem.

Rock debris fills the gorges, while erosion has sculptured awe-inspiring rock facades, like Solomon's Pillars near Timna, the Amram Columns, etc.

The Arabah Valley, the Rift's southern section in Israel, stretches from the Dead Sea to Eilat over a distance of 105 mi. (170 km.) between the Negev Highlands in the west and the Edom Mountains in the east. Particularly in its south, landscape features typical of the Rift are even more spectacular than anywhere else in the country. A thick cover of alluvium, mostly coarse sand and gravel, everywhere obscures the valley's rock foundations. The Arabah has a number of springs, brackish in various degrees, on its western and, more so, on its eastern side. Deep well drillings, particularly in the Ḥazevah area, have yielded water in previously unsuspected quantities.

Only the northwestern corner of the Negev has a climate that can, at best, be described as semiarid; all the other parts are desert proper. While peak temperatures, with the exception of the Arabah Valley, hardly exceed those of 265 other parts of the country, there is a large diurnal span of temperatures, typical of continental climates. Humidity decreases in southern and eastern directions, as does rainfall, which is extremely capricious; entire years may pass without any rain, and a thunderstorm lasting a few hours at a desert spot may yield the total annual average. Only the northern half of the Beersheba region and the highest reaches of the Negev hills belong to the Irano-Turanian dry-steppe vegetation zone. All the rest of the Negev belongs to the Saharo-Arabian desert zone, where the vegetation cover is extremely sparse or totally absent over long distances.

Basically, the Negev always seems to have been the nomad's domain, but other forms of human presence and activity appeared in certain periods, conditioned by the exploitation of minerals, the development and maintenance of lines of communications, and the holding of defense posts of the sown land against the wilderness. While prehistoric artifacts found over wide areas and in considerable number possibly testify to periods of greater rainfall in the earlier Stone Age, it is certain that the impressive achievements of the Chalcolithic period, which included manufacturing near Beersheba (Tell Abu Matar) and copper mining and transporting in the Arabah Valley, coincided with climatic conditions hardly different from those of the present. For a millennium the Negev had no sedentary population after the period of the Nabateans, who made enormous efforts in Roman and Byzantine times to conserve water for farming and town dwelling. Only in 1900 did the Turks decide to build Beersheba as an administrative center. Even in the 1930s, no other towns or villages existed south and east of the Rafa–Gaza–Bet Guvrin–Zāhiraiya–Samūʿ (Eshtemoʿa) line. Bedouin, affiliated with five large tribal associations—Tarābīn, al-Tiyāha, ʿAzāzma, al-Ḥanājira and al-Jabārāt, roamed the Negev, mainly subsisting on their goat flocks and camel herds and occasionally, in rainy winters, sowing some wheat or barley.

Early Jewish settlers visualized the Negev as a field for

future development. Z. D. Levontin's plan, around 1882, to found Rishon le-Zion south of Gaza, as well as later attempts at purchasing holdings near Rafa and elsewhere in the northern Negev, came to naught, however, mainly because Bedouin would-be vendors did not have their ownership rights entered in the land registry. In the first decade of the 20th century, the idea of Jewish settlement in the Negev was brought up again, first as a daring plan for a Jewish-Bedouin alliance, then as a project to be assisted by the Turkish authorities, in connection with Herzl's El-Arish project. After World War I, veterans of the Jewish Legion tried to settle on state land offered by the British authorities at Arad, but despaired when no water was found. In the 1920s and 1930s, Jewish individuals and groups acquired isolated holdings in the Negev, which were taken over by the J.N.F. and secured and enlarged after the end of the 1930s. This made it possible to set up the three "observation outposts" of Gevulot, Revivim, and Bet Eshel in the spring and summer of 1943, and three years later 11 more villages in the south and Negev, on the night following the Day of Atonement (Oct. 6, 1946). By the outbreak of hostilities after the U.N. partition resolution of Nov. 29, 1947, the number of Negev settlements had grown to 18, and two pipelines drawn from the Nir Am and Gevaram wells supplied them with drinking water and a limited quantity of irrigation water.

In the years 1949–51, settlement activity was energetically pursued. Fifteen thousand of the Bedouin population, estimated at 50,000 before 1947, remained (their number increased to about 25,000 in 1971, when nearly all of them lived in the Arad region). Whereas farming villages are concentrated northwest of Beersheba, since the 1950s outposts have begun to be established in the Negev Hills and the Arabah Valley. Urban nuclei were started in the central and eastern Negev (Yeroham, 1951; Mizpeh Ramon, 1954; Dimonah, 1955; Arad, 1961), and the development of Eilat became feasible after the 1956 Sinai Campaign. In the northwest, Ofakim and Netivot were built as immigrant towns. All these made the Negev an integral part of Israel demographically as well as politically. Beersheba became Israel's sixth-largest city, and mineral quarrying and processing (Dead Sea minerals, phosphates, methane gas, copper, ceramic clays, glass sands, etc.) furnished the basis for industrialization. Important were the traffic arteries that came into being after 1948; previously, the only one was the Gaza-Beersheba-Niẓẓanah road, with a branch leading up to the present-day Yeroḥam. Among these are the Beersheba–Dimonah–Sodom road (continuing to En-Gedi), the Beersheba–Miẓpeh Ramon–Eilat and Tel Shoket–Arad–Shefekh Zohar roads, and the Sodom–Eilat highway. To these was added the Tel Aviv–Beersheba railroad, which was later continued to Dimonah, Oron, and Ẓefa-Efeh.

The entire Negev is included in the sub-district of Beersheba which extends over 4,956 sq. mi. (12,835 sq. km.). The sub-district has 198,700 inhabitants: 168,500 Jews and 30,200 Arabs. Practically all the latter are Bedouin, living as nomads or in transition to sedentary life, mostly in the area between Beersheba and Arad. The population density has increased from 2.85 per sq. mi. (1.1 per sq. km.) in 1948 to 40.1 per sq. mi. (15.5 per sq. km.) in 1971.

NORTHWESTERN NEGEV. This region, which includes the Gerar and Besor regions, has an area of 549 sq. mi. (1,423 sq. km.). Farming is almost entirely dependent on irrigation, mainly with water from the National Water Carrier. Out-of-season vegetables for export, flowers, deciduous and subtropical fruit trees, cotton, and fodder crops are characteristic. A beginning has been made with auxiliary irrigation to secure the grain harvest in the rain-deficient years. Citrus groves have begun to appear in the northwestern Negev since the 1960s. Out of the 82 inhabited places in the Negev, 57 lie in this relatively small area; most are moshavim, grouped in the settlement regions of Benei Shimon, Merḥavim, and Eshkol. The development towns of Ofakim and Netivot are based on various industries. The total population of the region, all of them Jewish, numbers 31,700.

BEERSHEBA REGION. The Beersheba region, measuring 614 sq. mi. (1,589 sq. km.), has only seven inhabited places, among them the city of Beersheba and the town of Arad, where over 95% of the region's 88,500 Jewish inhabitants live; the rest of the population, numbering 29,600, are Bedouin. The principal economic activity is industry, concentrated in the two towns and partly based on Negev minerals. Beersheba's academic and research institutes have had a mounting impact on the life of the city and its vicinity. Dry farming (mostly barley and wheat fields) is practiced on relatively small areas. While the Bedouin used to wait until the first rains had come down in promising quantity before sowing, auxiliary irrigation has been introduced with the aid of small storage dams that retain occasional flash-flood waters.

NEGEV HILLS, PARAN PLATEAU, AND ARABAH VALLEY. The vast area, extending over 3,793 sq. mi. (9,823 sq. km.), comprises the Negev Hills, Paran Plateau, and Arabah Valley (including the southern section of the Judean Desert and the west shore of the Dead Sea). It has 18 inhabited places, among them the towns of Dimonah and Eilat and the development centers of Yeroḥam and Miẓpeh Ramon. In addition, there are important mining and industrial sites (e.g., Oron, Ẓefa-Efeh, Timna, Sodom, etc.) with no resident population. Phosphates, copper, clay minerals, and the Dead Sea minerals are extracted and treated. Oasis-type farming is to be found in the Arabah Valley settlements (numbering ten in 1972), where tropical fruit (dates, mangoes, etc.) and out-of-season export vegetables and flowers are prominent. The region contains 48,800 inhabitants (48,300 Jews and 500 Arabs), two-thirds of them in Dimonah and Eilat.

Golan. This region forms the western section of the Bashan in northern Transjordan. Ramat ha-Golan borders on the upper Jordan Rift Valley and Lake Kinneret in the west, on the Yarmuk Valley in the south, on the Ruqqād 269

Part of the residential zone of Arad, in the Negev, with apartment blocks built around courtyards. Courtesy Government Press Office, Tel Aviv.

stream in the east, and on the Hermon Massif in the north. Together with the southeast portion of Mount Hermon the region under Israel administration since 1967 measures 444 sq. mi. (1,150 sq. km.).

Two subregions are distinguished: the Lower Golan in the south, with altitudes between 600 and 1,900 ft. (185–600 m.) above sea level, and the Upper Golan in the north, rising to altitudes of 2,000–3,000 ft. (600–900 m.), with a number of hilltops attaining 3,600–4,040 ft. (1,100–1,226 m.). The dominant characteristics of the Golan's topography were created through volcanism, which continued into the Middle Pleistocene period, i.e., until approximately 500,000 years ago, with lava pouring out from fissures and craters and covering the plateau with a continuous layer of basalt and strings of volcanic cones, the largest being Tel

The Yarmuk River flowing through the southern hills of the Golan Heights. Photo Zev Radovan, Jerusalem.

Avital (Tell Abu al-Nadā', 1,204 m.). The plateau rises gently from south to north and dominates the rift valley to the west and south with abrupt escarpments. Stream courses, mainly in the southern section, have cut deep ravines, laid bare light-colored chalks, marls, and limestones underneath the black basalt, and separated small portions of the plateau from each other. Soils are mostly dark, fertile, and deep grumusols and are covered with basalt boulders in the north.

The northern Golan's climate is perceptibly cooler than that of other parts of Israel. While annual precipitation near the southern border of the Golan averages 16 in. (400 mm.), it amounts to 36–40 in. (900–1000 mm.) and more in the north. The Lower Golan has been farming country throughout most of its historic past, with grain crops as the principal branch; the ample rainfall and resulting stronger erosion make the Upper Golan a region of brush, forest, and pastures, rather than tilled fields, and biblical expressions such as the "cows" or "cattle of Bashan" (Amos 4:1;

Ezek. 39:18) and "oaks of Bashan" (Isa. 2:13; Ezek. 27:6) seem to refer to this section. Deforestation by man has left only stunted remnants of ancient forests in the northern Golan; flocks of sheep and herds of cattle, however, continued to be the region's economic mainstay until the recent past.

The Golan, which was one of Syria's backward provinces, entered modern history in the 1880s, when the Turkish authorities settled Circassians there to ward off Bedouin robbers. The regional center, al–Quneitra, came into being at that time. Shortly afterward, Jews made attempts to found settlements in the Golan, initially at Rumsaniyya, south of al-Quneitra; then at Benei Yehudah east of Lake Kinneret; and finally, in 1908, in the Bet Zayyada (al-Buṭayḥa) Valley (a much larger enterprise, at Benei Binyamin and Jilīn, was undertaken with Baron E. de Rothschild's aid in the Bashan, further east). Prior to 1967, the Golan's population included Sunnite Muslims, as well as Circassians, Druze, Alawids (Nusayris), a small Christian minority, and others. In the 1950s and 1960s, the Syrians covered the Golan with a network of artillery positions and fortifications to harass Israel settlements in Upper Galilee and the Lake Kinneret area, and geared the region's entire economy to military needs. In the last two days of the Six-Day War (June 9–10), nearly the entire region was occupied by the Israel army and came under Israel administration. Almost all the population took to flight together with the Syrian army, with the exception of the Druze who stayed on in six villages in the north (in the September 1967 census they numbered over 6,000). The remaining Druze villagers in the area quickly made contact with their kinsmen in Israel and developed friendly relations with the Israel administration and their new Jewish neighbors.

The first initiative for new Jewish settlement in the region was taken in July 1967 by a group of Ha-Kibbutz ha-Me'uḥad, which founded the village Merom Golan. By 1972 the number of Golan settlements had increased to 15,

First vegetable harvest at Givat Yo'av, a Naḥal outpost on the Golan Heights, 1968. Courtesy Government Press Office, Tel Aviv.

including Ramat Banias (Senir; of Ha-Shomer ha-Ẓa'ir), Merom Golan and Ein Zivan (Ha-Kibbutz ha-Me'uḥad) in the north; Naḥal Geshur (Ha-Shomer ha-Ẓa'ir) in the center; Ramot Magshimim (moshav shittufi of Ha-Po'el ha-Mizrachi), Givat Yo'av (Tenu'at ha-Moshavim), Ne'ot Golan (moshav shittufi of Ha-Oved ha-Ẓiyyoni), El Al (Tenu'at ha-Moshavim), Mevo Ḥammah (Iḥud ha-Kibbutzim), Naḥal Golan, and Ramot (Tenu'at ha-Moshavim) in the south Hermon. After 1967, land reclamation was **273**

GLOSSARY

Aḥdut ha-Avodah, Israel socialist party, seceded from Mapai in 1944; reunited in 1968 as part of Israel Labor Party.

Aḥdut ha-Avodah, Zionist Socialist Labor Party in Palestine founded in 1919; in 1930 merged with Ha-Po'el ha-Ẓa'ir and formed Mapai.

Aliyah, (1) immigration to Ereẓ Israel; (2) one of the waves of immigration to Ereẓ Israel from the early 1880s.

Arabah ("steppe", "desert"), a stretch of depressed ground between the Dead Sea and the Gulf of Elath.

Asefat ha-Nivḥarim, representative assembly elected by Jews in Palestine during the period of the British Mandate (1920–48).

Ashkenazi (pl. **Ashkenazim**), German or West-, Central-, or East-European Jew(s), as contrasted with Sephardi(m).

Av, fifth month of the Jewish religious year, eleventh of the civil, approximating to July-August.

Baḥad, a religious youth organization founded in Germany in 1928.

Bank ha-Poalim, the central financial institute of the Histadrut founded 1921.

Bet din (pl. **battei din**), rabbinic court of law.

Diaspora, Jews living in the "dispersion" outside Ereẓ Israel; area of Jewish settlement outside Ereẓ Israel.

Dor De'ah ("generation of wisdom"), religious movement in Yemen opposed to mystical trends.

Druze, a religio-political sect deriving from Islam, with communi- ties in Syria, Lebanon, and Israel.

Dunam, unit of land area (1,000 sq. m., c. 1/4 acre), used in Israel.

Ereẓ Israel, Land of Israel; Palestine.

Gaḥal, Israel party established in 1965 by two opposition parties Ḥerut and the Liberal Party.

Gedud ha-Avodah, first countrywide commune of Jewish workers in Palestine, founded 1920.

Hadassah, the Women's Zionist Organization of America, founded in 1912, and started its medical work in Palestine in 1918. 275

Haftarah (pl. **haftarot**), designation of the portion from the prophetical books of the Bible recited after the synagogue reading from the Pentateuch on Sabbaths and holidays.

Haganah, clandestine Jewish organization for armed self-defense in Erez Israel under the British Mandate, which eventually evolved into a people's militia.

Hakham bashi, title in the 15th century and modern times of the chief rabbi in the Ottoman Empire, residing in Constantinople (Istanbul), also applied to principal rabbis in provincial towns.

Halakhah (pl. **halakhot**), an accepted decision in rabbinic law. Also refers to those parts of the Talmud concerned with legal matters.

Halizah, biblical prescribed ceremony (Deut. 25:9-10) performed when a man refuses to marry his brother's childless widow.

Halutz (pl. **halutzim**), pioneer, especially in agriculture, in Erez Israel.

Halutziyyut, pioneering.

Hamashbir Hamerkazi, the main wholesale supplier for consumers' cooperatives and labor settlements in Israel, founded (as Hamashbir) in 1916.

Ha-Olam ha-Zeh—Koah Hadash, political party in Erez Israel founded 1965.

Ha-Oved ha-Dati, a religious workers faction in the Histadrut founded 1943.

Ha-Oved ha-Ziyyoni ("The Zionist Worker"), Israel labor movement founded as a Histadrut faction in 1935.

Ha-Po'el ha-Mizrachi, religious pioneering and labor movement in Erez Israel, founded in 1922.

Ha-Po'el Ha-Zair, Erez Israel labor party founded in 1905, merged in 1929 with Ahdut ha-Avodah and in 1930 created Mapai.

Ha-Shomer Ha-Za'ir, Zionist socialist pioneering youth movement founded 1916 in Vienna, and in the long run it spread to most countries of the world.

Hasidism, (1) religious revivalist movement of popular mysticism among Jews of Germany in the Middle Ages; (2) religious movement founded by Israel ben Eliezer Ba'al Shem Tov in the first half of the 18th century.

He-Halutz, an association of Jewish youth whose aim was to train its members to settle on the land in Erez Israel.

Herut, political movement in Erez Israel established in 1948, by the Irgun-Zevai Le'ummi, to continue as a parliamentary party with ideals of Vladimir Jabotinsky.

Ḥevra kaddisha, title applied to charitable confraternity (*ḥevrah*), now generally limited to associations for burial of the dead.

Ḥevrat ha-Ovdim, roof organization of all the cooperative and independent economic enterprises of the Histadrut founded in 1928.

Histadrut (abbr. for Heb. **Ha-Histadrut ha-Kelalit shel ha-Ovedim ha-Ivriyyim be-Erez Israel**), Erez Israel Jewish Labor Federation, founded in 1920; subsequently renamed Histadrut ha-Ovedim be-Erez Israel.

Holocaust, the organized mass persecution and annihilation of European Jewry by the Nazis (1933–1945).

I.Z.L. (initials of Heb. **Irgun Zevai Le'ummi;** "National Military Organization"), underground Jewish organization in Erez Israel founded in 1931, which engaged from 1937 in retaliatory acts against Arab attacks and later against the British mandatory authorities.

Jewish Agency, international, nongovernment body, centered in Jerusalem, which is the executive and representative of the World Zionist Organization, founded 1929.

Jewish Brigade Group, military unit serving in World War II in the British army, formed in 1944.

Jewish Legion, Jewish units in British army during World War I.

Jewish National Fund, the land purchase and development fund of the World Zionist Organization founded 1920.

Kabbalah, the Jewish mystical tradition.

Karaite, member of a Jewish sect originating in the eighth century which rejected rabbinic (Rabbanite) Judaism and accepted only Scripture as authoratative.

Keren Hayesod (Palestine Foundation Fund), the financial arm of the World Zionist Organization found 1920.

Kevuzah, small commune of pioneers constituting an agricultural settlement in Erez Israel (evolved later into kibbutz).

Kibbutz (pl. **kibbutzim**), larger-size commune constituting a settlement in Erez Israel based mainly on agriculture but engaging also in industry.

Knesset, parliament of the State of Israel.

Kuppat Ḥolim, the medical insurance fund of the Histadrut founded 1912.

Lag ba-Omer, 33rd (Heb. **lag**) day of the *Omer* period falling on the 18th of Iyyar; a semi-holiday.

Leḥi (abbr. for Heb. **Loḥamei Ḥerut Israel,** "Fighters for the Freedom of Israel" also L.H.Y.), radically anti-British armed 277 underground organization in Palestine, founded in 1940 by dissidents from I.Z.L.

Ma'barah, transition camp; temporary settlement for newcomers in Israel during the period of mass immigration following 1948.

Mamzer, the offspring of a relationship which is forbidden according to the Torah.

Mandate, Palestine, responsibility for the administration of Palestine conferred on Britain by the League of Nations in 1922; mandatory government: the British administration of Palestine.

Mapai, a labor party in Erez Israel founded in 1930 by the union of Aḥdut ha-Avodah and Ha-Poel ha-Za'ir.

Mapam, a pioneering, left-wing, labor-Zionist Israel party, founded 1948, when Ha-Shomer ha-Za'ir merged with Aḥdut ha-Avodah–Po'alei Zion.

Minyan, group of ten male adult Jews, the minimum required for communal prayer.

Moshav, smallholders' cooperative agricultural settlement in Israel, see moshav ovedim.

Moshavah, earliest type of Jewish village in modern Erez Israel in which farming is conducted on individual farms mostly on privately owned land.

Moshav ovedim ("workers' moshav"), agricultural village in Israel whose inhabitants possess individual homes and holdings but cooperate in the purchase of equipment, sale of produce, mutual aid, etc.

Moshav shittufi ("collective moshav"), agricultural village in Israel whose members possess individual homesteads but where the agriculture and economy are conducted as a collective unit.

Musta'rab, Arab-speaking, old, established Jewish communities and residents in the Middle East.

Naḥal, a regular unit of Israel Defense Forces training cadres for agricultural settlements.

Negev, the southern, mostly arid, area of Israel.

Nir Company, a credit, financial institute of the labor settlements founded 1934.

Palmaḥ (abbr. for Heb. *peluggot maḥaz;* "shock companies"), striking arm of the Haganah.

Partition plan(s), proposals for dividing Erez Israel into autonomous areas.

Peel Commission, British Royal Commission appointed by the British government in 1936 to inquire into the Palestine problem and make recommendations for its solution.

Perushim, a community of Ashkenazim, opponents of the Ḥasidim, organized in Jerusalem in 1816.

Po'alei Agudat Israel (P.A.I.), religious labor movement, affiliate of Agudat Israel, founded in Poland in 1922, active in Ereẓ Israel from 1925.

Po'alei Ẓion, movement whose ideology combines Zionism and socialism.

Rabbanite, adherent of rabbinic Judaism. In contradistinction to Karaite.

Rafi, a socialist political party founded in 1965 by David Ben-Gurion and members of Mapai as a result of a split in Mapai: since 1968 part of Israel Labor Party.

Revisionists, party of maximalist political Zionists founded 1925 and led by Vladimir Jabotinsky.

Rishon le-Zion, title given to Sephardi chief rabbi of Ereẓ Israel.

Rosh Ha-Shanah, two-day holiday (one day in biblical and early mishnaic times) at the beginning of the month of Tishri (September-October), traditionally the New Year.

Sefer Torah, manuscript scroll of the Pentateuch for public reading in synagogue.

Sephardi (pl. **Sephardim**), Jew(s) of Spain and Portugal and their descendants, wherever resident, as contrasted with Ashkenazi(m).

Shavuot, Pentecost; Festival of Weeks; second of the three annual pilgrim festivals, commemorating the receiving of the Torah at Mt. Sinai.

Shemittah, Sabbatical year.

Shephelah, southern part of the coastal plain of Ereẓ Israel.

Shomer, Ha-Shomer, organization of Jewish workers in Ereẓ Israel founded in 1909 to defend Jewish settlements.

Sinai Campaign, brief campaign in October-November 1956 when Israel army reacted to Egyptian terrorist attacks and blockade by occupying the Sinai peninsula.

Six-Day War, brief war in June 1967 when Israel reacted to Arab threats and blockade by defeating the Egyptian, Jordanian, and Syrian armies.

Solel Boneh, Histadrut concern for building, public works, and industry founded 1924.

Stockade and Watchtower, type of settlement established in Palestine between 1936 and 1947 in planned surprise operation to provide immediate security against Arab attacks.

Sukkot, festival of Tabernacles; last of the three pilgrim festivals, beginning on the 15th of Tishri.

Talmud, "teaching"; compendium of discussions on the Mishnah by generations of scholars and jurists in many academies over a period of several centuries. The Jerusalem (or Palestinian) Talmud mainly contained the discussions of the Palestinian sages. The Babylonian Talmud incorporates the parallel discussion in the Babylonian academies.

Talmud torah, term generally applied to Jewish religious (and ultimately to talmudic) study; also to traditional Jewish religious public schools.

Tammuz, fourth month of the Jewish religious year, tenth of the civil, approximating to June-July.

Targum, Aramaic translation of the Bible.

Templer, German sect which founded settlements in Palestine in the 19th and 20th centuries.

Tishav be-Av, Ninth of Av, fast day commemorating the destruction of the First and Second Temples.

Tnuva, a cooperative association affiliated to the Histadrut, marketing agricultural produce.

Torah, Pentateuch or the Pentateuch scroll for reading in synagogue; entire body of traditional Jewish teaching and literature.

Va'ad Le'ummi, national council of the Jewish community in Erez Israel during the period of the British Mandate.

Waqf (Ar.), (1) a Muslim charitable pious foundation; (2) state lands and other property passed to the Muslim community for public welfare.

War of Independence, war of 1947-49 when the Jews of Israel fought off invading Arab armies and ensured the establishment of the new state.

Wizo, Women's International Zionist Organization founded in 1920, rescuing Jewish children and young people and giving them care and education in Erez Israel.

Yeshivah, Jewish traditional academy devoted primarily to study of rabbinic literature; *rosh yeshivah,* head of the yeshivah.

Yishuv, settlement; more specifically, the Jewish community of Erez Israel in the pre-State period. The pre-Zionist community is generally designated the "old yishuv" and the community evolving from 1880, the "new yishuv."

Youth Aliyah, organization founded in 1932 for the purpose of rescuing Jewish children and young people and giving them care and education in Erez Israel.

Ze'irei Zion, moderate Zionist socialist labor movement, active mainly in Russia, established in 1903.

Zohar, mystical commentary on the Pentateuch; main textbook of Kabbalah.

BIBLIOGRAPHY

Population: *Census of Palestine* (1931, 1933); *Survey of Palestine,* 3 vols. (1946); *Statistical Abstracts of Palestine* (1936–45); Israel, Central Bureau of Statistics, *Statistical Abstracts of Israel* (1950–1970); idem, *Special Publications,* nos. 36 and 53 (Registration of Population Nov. 8, 1948); no. 194 (Marriages of Jews in Israel 1947–62); no. 242 (Projection of the Population in Israel up to 1985); no. 268 (Vital Statistics 1965–66); no. 262 (Internal Migration of Jews in Israel 1965–1966); no. 276 (Demographic Characteristics of the Jewish Population in Israel 1965–67); idem, *Publication* no. 42 (Main Data of the Census 1961); nos. 36 and 39 (Census 1961, Families in Israel); R. Bachi, in: *Proceedings, World Population Conference* (1954); idem, in: *Challenge of Development* (1958), 41–80; idem, in: JJSO, 8 (1966), 142–9; idem, in: *International Symposium on Automation of Population Register System, Proceedings* (1967); idem, in: *Sydney Conference of the International Union for the Scientific Study of Population* (1967); R. Bachi and J. Matras, in: *Milbank Memorial Fund Quarterly,* 40 (1962); R. Bachi, *Ha-Nohag ba-Nissu'in u-va-Yeludah be-Kerev ha-Shekhavot ha-Shonot shel ha-Yishuv ve-Hashpa'ato al Atido* (1944); *Din ve-Ḥeshbon shel ha-Va'adah li-Ve'ayot ha-Yeludah Muggash le-Rosh ha-Memshalah* (1966); D.H.K. Amiram and A. Shachar, *Development Towns in Israel* (1969). Izhak Ben-Zvi, *The Exiled and the Redeemed* (1961); idem, *Israel under Ottoman Rule 1517–1917* (1960), also in: L. Finkelstein, *The Jews,* 1 (1960³), 602–89; D. and M. Hacohen, *Our People* (1969); A. M. Luncz, *Jerusalem,* 1 (Eng., 1882), 20–114; H. Mizraḥi, *Yehudei Paras* ... (1959); R. H. Hacohen, *Avanim ba-Ḥomah* (1970); A. Ben-Jacob, *Yehudei Bavel* ... (1965); idem, *Kehillot Yehudei Kurdistan* (1961); idem, *Yalkut Minhagim: Miminhagei Shivtei Yisrael* (1967); D. Bensimon-Donath, *Immigrants d'Afrique du Nord en Israel. Evolution et Adaptation* (1970); S. N. Eisenstadt, *Israeli Society* (1967), incl. bibl.; S. N. Eisenstadt, R. Bar Yosef and Ch. Adler, *Integration and Development in Israel*

(1970), incl. bibl.; M. Sicron, *Immigration to Israel 1948–1953* (1957); A. A. Weinberg, *Immigration and Belonging* (1961); J. Shuval, *Immigrants on the Threshold* (1963).

Kibbutz Movement: A. Bein, *The Return to the Soil* (1952); Y. Baratz, *A Village by the Jordan* (1954); M. Weingarten, *Life in a Kibbutz* (1955); M. E. Spiro, *Kibbutz, Venture in Utopia* (1956); idem, *Children of the Kibbutz* (1958); H. Darin-Drabkin, *The Other Society* (1962); B. Bettelheim, *Children of the Dream* (1969). KIBBUTZ ARẒI: D. Leon, *The Kibbutz* (1964); E. H. Samuel, *The Children's Community of the Hashomer Hatẓair at Mishmar Haemek* (1962); L. Dror et al. (ed.), *Sefer ha-Shomer ha-Ẓa'ir,* 3 vols. (1956–64), passim. KIBBUTZ DATI: M. Unna, *Shutafut shel Emet* (1965); M. Krone, *From Rodges to Yavne* (1945); A. Fishman, *The Religious Kibbutz Movement* (1957); Bnei Akiva, *The Religious Kvuẓah* (1960); J. Walk, in: YLBI (1961), 236–56.

Moshav: H. Viteles, *A History of the Cooperative Movement in Israel,* 4 (1968), incl. bibl.; I. M. Klayman, *The Moshav in Israel* (1970); D. Weintraub, M. Lissak, and Y. Azmon, *Moshava, Kibbutz and Moshav . . .* (1969); R. Tamsma, *De Moshav Ovdiem* (Dutch, 1966), English summary; *ibid.,* 342–91, incl. bibl.; H. Darin-Drabkin, *Patterns of Cooperative Agriculture in Israel* (1962); S. Dayan, *Man and the Soil* (1965); E. Meyer, *Der Moshav 1948–1963* (1967); E. Joffe, *Ketavim,* 2 vols. (1947); idem, *Yissud Moshevei Ovedim* (1919); A. Assaf, *Moshevei ha-Ovedim be-Yisrael* (1954); Y. Uri, *Bi-Netivei Moshav ha-Ovedim* (1950); I. Korn, *Kibbutz ha-Galuyyot be-Hitnahaluto* (1964); R. Weitz, *Darkenu ba-Ḥakla'ut u-va-Hityashevut* (1959); Y. Shapira (ed.), *Nahalal . . .* (1947); *Kefar Yeḥezkel* (Heb. anthol., 1948); E. Labes, *Handbook of the Moshav* (1959); D. Weintraub, *Immigration and Social Change* (1971).

Jewish Labor Organization: W. Preuss. *The Labour Movement in Israel* (1965[3]); F. Zweig, *The Israeli Worker . . .* (1959); N. Malkosh, *Histadrut in Israel* (1962[2]); I. Sobel, in: W. Galenson (ed.), *Labor in Developing Economies* (1963), 187–250; M. Braslavsky, *Tenu'at ha-Po'alim ha-Ereẓ-Yisre'elit,* 4 vols. (1955–63), includes bibliography; P. Merḥav, *Toledot Tenu'at ha-Po'alim* 283 *be-Ereẓ Yisrael* . . . (1967); G. Kressel, *Ha-Histadrut, Madrikh Bibliografi* (1970); Ha-Histadrut ha-Kelalit shel ha-Ovedim ha-Ivryyim be-Ereẓ Israel, *Ḥukkot ha-Histadrut* (1952); idem, *Ha-Histadrut mi-Yom Kum ha-Medinah* (1969–), statistics; S. Kurland, *Cooperative Palestine* (1947); G. Muenzer, *Labor Enterprise in Palestine* (1947); Z. Even Shoshan, *Toledot Tenu'at ha-Po'alim be-Ereẓ-Yisrael*, 3 vols. (1955–66).

Labor Relations: Israel, Ministry of Labor, Manpower Planning Authority, *Annual Reports* (Heb. and Eng., 1964–); Israel, Central Bureau of Statistics, *Statistical Abstract of Israel* (Heb. and Eng., 1950–).

Health Services, Social Security and Welfare: T. Grushka (ed.), *Health Services in Israel* (1968²); G. Lotan, *Social Insurance in Israel* (1960); idem, *Eser Shenot Bittu'aḥ Le'ummi* (1964).

Human Geography: E. Orni and E. Efrat, *Geography of Israel* (1971³); E. Huntington, *Palestine and its Transformation* (1911); A. Ruppin, *The Agricultural Colonization of the Zionist Organization in Palestine* (1926); A. A. Reifenberg, *The Struggle between the Desert and the Sown* (1950); N. Glueck, *Rivers in the Desert: The Exploration of the Desert* (1959); E. Orni, *Huleh, Background and Development* (1952); idem, *Forms of Settlement* (1963⁵); idem, *Agrarian Reform and Social Progress in Israel,* (1972). A. Bein, *The Return to the Soil* (1952); E. Efrat and E. Gaybrieli, *Physical Master Plan of the Coastal Strip* (1966); Jewish Agency Agricultural Settlement Dept., *The Composite Rural Structure. A Settlement Pattern in Israel* (1960); A. Granott, *The Land System of Palestine* (1952); idem, *Agrarian Reform and the Record of Israel* (1956); D. H. K. Amiran and A. Shaḥar, *The Towns of Israel. Principles of Their Urban Geography* (1961); E. Brutzkus, *Physical Planning in Israel* (1964); J. Dash and E. Efrat, *The Israel Physical Master Plan* (1964); E. Efrat, *Judea and Samaria, Guidelines for Regional and Physical Planning* (1971).

INDEX

294